Corel® Paint Shop Pro® X:

The Official Guide

The easiest way to turn your pictures into professional-looking **photos**—fast!

CORE Paint Shop Pro X

Adjust & Retouch	Create & Collage	Graphics & Effects	Organize & Share
Fix any flaw	Erase backgrounds	Convert to black & white	Find any photo fast
Rotate, resize and crop	Add frames and edges	Paint with realistic art tools	Organize photo collections
Repair faded, damaged or scratched photos	Create calendars, cards, books picture CDs & more	Add text and shapes	Show off photo creations

Corel® Paint Shop Pro® X:
The Official Guide

Dave Huss
Lori J. Davis

McGraw-Hill

New York   Chicago   San Francisco   Lisbon
London   Madrid   Mexico City   Milan   New Delhi
San Juan   Seoul   Singapore   Sydney   Toronto

McGraw-Hill books are available at special quantity discounts to use as premiums and sales promotions, or for use in corporate training programs. For more information, please write to the Director of Special Sales, Professional Publishing, McGraw-Hill, Two Penn Plaza, New York, NY 10121-2298. Or contact your local bookstore.

Corel® Paint Shop Pro® X: The Official Guide

1234567890 DOC DOC 019876

ISBN 0-07-226262-1

Sponsoring Editor: Megg Morin
Editorial Supervisor: Patty Mon
Project Editor: Claire Splan
Acquisitions Coordinator: Agatha Kim
Technical Editor: David Plotkin
Copy Editor/Indexer: Claire Splan
Proofreader: Paul Tyler
Production Supervisor: Jean Bodeaux
Composition: Apollo Publishing Services
Cover Designer: Pattie Lee
Color Insert: Lyssa Wald

Dedicated to Cooper Morin. A fine young man who has done such a splendid job of raising his mom and dad.

About the Authors

Dave Huss has authored over 28 books on digital photo editing and photography that have been translated into eight languages. A photographer for over 40 years, Dave was one of the early adopters of digital photography. A popular conference speaker, Dave has taught workshops in both the U.S. and Europe and has been seen on CNN and TechTV.

Lori J. Davis is the author of several books on Paint Shop Pro and the coauthor of a book on digital scrapbooking. She has been teaching graphics classes online for about ten years and has contributed to online publications and to *Digital Camera Magazine*. When she isn't exploring computer graphics, Lori enjoys painting, photography, knitting, gardening, and birding.

CONTENTS AT A GLANCE

CONTENTS

ACKNOWLEDGMENTS

All books are a team effort, and this book is no exception. First of all, there are several people at Corel who were of immeasurable assistance as I worked with Paint Shop Pro X. Doug Meisner and his crew worked so hard to ensure that Paint Shop Pro X was the world class product that they had envisioned. Allison Pankratz went to bat to get the book's cover into shape. Nancy Peterson was amazing in somehow finding the time to provide me with answers to some of my seemingly endless questions about the product, all while heading up both the private and public beta testing. I especially appreciated all of the gracious hospitality afforded this author when visiting the Corel facility in Minnesota. I still use my Minnesota coffee cup!

From the Osborne team, there are many people to thank. Many of these people have worked with me on other books. At the top of my list is Megg Morin, my acquisitions editor and friend, who has seen me through more books than either of us will admit to.

As usual, I am deeply indebted to my friend and technical editor, David Plotkin, who is himself a best-selling author. I appreciate all of his efforts in not only making sure the materials and techniques described in the book are accurate but also lending his considerable wealth of graphics knowledge in the form of suggestions and recommendations about topics.

I would be remiss if I didn't thank all of the people in my church who let me take photos of them and use them in the book. Last on this list, but first in my life, is my lovely wife of almost 34 years* Elizabeth, who must put up with continued and repeated absences of her hubby as he buries himself in his laptop or runs off to some remote location to get some photos for the book.

—Dave Huss

---

* I am often asked what it takes to stay married for more than three decades—it is just two little words—Yes, dear. Everything else is details.

INTRODUCTION

How to Do Everything with Paint Shop Pro X

By the mere fact that you are reading this introduction, you are in a minority. Most computer book readers immediately jump into the middle of the book, after which the reader gets lost and sheepishly returns to Chapter 1. Because you are reading the introduction, we congratulate you and, because it is just the few of us here, let's get informal and talk about what is and what is not between the covers of this book.

Who Should Read This Book?

The purpose of this book is to show you how to do things with Paint Shop Pro X. While writing this book we used several major assumptions:

■ You, the reader, may not have ever worked with photo editing software before but you want to use it to make your photos look better.

■ You haven't won a Nobel Prize but you also are not a dummy or an idiot*.

■ You are more interested in discovering what you can do with a tool or feature than reading a detailed explanation of how it works.

| TIP | *If you are interested in a book that offers detailed explanations of every tool, always go for the heaviest one.* |

---

* *"Suppose you were an idiot. And suppose you were a member of Congress. But I repeat myself."*
—Mark Twain, a Biography

You will discover that our approach to Paint Shop Pro X is more focused on using it to work with photographs rather than draw heart-shaped vector objects or as a paint tool to create semi-realistic flowers. Most of these pages are dedicated to improving, preserving, and printing photos and having some fun in the process. There are also tips scattered throughout on how to prevent some of the more common problems that photographers face. Did you know people who have had too much to drink are much more susceptible to red-eye? One of the many reasons flash photography and bars rarely mix.

You'll be impressed with the vast array of digital image correction tools that up until now have only been available as expensive Photoshop plug-ins. For example, one of the inherent problems with digital cameras is the distortion created by the wide-angle lenses used by the cameras. In this book, you will discover that Paint Shop Pro X includes a set of tools to correct perspective distortion (the distortion that makes the top of a building appear smaller than the bottom), as well as the rounded corner distortion produced by wide-angle lenses.

Paint Shop Pro is also about having fun with your photos and while Corel improved the performance, they didn't forget about important features such as the Makeover brush, which can give you a facial and a tan with a few brushstrokes. You will discover how to use the wide assortment of really cool picture-edge effects so that your next Christmas newsletter might end up as a Pulitzer candidate.

If you just want to make photos look better, you will learn how to use the powerful set of image enhancement tools to give both beginners and power users the ability to make even poor quality photos look great with only a few keystrokes.

One of the benefits of digital cameras—that you can take as many pictures as you want—can really become a nuisance when you return from your family vacation with 600 images instead of the usual 60. This is probably why the folks at Corel have added a lot of new scripting features for commonly repeated tasks in addition to some great new, easy-to-use batch processing features.

Corel Paint Shop Pro X: The Official Guide is written in nontechnical, everyday language for the beginner-to-intermediate user. A special effort was made to focus on the realistic use of program features on real-world projects and problems. We take issue with authors and others who demonstrate how a feature works with an example that leaves the reader wondering why in the world they would ever want to do that. We also do not believe in wasting precious pages providing detailed information about how every tool works. If you want to learn how a tool or feature works, Corel has included an excellent printed user manual that can also be accessed by clicking the Help button in Paint Shop Pro X. If you are not a beginner, we have included a wealth of techniques, ideas, and suggestions for the advanced user, digital photographer, or photo editor.

Conventions Used in This Book

As you follow the procedures contained in this book, you're bound to encounter terms specific to manipulating tools, using shortcuts, or applying or accessing commands. The following brief list may help define some of these terms:

■ **Click-drag**   This action involves clicking the left mouse button and subsequently dragging the tool or cursor while holding down the button. You often find this action described as simply a "drag." Click-dragging is often used for moving objects, manipulating control or object handles, or drawing with tools.

■ **CTRL-click**   This term describes the action of holding the CTRL (Control) key in combination with a mouse click.

■ **CTRL-SHIFT-drag**   This action describes holding the CTRL (Control) and SHIFT keys together, while dragging an object or tool cursor.

■ **CTRL-drag**   This term describes holding the CTRL (Control) key while dragging, which can have different effects depending on which tool you are using and the action you are performing.

■ **Menu | Submenu | Submenu**   This commonly found annotation is used to describe the action of accessing application menus and further selecting submenus. The first entry describes the main application menu, while subsequent entries describe further menu access with each menu/submenu name separated by a vertical bar.

■ **Right-click**   This term is used to describe the action of clicking your *right* mouse button as opposed to the typical left mouse button; this action is most often used for accessing context-sensitive commands contained in the pop-up menu. The pop-up menu offers shortcuts to commands or dialogs.

How This Book Is Organized

Corel Paint Shop Pro X: The Official Guide includes 14 chapters organized into five parts. Each chapter is designed to guide you through how to use Paint Shop Pro's tools, features, and/or resources. The parts are structured in a sequence for reference and in logical progression, much like a typical learning sequence.

Part I: Getting Acquainted with Paint Shop Pro X

Whether you're just getting acquainted with Paint Shop Pro X as a first-time user or you're revisiting this latest version, Part I is designed to cover the basics. If you're new to Paint Shop Pro, Chapter 1, "Meet Paint Shop Pro for the First Time," provides brief summaries of the new tools and features available in Paint Shop Pro X and familiarizes you with how to use various application and document window components including palettes, toolbars, the status bar, and workspace features. Chapter 2, "Set Up Shop," teaches you how to set up, configure, and customize the program to fit you and your working environment. To round off the quick-start reference, Chapter 3, "Getting Pictures into Paint Shop Pro," covers essential skills and techniques necessary to capture both digital and non-digital images using a scanner. Once these images are captured you will discover how to manage the vast number of images that either do or will soon exist in your computer.

Part II: Photo Editing

For users somewhat more familiar with Paint Shop Pro, Part II covers basic skills for working with digital photos, how to fix minor photo problems, and how to add text to photos. Chapter 4, "Simple Image Editing and Printing," offers basic instruction as well as tips and tricks used by professionals to make your photos look their best in e-mails, Web pages, or printed documents. Chapter 5 is "Correcting Photographic Problems." All photographs have problems—too much light, too much darkness, color casts caused by cloudy days. This chapter shows you how to correct most of these common photographic problems. Chapter 6, "Repairing and Restoring Photographs," offers techniques on how to scan, repair, and preserve damaged photos and other important documents.

Part III: Creating Original Images Using Paint Shop Pro X

Part III features two chapters specifically dealing with using Paint Shop Pro X's powerful selection tools to create exciting photo compositions from images drawn from many sources and teaches you how to add dazzling effects to your photos using the fantastic effects filters and other features built into Paint Shop Pro. Chapter 7, "Create a Photo Montage," covers a lot of ground by explaining in detail how to select, add, remove, and manipulate people and objects from photos. Chapter 8, "Add Text to Your Images," details many of the different ways you can use text to add more impact to your photos. You will learn how to create different types of text effects, from adding cartoon-like caption balloons to making text flow around or along a curve.

Part IV: Getting Creative with Paint Shop Pro X

Learn to add special, cool effects to your photos in Chapter 9, "Add Dazzling Effects to Your Photos." You will learn how to add photo edges and photo frames to your photos, how to create stunning effects with the Picture Tube brush, and much more. In Chapter 10, "Understanding the Vector Tools," you leave the world of pixel manipulation and enter the realm of vector drawing. With vectors, you can create simple or complex shapes that can be precisely manipulated or resized with no image distortion. You'll learn the ins and outs of vectors, from using preset shapes to node editing.

Scrapbooking is taking the world by storm, and in Chapter 11, "Digital Scrapbooking," you'll learn what you need to know about creating your own digital scrapbook layouts, which you can print or share in digital form. You'll even see how easy it is to create some of your own digital scrapping embellishments.

Digital drawing and painting is a snap with Paint Shop Pro's special Art Media tools and layers, which you'll explore in Chapter 12, "Art Media." Create a new digital piece of art from scratch, or use Art Media's Trace feature to transform a photo into a painting.

Part V: Customizing and Automation

People work in different ways, and different kinds of projects require different tools and commands. In Chapter 13, "Customizing the Paint Shop Pro Workspace," you'll see how to modify Paint Shop Pro's workspace so that the tools, palettes, toolbars, and commands that you need are readily available and within easy reach.

Sometimes it's handy to record image editing steps for future use or to automate a repetitive process. In Chapter 14, "Script and Batch Processing," you'll learn the basics of scripting and batch processing, so you can spend less time on mechanics and more time on creativity.

PART I

Getting Acquainted with Paint Shop Pro X

CHAPTER 1

Meet Paint Shop Pro for the First Time

Paint Shop Pro X offers powerful digital-imaging tools that enable you to create eye-catching images, dazzling effects, and exciting photo enhancements in a short amount of time. Because this program is very easy to learn and use, it is perfect for the scrapbooking hobbyist as well as for the digital-imaging entrepreneur. In this chapter, you'll learn some tricks about installing Paint Shop Pro as well as downloading and installing updates. You will also discover the new features and improved ones included in this release, become acquainted with the Paint Shop Pro X workspace, and gain an overview of how to create some digital magic.

What Computer Hardware Do I Need?

Paint Shop Pro X doesn't require the most powerful computer on the planet to allow you to create photographic masterpieces. As with all photo editors, there are minimum hardware requirements to be able to use the application. Corel lists the following as the minimum system requirements:

- 500 MHz processor
- Windows 2000 (SP4) or Windows XP
- 256MB of RAM
- 500MB of free hard drive space
- 1024 x 768 resolution display, 16-bit color
- Macromedia Flash™ Player 7 (included)

If your computer meets these minimum requirements then Paint Shop Pro X will work on your machine. If your computer doesn't meet these requirements, you have a choice to upgrade or to replace the computer to have hardware that will not only perform photo editing more quickly but make your creative efforts more fun and productive. Corel also has provided a list of what is described as the recommended system configuration as follows:

- 1 GHz or faster processor
- Windows XP
- 512MB of RAM
- 500MB of free hard drive space
- 1024 x 768 resolution display, 32-bit color

Should I Upgrade or Replace My Hardware?

To upgrade or not to upgrade, that is the question. Here are some suggestions if you are facing that question at the moment. If your computer's processor speed is less than 1 GHz, you may want to consider replacing it with a newer unit because computer prices have plummeted over the past few years and it is very likely it is cheaper to replace the unit than to buy the components necessary to upgrade it. When you go shopping for a new computer, you will discover that many new computers advertise that they contain expensive high-power graphics cards. You should be aware that these graphical wonder cards make computer games really fly but have zero impact on anything you will do with Paint Shop Pro.

If your computer processor speed is 1 GHz or greater then you should consider upgrading rather than replacement. The most important area that you should consider upgrading is the amount of memory, called RAM (random access memory). Corel recommends 512MB as the minimum amount. If you will be doing a lot of graphics with images taken with one of the newer cameras using a 5–8 megapixel sensor, you may even want to consider getting 1 GB of RAM (also called SDRAM). Besides memory, the other easily changed computer component is the hard drive. Hard drives are really inexpensive these days so buying an extra drive doesn't cost much at all. If you don't want to go through the hassle of adding or replacing an internal drive, you can buy an external drive that attaches to your computer using a USB connection. These don't cost very much and provide the easiest way to add a bigger hard drive to your system.

Installing Paint Shop Pro X

As with most Windows programs, the installation of Paint Shop Pro uses a wizard-style approach. On the opening screen (see Figure 1-1) that launches after you insert the CD, you can choose from the following:

- Install Corel Paint Shop Pro X

- Install Photo Album 6 Standard Edition

- View Lynda.com Training Videos

- Install Pixmantec RawShooter essentials

- Install MyPublisher BookMaker

- Explore the CD

Choosing to install Paint Shop Pro launches the installation wizard. If you installed earlier versions of this program you might be surprised to find that PSP X now requires the use of a serial number. If you purchased a boxed version of the product, the serial number is on a card included in the box, and if you downloaded it, your serial number came with your e-mail message.

When you come to the File Format Associations dialog box during the installation, review your choices before taking the default selections. There are a lot of choices on the screen but the important one is the association of JPEG images. If the default setting has Paint Shop Pro associated with JPEG, it means that anytime you double-click a JPEG

FIGURE 1-1   The opening screen offers several installation choices.

file, Paint Shop Pro launches. If you receive a lot of JPEG images attached to e-mails, consider not checking a JPEG association because it is faster and easier to view images using the Windows Picture and Fax Viewer.

Changing the File Format Associations

If you have already installed Paint Shop Pro and have chosen JPEG by default, here is how to change it.

1. Launch Paint Shop Pro.

2. From the Menu bar choose File | Preferences | File Format Associations.

3. When the File Format Associations dialog box appears (see Figure 1-2), scroll down and uncheck the file format that you do not want to launch Paint Shop Pro. In this case you should uncheck the one marked JPG JPEG. There are two types of JPEG files in the list: JPG2 and JPG. You only need uncheck JPG.

NOTE   *Unchecking JPEG in the File Format Associations dialog box does not prevent Paint Shop Pro from opening JPEG files.*

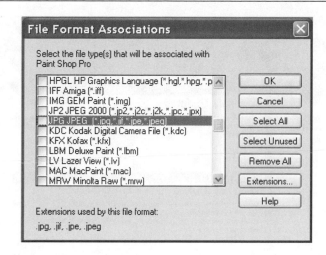

FIGURE 1-2   Modify file associations if necessary.

Installing the Other Programs on the CD

When you have finished installing Paint Shop Pro you can return to the install menu (shown earlier in Figure 1-1) and either install the remainder of the programs at this time or install them as you need them at a later time by reinserting the CD in your computer and choosing the desired program.

Keeping Paint Shop Pro Up to Date

When you launch Paint Shop Pro for the first time, you will be asked to register the program. This requires Internet access and it is important to do it so that Corel can work with your computer to keep your software up to date. Corel does this through the Corel Update Service, which was installed at the same time you installed Paint Shop Pro.

The first time that you launch Paint Shop Pro it automatically checks with Corel via the Internet to ensure that you have the most current version of the software. Like all software updates done by professional software companies, no information is communicated between Corel and the update software on your computer. It only checks the version of your copy of Paint Shop Pro and compares it to the latest version information at Corel. If there is a newer version, an Update Service screen similar to the one shown in Figure 1-3 will appear advising you that there is an updated version of the software available. To upgrade your software, click the Add button and then when the Next button (above the update description) is no longer grayed out, click it. The update will be downloaded from Corel and installed.

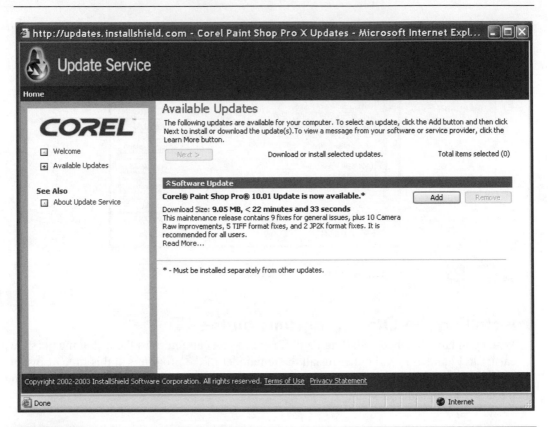

FIGURE 1-3   A software update ready to install

The Corel Update Service and Paint Shop Pro are separate programs. While the update is downloading, close Paint Shop Pro because it needs to be closed to apply the update. After Paint Shop Pro has been updated, it may appear unchanged when you launch it, but if you look carefully at the opening screen you can see the version number has changed. If you missed the screen when the program opened, you can always view it by clicking Help in the menu bar and selecting About Paint Shop Pro, which opens the splash screen shown in Figure 1-4. In this screenshot the original 10.0 release was updated to 10.01. Click OK to return to Paint Shop Pro.

Version number

FIGURE 1-4   Updated version information

New Features of Paint Shop Pro X

Regardless of what version you have, there are new features to explore. If you're familiar
with previous versions of Paint Shop Pro, you're going to be pleasantly surprised with what
Paint Shop Pro X has to offer. So let's take a peek at what's in store for your digital-imaging
potential.

A New Learning Center

With the new Learning Center (see Figure 1-5), Paint Shop Pro will actually teach you how to edit your photos, remove objects from your photos, create collages, discover how to make the most of the Text tool, and so much more. Finally, you can learn how to do all the things you've always wanted to do with Paint Shop Pro, but never knew how.

New Photo Features

Paint Shop Pro X has added a host of new photo features beginning with the Smart Photo Fix feature that automatically corrects color, brightness, sharpness, and saturation while also letting you fine-tune the suggested settings. Corel has also added Makeover tools (Blemish

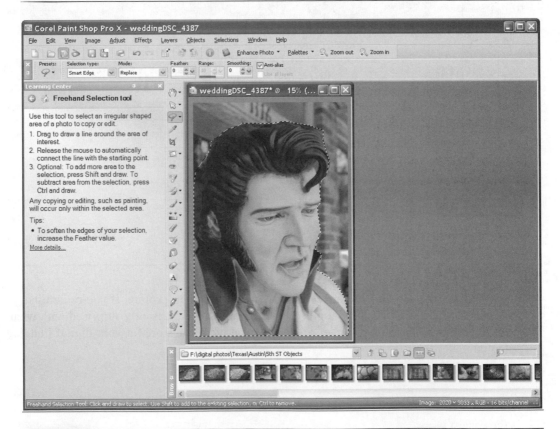

FIGURE 1-5   The Learning Center describes how to do many tasks using Paint Shop Pro.

Fixer, the Toothbrush, and the Suntan Modes) that allow you to retouch the faces in your photos to remove flaws, just like the airbrushing done by magazine photo editors for their models. Paint Shop Pro now has a fast Red-Eye Remover that allows you to quickly zap red-eye from your photos with the click of a mouse. Now you can easily remove an unwanted portion of a photo and it uses portions of the remaining photo to fill in the area removed using the Object Remover. The One-Step Purple Fringe Fix lets you remove the purple glow that surrounds high-contrast edges of objects in many digital camera photos while the High Pass Sharpen command provides a new, powerful way to sharpen digital photos. The One-Step Noise Fix feature lets you remove the grainy digital camera noise with one click.

For those users wanting to create studio artistic effects Paint Shop Pro X now has Black & White Film and Black & White Infrared Film effects, which you can use to simulate IR film or black-and-white film taken with colored filters. Many professional photographers shoot in Raw format, which can produce 16-bit images (16 bits per channel rather than the normal 8 bits per channel). To allow Paint Shop Pro X users to work with these images, Paint Shop Pro X supports 16-bit-per-channel functionality.

A New User Interface

The redesigned Layers palette provides thumbnail views of each image layer, making it easier to use and understand. The Browser has been enhanced to offer more options, such as a Zoom slider for quickly adjusting the size of thumbnail previews, EXIF editing, an option to download photos from a digital camera, and the ability to dock the Browser in different workspace locations. The Pick tool has been completely overhauled. Now you can select, move, resize, and rotate both raster and vector objects.

What's New Under the Hood

Some changes to Paint Shop Pro X are not visually apparent, especially if you are new to Paint Shop Pro, but to users of earlier versions the speed of performance is exciting. The first improvement you will notice is a faster start-up speed that allows you to view your photos in a flash. Another major improvement is that Paint Shop Pro now saves undo and redo data, so you will benefit from faster Undo/Redo of multiple steps, and by using File Open Pre-Processing, you can run an automatic script to save time when opening single images or batches of photos.

Paint Shop Album 6

With the inclusion of Photo Album 6 Standard Edition in Paint Shop Pro X, Paint Shop Pro really is the most complete photo editor on the market. Photo Album, shown in Figure 1-6, is the easiest way to manage your photos, plus it gives you tons of fun and creative options for sharing and more. Best of all, you get it absolutely free!

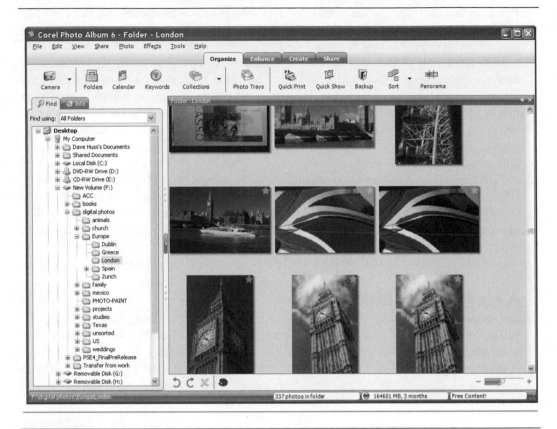

FIGURE 1-6 Paint Shop Album 6 is an essential tool for organizing and sharing your photos.

Video Tutorials

For those that are new to image editors or those who just want to see what else they can do, Corel included two hours' worth of Lynda.com video tutorials! These tutorials, included when you buy the upgrade, will show you how to make the most of this brand-new version.

Special Effects and Picture Tubes™

With over 500 special effects, Paint Shop Pro is sure to have the effect you need so you can create the look you want. And, of course, we haven't forgotten the Picture Tubes™. With Paint Shop Pro X you get a host of new Tubes that can only be found in this latest version.

Tour the Paint Shop Pro X Workspace

When you open Paint Shop Pro X the main program area, called the *workspace*, is displayed. Getting to know the Paint Shop Pro X workspace will save you time when it comes to getting a project done. There are a lot of items in the standard workspace, and if this is your first time using Paint Shop Pro it can seem a little daunting. At this point just learn the basic parts and don't concern yourself with what each part does. You will learn about these features as you use them in the step-by-step exercises throughout the book.

Depending on changes you may have already made to your workspace, when you start Paint Shop Pro X and open an image, your workspace resembles the one shown in Figure 1-7.

In the following sections we'll take a quick look at how some parts of the PSP workspace operate. For detailed information on how all of the many toolbar and palette options work, see Chapter 2 in the Paint Shop Pro X User Guide.

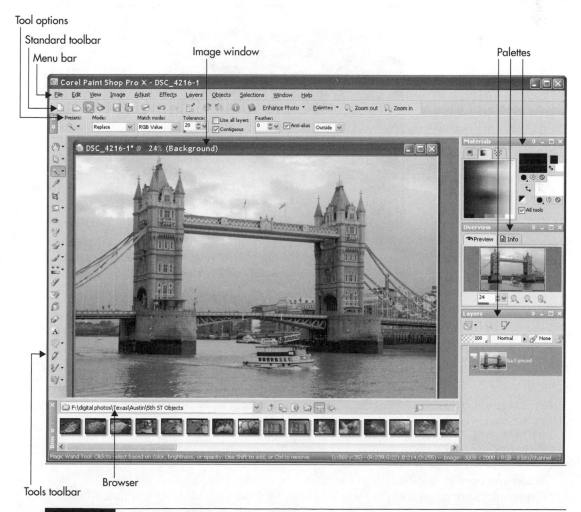

FIGURE 1-7   The Paint Shop Pro X workspace

Windows and Dialog Boxes

Throughout this book, you'll encounter terms such as windows and dialog boxes. So, what's the difference? A *window* is a display that allows you to do normal Windows functions such as change a file directory, select a file, and so on, but a window does not offer command buttons, such as OK or Cancel. Figure 1-8 shows an example of an image window.

Dialog boxes enable you to set options or specify text. To apply the choices you make, you are often given the chance to save the changes by clicking the OK button, or to ignore and discard your changes by clicking Cancel. Of course, other command buttons may be available, but OK and Cancel are the most common. The Page Curl dialog box (see Figure 1-9) is a good example.

FIGURE 1-8 The image window, like all other windows, doesn't offer command buttons or other choices.

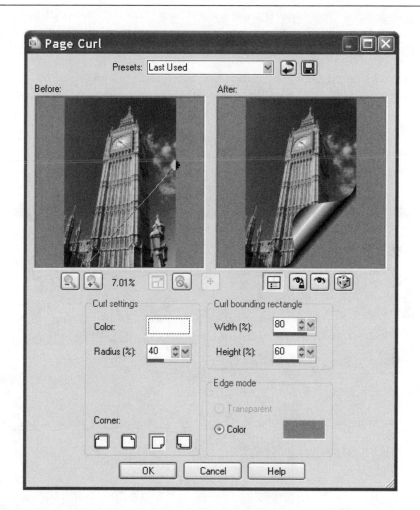

FIGURE 1-9   Unlike a window, a dialog box like this one offers you choices to make.

Toolbars

The toolbars offer icons that are associated to common functions. Of course, unless you use these icons frequently, it is easy to forget what each one does. To spark your memory, you can position your cursor over the icon and a screen tip displays the name of the tool (see Figure 1-10). And if that's not enough information, look at the left portion of the status bar to read a description of what the tool does.

NOTE *If the screen tip does not appear, choose View | Customize to open the Customize dialog box, click the Options tab, and ensure the Show Screen Tips on Toolbars checkbox is checked.*

Toolbars take up precious area in the workspace that could otherwise be used by the image window. You can dock a toolbar at the edge of a workspace, or float it anywhere on the screen. To give you the most room on your workspace, make a habit of closing infrequently used toolbars.

Screen tip

Status bar

FIGURE 1-10 Hold the cursor over an icon to display the screen tip and information about the tool in the status bar.

Moving and Hiding Toolbars

You can display or hide toolbars by one of the following ways:

- Choose View | Toolbars and toggle the toolbar on or off from the menu.

- Right-click any toolbar or palette, choose Toolbars, and then choose the toolbar from the context menu.

- To hide a specific toolbar or the palette that is floating, click the Close button on its title bar.

To move a docked toolbar, click and drag the toolbar handle to the desired location. The toolbar handle is depicted by a series of gray dotted lines.

> **NOTE** *When you are docking toolbars together they tend to snap in place, change sizes and shapes, and generally be a little bit of a challenge the first time you try it.*

The Standard and Tools Toolbars

Of the seven toolbars in Paint Shop Pro the two that you will use most often are the Standard and Tools toolbars. The Standard toolbar contains icons that are familiar to Windows users. The exceptions are the Undo and Redo buttons shown in Figure 1-11, which provide the quickest way to Undo and Redo actions you have done.

The Tools toolbar contains the basic tools required for most digital imaging. The down arrow at the right of an icon indicates the icon is part of a group of similar tools. When you click the down arrow, the group opens (see Figure 1-12) and you are able to select another tool from that group.

> **TIP** *When you select a tool, the options in the Tool Options palette change to reflect the options available for the selected tool.*

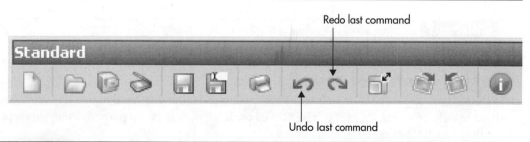

FIGURE 1-11   The Undo and Redo buttons in the Standard toolbar provide a fast way to undo and redo any action.

Preset Shape			P
Rectangle			G
Ellipse			Q
Symmetric Shape			H

FIGURE 1-12   Some tools in the Tools toolbar contain many different tools.

Taking Control of Your Palettes

Palettes may appear to take up a lot of your workspace, but they really are excellent tools to have readily available. Palettes can be docked on the right, left, or top portions of the workspace, or they can float over the workspace area.

To view a palette that is hidden, select View | Palettes and click the palette name you want. You can also view a palette by pressing its associated function key. The list of function key assignments for the palettes appears when you choose View | Palettes, as shown here.

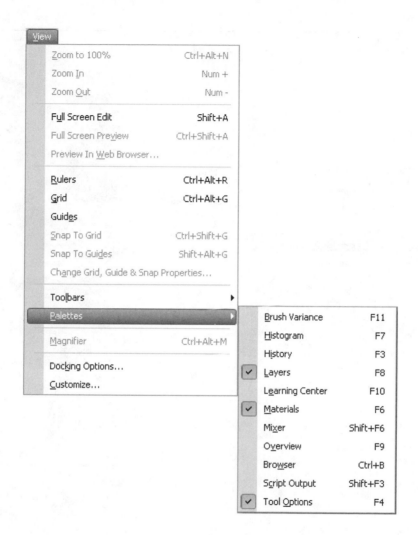

By default, the palettes are docked on the right side of the workspace (see Figure 1-13), with the exception of the Tool Options palette.

There are a lot of palettes. Only the palettes that are used most often are described in this chapter. The other palettes are described in Chapter 2 of the Paint Shop Pro User Guide and those palettes are also covered throughout this book in the step-by-step tutorials in which they are used.

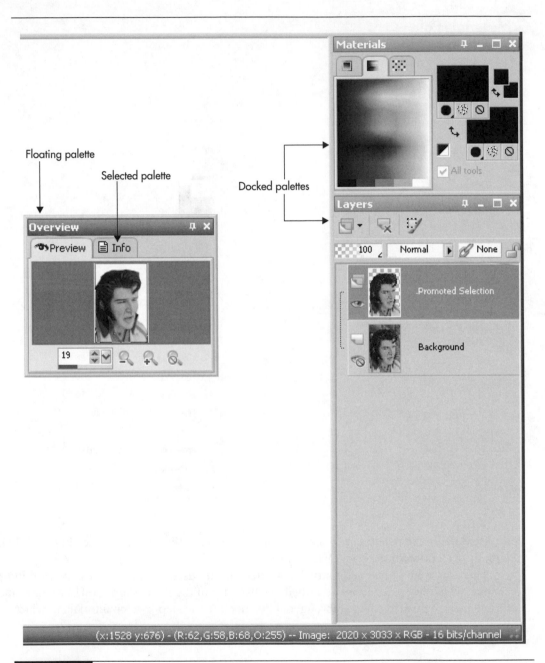

Floating palette

Selected palette

Docked palettes

FIGURE 1-13   Floating and docked palettes

Materials Palette

The Materials palette is where you choose your colors, canvas material, patterns, and styles. Think of it as your personal art supply store. Because there are so many options in this single palette, you may find it a little difficult to use. If so, don't worry—you'll get the hang of it in no time. This is definitely a palette you want to have available all the time.

> **TIP** *To show or hide the Materials palette, press* F6.

Layers Palette

The Layers palette displays the individual layers that make up an image. Layers are like sheets of clear plastic, each with a picture. When you lay the pieces of plastic on top of one another, they form a complete image. The fun thing about working with layers is that it allows you to make photo compositions with the ability to make changes to each individual layer. In the example shown in Figure 1-14, the photo of the young girl in the ball cap was pasted as a layer on top of a photo of the U.S. Supreme Court. Controlling the visibility of the layer allows her to become visible. As you learn to work with layers you will discover that you can also apply color correction to her layer and not the others, flip her layer so she is facing the other direction, and much more. You'll be using the Layers palette (shown here) quite a bit throughout the book.

> **TIP** *To show or hide the Layers palette, press* F8.

FIGURE 1-14   With the Layers palette you can turn layers on and off to change the photo. (Top) With layer visibility turned off, only the background can be seen. (Bottom) Making the top layer visible makes the girl visible and results in a completely different photo.

1

Tool Options Palette

The Tool Options palette is like a chameleon; its contents change to reflect the settings of the selected tool. Because different tools have different numbers of settings, the size of the palette can vary quite a bit. The undocked Tool Options palette shown here is for the Brush tool and is one of the largest Tool Options palettes in Paint Shop Pro X.

| **TIP** | *To show or hide the Tool Options palette, press* F4. |

Overview Palette

The Overview palette offers a thumbnail view of your entire image from which you can navigate. When you zoom in close to work on a specific area of a photo it is difficult to move to another part of the image without first zooming back out. With the Overview palette (shown here), a rectangle outlines the area you are currently working on. By clicking and dragging the rectangle you can instantly move to any part of the image. Click on the Info tab to see information about the image dimensions (height and width), color depth, memory used, and so on.

To show or hide the Overview palette, press F9.

Learning Center Palette

The Learning Center palette (see Figure 1-15) provides convenient access to simple tutorials designed to quickly get you started with common tasks. These tutorials not only tell you how to do a task or technique, but they have links you can click to run scripts that do the action for you. If you need to jump-start your creative juices, this may be a good place to begin.

 To show or hide the Learning Center palette, press F10.

Auto-Hiding Palettes and Toolbars

When it comes to saving space on your workspace, there is probably nothing better than the little-known feature built into palettes and toolbars called Auto-Hide. It is controlled by the tiny pushpin button icon in the toolbar/palette's title bar shown here.

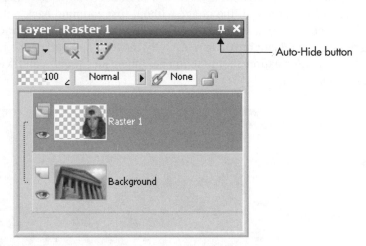

— Auto-Hide button

How the Auto-Hide feature operates changes based on whether the toolbar/palette is floating or docked. When the toolbar/palette is floating it works as follows:

- When the pushpin is pointing down, the toolbar/palette remains fully displayed when you move the cursor away from it.

- When the pushpin is pointing to the left (shown here), the toolbar/palette rolls up so that only its title bar is visible.

— Auto-Hide enabled

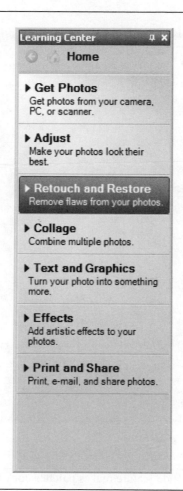

FIGURE 1-15   The Learning Center palette contains many tutorials organized by subject matter.

When the palette is docked the actions of Auto-Hide are different. Note that the following Auto-Hide actions only apply to docked palettes, not docked toolbars:

- When the pushpin button is pointing down, the palette operates normally and remains fully displayed in its docked position when you move the cursor away from it.

- When the pushpin is pointing to the left, the palette will slide into the workspace side as shown in Figure 1-16. To display the palette again, move the cursor over the tab.

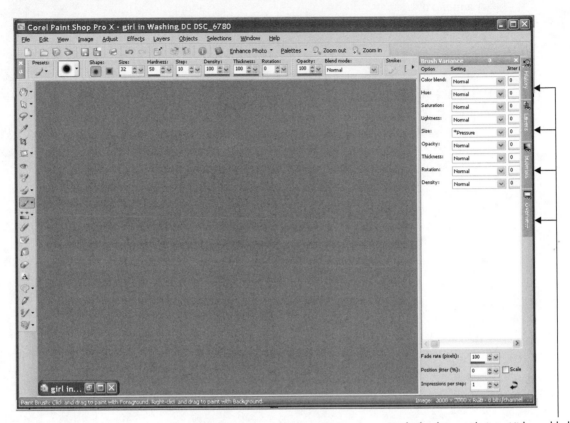

Docked palettes with Auto-Hide enabled

FIGURE 1-16 The Auto-Hide feature makes palettes dock fast against the side of the workspace out of the way.

> **TIP** *You can also animate the Auto-Hide action using an option in the Options tab of the Customize dialog.*

Menus

Menus offer the same options provided by the toolbar icons plus additional commands that are not as commonly used. Menus in Paint Shop Pro operate the same as menus in other Windows applications. If a menu item is grayed out, that option is not available. For example, if you open the Image menu and notice that the Crop to Selection option is grayed out, that's because a selection has not been defined in the image. The program doesn't know what you want to crop. Once you define a selection area, the Crop to Selection option will be available to you.

1

If a menu option is followed by an ellipsis (…), that option opens a dialog box. The dialog box enables you to specify parameters for a given action. For example, if you open the File menu and click Print, the Print dialog box appears. From there you can define specific output options for the image you want to print.

Shortcut Keys

Some frequently used menu options offer *shortcut keys*, also known as *hot keys*. Some hot keys are executed using a modifier key, such as the CTRL key (CTRL-S) or the ALT key (ALT-S).

That's all we're going to cover in this chapter. There is a lot more to learn about using the parts of PSP that we have seen, but you will find out as you go through the step-by-step tutorials in the following chapters. In the next chapter you will discover how to customize Paint Shop Pro and navigate your way through the maze of toolbars, palettes, and more.

The **easiest way** to turn your pictures into professional-looking **photos**—*fast!*

COREL®
Paint Shop™ Pro® X

Adjust & Retouch	Create & Collage	Graphics & Effects	Organize & Share
■ Fix any flaw	■ Erase backgrounds	■ Convert to black & white	■ Find any photo fast
■ Rotate, resize and crop	■ Add frames and edges	■ Paint with realistic art tools	■ Organize photo collections
■ Repair faded, damaged or scratched photos	■ Create calendars, cards, books picture CDs & more	■ Add text and shapes	■ Show off photo creations

CHAPTER 2

Set Up Shop

Corel has provided so many workspace customization options it can be a little bit daunting. In this chapter you'll learn how to set up a workspace that promotes creativity to the highest degree—or at least make your working experience a bit more relaxing. So grab a cup of your favorite beverage and let's get started.

Discover the Toolbars

In Chapter 1 you were introduced to menus, palettes, and toolbars. Before we go any further you need to understand that Paint Shop Pro X has seven toolbars displaying buttons that are useful for performing the most common tasks. When you position the pointer over a button, its name appears on a Tool Tip. The status bar displays additional information about the command. But just because a toolbar exists doesn't mean you have to use it. Having said that, let's see what toolbars are available and discover what each toolbar does. All of the toolbars in this section are shown in an undocked state.

The Standard Toolbar

Paint Shop Pro automatically displays this toolbar when you first run the program. Most of the icons on the Standard toolbar are familiar to Windows users. There are several icons that might be new to you: Browser palette, Scan Image (via TWAIN), Undo/Redo, Resize, and Rotate Left/Right. Clicking the Browser palette opens the Browser (a visual file organizer) at the bottom of the screen, while the TWAIN Acquire button activates the currently selected TWAIN device (usually a scanner). The place where you select a TWAIN device is buried pretty deep in the menu system (File | Import | TWAIN Source). Undo/Redo is self-explanatory, while Resize opens a dialog box with controls to change the size of the selected image. Rotate Left/Right offers a quick way to correct the orientation of the photo. Did your photo automatically rotate when you opened it? Some cameras add orientation information in the image file and Paint Shop Pro automatically detects it and rotates the image.

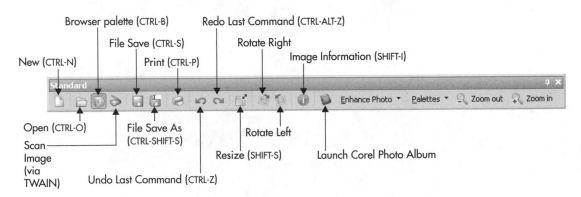

If you haven't installed any TWAIN devices, clicking the Scan Image (via TWAIN) button produces an error message.

We'll learn more about this toolbar in the next chapter, when we learn how to use a scanner to get images into Paint Shop Pro X.

The Tools Toolbar

Like the Standard toolbar, the Tools toolbar is essential for most operations in Paint Shop Pro. Typically, it is found docked on the left side of the screen but it can be docked anywhere in the workspace or left floating. On the Tools toolbar you will find many of the most commonly used tools. Please note that your Tools toolbar may look different from the one shown below because 10 of the 20 tool icons that appear on the toolbar may be displaying different tools. Let us explain.

Tool icons that have a black triangle next to them open to reveal a number of additional tools when the cursor is clicked on the black triangle. The number of tools each contains varies greatly as demonstrated by the two examples shown next.

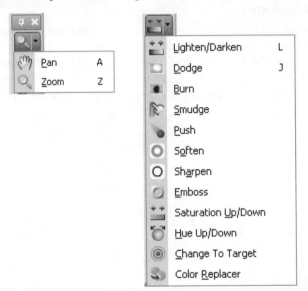

The Status Toolbar

The Status toolbar (also called the status bar) appears at the bottom of the screen as shown next. It displays the name of the currently selected tool and a brief description of what the tool does. The status bar is a unique toolbar. While you can toggle its display on and off via the View | Toolbars menu like the other toolbars, you cannot move it around (it can only appear at the bottom), nor can you customize it by adding or removing command icons to or from it.

Status toolbar

All of the previous toolbars are essential for most Paint Shop Pro operations. The next four toolbars only need to be open if you are working with that part of Paint Shop Pro they were designed to support, which brings up the obvious question—how do you open and close toolbars? Select View | Toolbars and a list of the seven toolbars appears, as shown next. Those toolbars that are already open have a checkmark beside them. Clicking on a toolbar name in this list toggles it on or off.

TIP   *You can also open the Toolbars menu by right-clicking any toolbar and selecting Toolbars.*

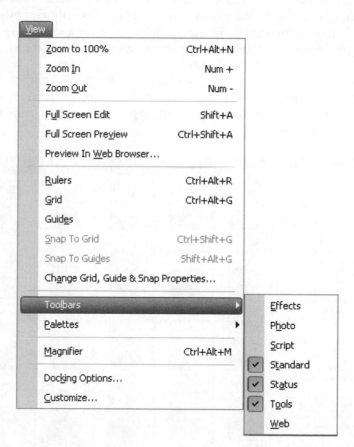

The Effects Toolbar

The Effects toolbar contains a mixed bag of useful and not-so-useful effects. For those who don't care for Corel's choice of effects included in this toolbar, you can customize it by removing rarely used effects (like Hot Wax) so it only contains effects that you use all of the time (like Drop Shadow or Gaussian Blur). The Effects toolbar, shown next, is one of the few toolbars that has a button that opens a large browser.

The Effect Browser, shown below, displays thumbnail previews of all of the Effects. Depending on your display settings, the thumbnails in the Effect Browser may appear to be too small. You can resize the thumbnail preview in the Effect Browser by choosing File | Preferences | General Program Preferences, clicking Display and Caching along the left side, and in the Effect Browser's Thumbnails group box setting a value in the Size (Pixels) control.

TIP   *There is a checkbox labeled Quick Render in the Effect Browser. If you are working with large images (3000 x 2000 pixels or larger) do not uncheck this box or the computer will begin processing all of the previews, which can tie up the program for several minutes.*

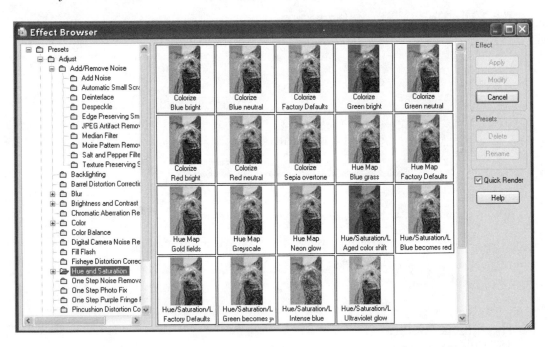

The Photo Toolbar

The Photo toolbar contains quick access to many of the more popular commands for enhancing your digital photos.

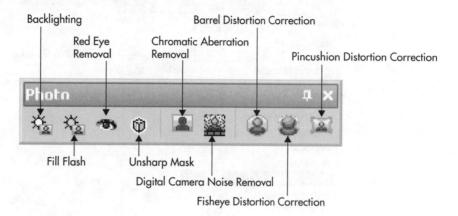

The Script Toolbar

The Script toolbar is a specialty toolbar that offers shortcuts for creating and running scripts. Scripts offer a way to automate often-used procedures and techniques so that they can be run at the click of a button.

Even if you never make a single script, you owe it to yourself to investigate the scripts that are already written for you. We're just introducing the toolbars in this chapter but here is a simple exercise that shows how powerful and easy to use these scripts can be.

Adding a Caption to a Photo Using a Script

You can use any photo you like for this exercise, but the photo Dog in Backpack.JPG is available from www.osborne.com if you want to use it.

1. Open the photo you will be using (File | Open).

2. Locate the Script toolbar and click the down arrow to open the list of stored scripts. Click on the SimpleCaption script as shown below.

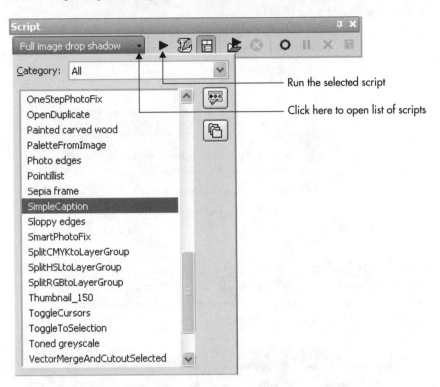

3. Click the Run Selected Script button, which opens the Enter Image Caption dialog box as shown next. Enter text that you want to appear as a caption to the photo and click OK. The result is shown in Figure 2-1.

Web Toolbar

The Web toolbar, which is divided into three sets of three tools, provides a quick way to access tools that are commonly used when working with Web graphics. In this day and age,

Dog in a Backpack.

FIGURE 2-1   Built-in scripts allow you to create projects like this with a single keystroke.

many people use software specifically designed to create Web pages, but it you like to roll your own, the Web toolbar will make the task easier.

The first three tools (beginning on the left) are the JPEG Optimizer tool, which exports (saves) a JPEG file with controllable compression; the GIF Optimizer tool, which exports (saves) a Compuserve GIF with transparency; and the PNG Optimizer tool, which exports (saves) an optimizer PNG file. Of the three tools, the one you will use most often is the JPEG Optimizer tool.

In the next set, the Preview in Web Browser tool is used to preview the currently selected image in a Web browser. The Image Slicer tool applies image slicing and rollovers. The last tool in the middle section is the Image Mapper tool, which applies image mapping.

The last set of tools begins with the Offset tool, which is used to offset an image. The Seamless Tiling tool creates an image suitable for seamless tiles. The last tool on the right is the Buttonizer tool, which applies a button effect to an image.

Customizing Paint Shop Pro

Let's learn how to optimize your workspace. Think of it as rearranging the equipment in your virtual digital-imaging lab to make it more efficient for your specific needs. This is just an introduction to customizing. See Chapter 13 for more information.

Customizing the Toolbars

As you become more proficient at using the toolbars and buttons, you'll find that you use certain buttons more than others. For this reason, Paint Shop Pro enables you to customize the buttons on each toolbar. Don't worry about messing up the toolbars in your copy of Paint Shop Pro. At any time you can return the toolbars to their default states. Corel has made this ability to customize toolbars a relatively simple process. You have the ability to do the following:

- **Remove Command Buttons from Existing Toolbars**   You may find it necessary to remove buttons that you don't use very often to make the toolbar smaller or less cluttered. Don't worry; you can always add them at a later time.

- **Customize Command Buttons of Existing Toolbars**   There are several toolbars that have buttons that might make you wonder what the designers were thinking when they made them. So, after you work with a toolbar a while and realize that a particular button isn't something you'll ever use, you should remove it.

Corel has provided detailed, step-by-step directions for adding and removing buttons from toolbars in the User Guide (Chapter 4: Customizing Paint Shop Pro).

Creating Your Own Custom Toolbar

If you want to make your own toolbar from scratch, you can do that as well. This is extremely helpful when you work on specific tasks and only want to deal with one toolbar instead of several.

To create your own toolbar, open the step-by-step directions for adding and removing buttons from toolbars in the online User Guide. Press F1 key to launch Help, click on the Contents tab, and click on the plus sign next to Customizing Paint Shop Pro. When the list of topics appear, choose Customizing Toolbars and Menus.

Deleting a Custom Toolbar

You cannot remove any of the default toolbars that came with Paint Shop Pro; you can only remove custom toolbars that you created. To remove a custom toolbar, complete the following steps:

1. Select View | Customize.

2. Click the Toolbars tab.

3. From the Toolbars list, select the toolbar you want to remove, and then click Delete.

4. To close the Customize dialog box, click Close.

Customizing the Menus

The command menus can be as personalized as your filing system at home: you can arrange things so you can find them when you need them without having to remember another person's logic. So customize away, and make those menus your own.

Additional Toolbar and Menu Options

You can control how your command icons and menus appear in Paint Shop Pro. You can even disable the Tool Tips from popping up each time you move your cursor over an item, although we recommend not turning them off.

To set additional toolbar and menu options, do the following:

1. Select View | Customize.

2. Click the Options tab.

3. Under the Toolbars and Palettes section (shown next), you can select one or more of the following options:

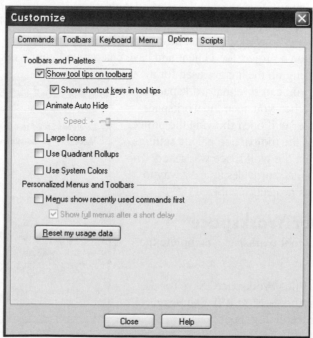

■ **Show Tool Tips on Toolbars** Displays a pop-up tip about the tool your cursor is currently suspended over. There is a chance that your copy of Paint Shop Pro will say Screen Tips instead of Tool Tips. The correct name is Tool Tips and early editions of Paint Shop Pro display the older (incorrect) name Screen Tips.

■ **Show Shortcut Keys in Tool Tips** When enabled, this causes any shortcut key that is assigned to be displayed along with the Tool Tips.

■ **Large Icons** Makes the icons in each toolbar larger and easier to see.

4. Under the Personalized Menus and Toolbars section, you can choose to have your most recently used commands appear first on a given menu by checking the Menus Show Recently Used Commands First option. If you select this option, the first time you open a drop-down menu the rest of the commands on a menu are hidden until you click the expansion button at the bottom of the abbreviated menu. If you enable the Show Full Menus After a Short Delay option, the rest of the menu drops down automatically after a few seconds. Sometimes, if you use a particular set of commands a lot for a project you end up with commands in the abbreviated menu that you no longer use. Clicking the Reset My Usage Data button erases the memory of your recently used menu commands.

5. To close the Customize dialog box, click Close.

Creating Your Own Workspace

The Paint Shop Pro workspace is made up of all the program's palettes, toolbars, and open images. Paint Shop Pro allows you to save any number of workspace arrangements, allowing you to load the specific workspace that best suits the work you intend to do. For example, if you are working on a project for a client and have customized your workspace with the Image Browser set to bring up the images used for a specific project, you can save that workspace and recall it at will. When you open the workspace, the Image Browser will open showing the project images and all of the toolbar and palette settings as they were when the workspace was saved. This not only saves time, it provides an easy way to keep your various projects organized.

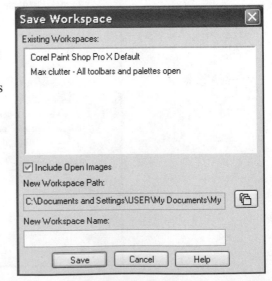

Saving Your Workspace

To save your current workspace, complete the following steps:

1. Choose File | Workspace | Save (or use the shortcut SHIFT-ALT-S). The Save Workspace dialog box opens.

2. To change the path to where the workspace settings are saved, click the Edit Paths button and specify the path in the Save To field. However, we recommend that you use the default path so all of your saved workspaces are in the same location. In the New Workspace Name text box, type the name you want to give to your workspace, and then click Save.

Loading a Custom Workspace

To load a custom workspace, complete the following steps:

1. Choose File | Workspace. You have two choices at this point. If the workspace you want is one of the last three workspaces you have opened, it appears on the drop-down list as shown next. If it isn't on the list select Load (SHIFT-ALT-L).

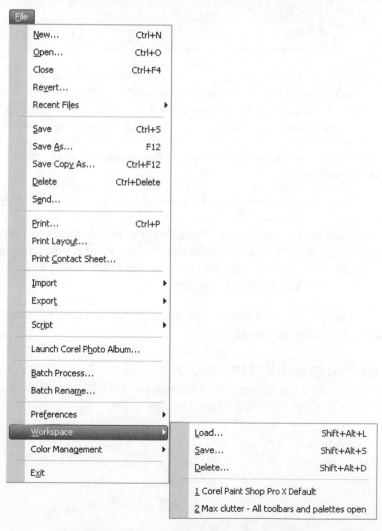

2. After selecting Load, a warning message appears (shown next) saying that any modifications you have made to the current workspace will be lost and asking if you want to save your current workspace. If you click the Yes button, you will open the Save Workspace dialog box. If you don't want to save the current workspace, click No.

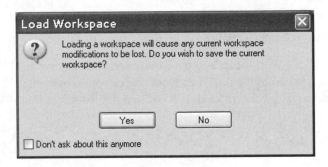

The workflow when loading workspaces is a little awkward. Unless you have customized your current workspace, you won't need to save it. To save time, you should consider checking Don't Ask About This Anymore, which lets you load a new workspace without the option to save the current workspace.

3. From the dialog box, select the name of the workspace you want to load, and then click Load.

Preferences

When you set preferences, you instruct Paint Shop Pro how to handle various aspects of your image-editing needs. Specify default file locations, color settings, format preferences, and much, much more. These preferences become part of the workspace environment and can be set for each workspace you have saved.

If you want your preferences saved, make certain you save the workspace when you are done making changes.

General Program Preferences

When you open the File menu and click Preferences, you will find seven categories of preferences that you can customize (shown next).

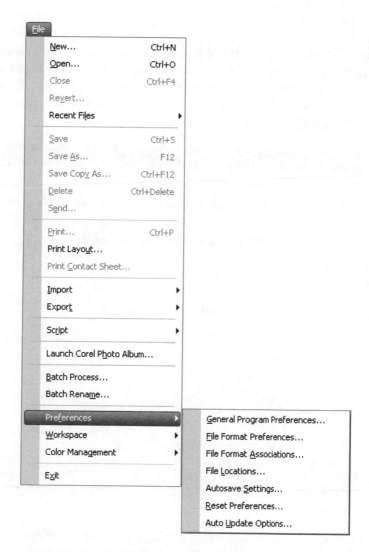

There are so many settings in the Preferences settings that it would take a few hours just to read all about them, much less understand them. The good news is that most of the preferences that will be of interest to you are found in the General Program Preferences dialog, whose tabs are described in the following sections.

Undo Tab

Click this tab to specify undo limits and how much command history memory you want to reserve for each open image. The higher the limit, the more commands can be stored. You can also compress the undo information to save memory. Depending on the speed of your system, this may or may not be a convenient choice. Unless you have extremely limited memory, we strongly suggest you do not disable the Undo feature.

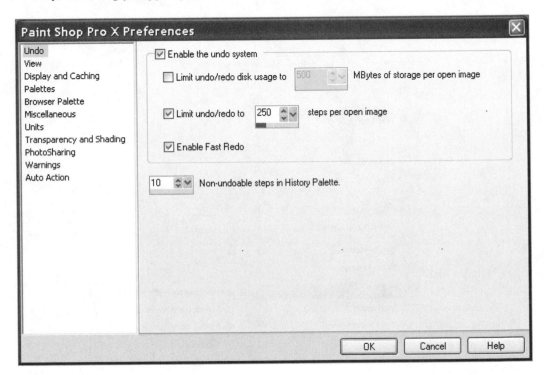

View Tab

Click this tab to specify zoom and image display preferences. For example, you may want the image to fill the screen rather than fit into a predefined window size. These are just the default settings; you can always change these settings in the program when you need to.

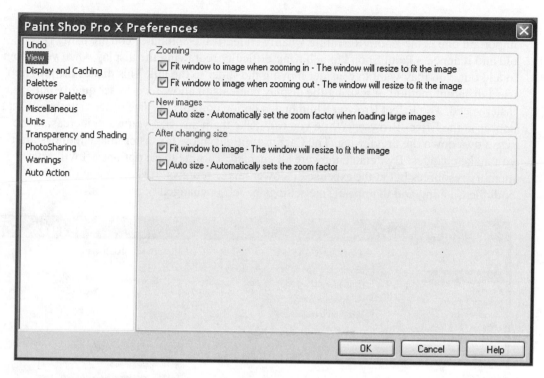

Display and Caching Tab

Click this tab to control the appearance of cursors and to access other controls that affect how fast the display is updated. The first checkbox, Re-use Last Type in File Save-As Dialog, determines the file type to default to when saving a file. If checked, every time you go to save a file Paint Shop Pro will attempt to save it in the last-used file format instead of the file format of the open file. For example, if you are working on a JPEG format file and go to save it, the program will offer to save it in the last file format that you saved instead of JPEG. You can still override this default behavior, but unless you have a specific need for this feature you should keep it unchecked (which is the default setting). The next settings of interest affect how your cursor appears on the screen. If you check Use Precise Cursors the shape of the cursor is not determined by the tool selected but rather always appears as a crosshair icon. It is off by default and probably best left that way. If the Show Brush Outlines option is unchecked the cursor size no longer changes to reflect the brush size being used. It is strongly recommend that you keep the default (brush outline) setting.

The other sections control how Paint Shop Pro regenerates the display. The most important one is the Zoom/Rescaling Quality slider. If the computer you are using is very old and it appears Paint Shop Pro is having difficulty redrawing the display when you zoom in and out, you may want to consider moving the slider to the left. This makes the program use a different method of resizing the display contents to allow for a lesser quality but a faster speed. The Effect Browser Thumbnails option controls the size of the thumbnails that appear in the Effect Browser. While you can make them any size you want, increasing the size slows down the previewing. The Caching options allow for faster image redraws after you make changes. By default, they are all enabled. Turning these options off will save memory resources but at the expense of slower image redraws. It is recommended that both the Caching and thumbnail size settings be left unchanged.

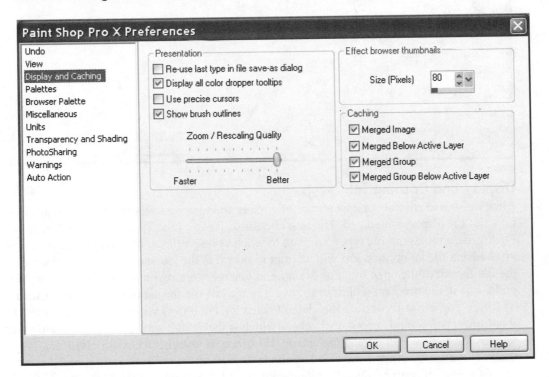

Palettes

Click this tab to specify how your color palette in the Materials palette displays colors and also to set which palettes can and cannot be docked. These options are helpful in rare situations when you need to specify color in HSL rather than the standard RGB. You can specify how you want the color palette to present the colors. Unless you have a specific reason to change it, leave it alone. The default setting for palette docking doesn't allow the Histogram to be docked. It isn't that Corel doesn't like the Histogram; this is its default setting because when you dock the Histogram it is very hard to read. If you are using the Histogram we recommend that you set it to Auto-Hide (see Chapter 1).

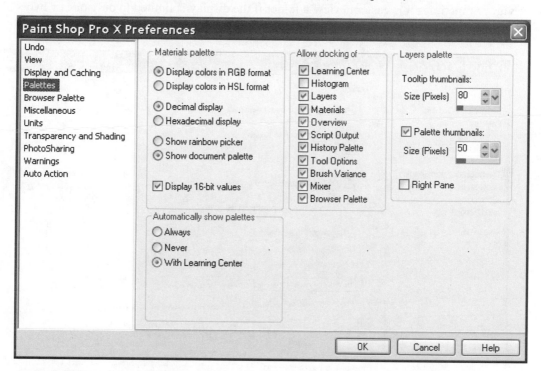

Browser Palette Options

Click this tab to specify how your Browser palette displays image thumbnails. You can change the size of the thumbnail using the control at the top-right corner of the Browser palette (it has a magnifying glass icon) and choose whether to show the thumbnails as a filmstrip or not by clicking the Photostrip View button in the set of controls just to the right of the path field in the Browser palette. If you use the Browser a lot there are a few settings that are recommended. First, make sure the Save Browser Files to Disk option is checked. When the Browser generates thumbnails, it saves the thumbnails in a special cache file along with the other images in the folder. If this feature should get unchecked (it is checked by default), every time you open a file folder the Browser will take several minutes to generate the thumbnails.

TIP *The only time you should turn the Save Browser Files to Disk feature off is when using the Image Browser to read images from a digital camera or card reader. These devices are very slow and if the memory card is full it may cause an error when Paint Shop Pro attempts to write a cache file to the card.*

The other setting that is often ignored is the File Format Exclusions button. From here you can pick what file extensions you want the Browser to ignore when opening a folder to view. Sometimes it is easier to view a folder if the display is limited to only one or two specific files formats.

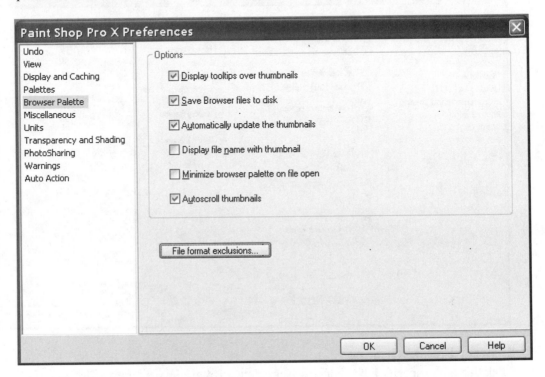

The settings of the remaining tabs on the General Preferences, covered in the following sections, should be left in their default state.

Miscellaneous
Click this tab to specify the number of recently used files you want to list, and how to handle images stored on the Clipboard when exiting the program.

Units
Click this tab to specify how to show units of measure. There may be times when inches work better than pixels. You can also specify the default resolution, which is very useful when designing Web elements versus printable images.

Transparency and Shading
Click this tab to specify how to handle transparent backgrounds. The default setting is adequate for most situations. Change the colors if the default colors are too close to a dominant color in the image you are working on.

PhotoSharing

This page defines what photo sharing service is used when it is accessed from within Paint Shop Pro. By default, the two most popular photo sharing services are listed. There is a Check for Updates link that takes you to the Corel Web site to see if there are additional photo sharing services that have been added.

Warnings

Click this tab to specify the types of warnings you want displayed in given circumstances.

Auto Action

Click this tab to specify which actions you want performed automatically and when they should occur.

File Format Preferences

This dialog box (File | File Format Preferences) specifies how Paint Shop Pro will handle or display specific types of files. While this offers a great deal of control over how the metadata in a file is managed, the settings are another batch of settings that should remain unchanged.

File Format Associations

To select the types of files you want to associate with Paint Shop Pro, choose File | Preferences | File Format Associations. The following dialog appears:

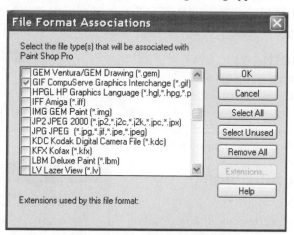

After you make your selections, whenever you double-click files with any of the selected file extensions, they will automatically open in Paint Shop Pro. In most situations you do not want JPEG associated with Paint Shop Pro. This was also covered in Chapter 1 in the installation section, but it is worth repeating. If JPEG is associated with Paint Shop Pro, then anytime that you double-click a photo in an e-mail it will launch Paint Shop Pro rather than the Microsoft Photo Fax Viewer. Paint Shop Pro takes some time to launch before it can display the photo whereas the Microsoft Photo Fax Viewer opens instantly.

File Locations

To specify the preferred locations for specific types of files, choose File | Preferences | File Locations. The following dialog appears:

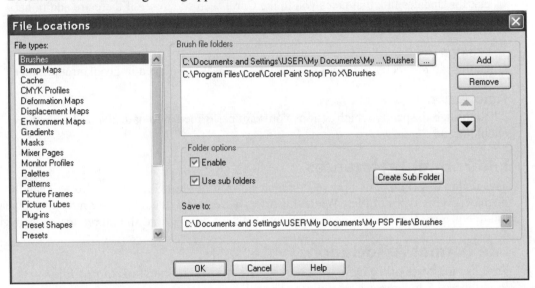

If you are working on a particular project, it is helpful to create a directory for that project and store all associated files under that directory.

Autosave Settings

To specify how often you want Paint Shop Pro to save your work, choose File | Preferences | Autosave Settings. The dialog appears as shown at right.

If you are not disciplined at remembering to save your work periodically, this feature is a real treasure.

Resetting Application Preferences

To reset various preferences to their original factory settings, choose File | Preferences | Reset Preferences. The dialog appears as shown at right.

This is a good way to start from scratch if you make many changes that you are not thrilled about.

Color Management

The purpose of color management is to try and get the printed photos as close as possible to the colors displayed on your monitor. We say get as close as possible because the colors will always be different because the colors on your monitor are backlit—they radiate light. Colors in your printed photos are illuminated by reflected light (sun, lamps, etc.). Paint Shop Pro offers some features that allow you to calibrate how colors in your monitor appear.

When you choose File | Color Management, the following three choices appear: Color Management, Color Working Space, and Monitor Calibration.

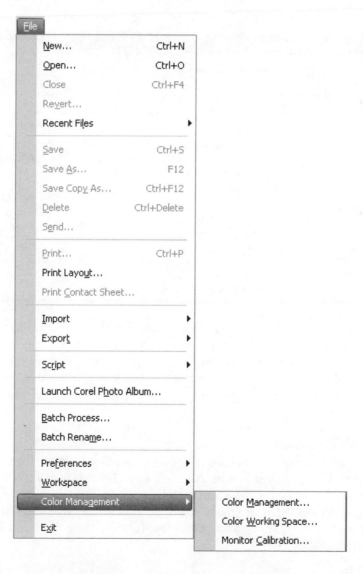

Color Management Dialog Box

When you open the Color Management dialog box (shown next) Paint Shop Pro offers the option to Enable Color Management (by default it is disabled). This option allows the use of the color management built into Windows in conjunction with specific printer and monitor color profiles. If you are preparing professional quality digital images, you can enable or disable color management settings. You can set your printer to simulate a printing press by choosing the Proofing option, choosing a device in the Emulated Device Profile drop-down list, and choosing the appropriate option in the Rendering Intent drop-down list.

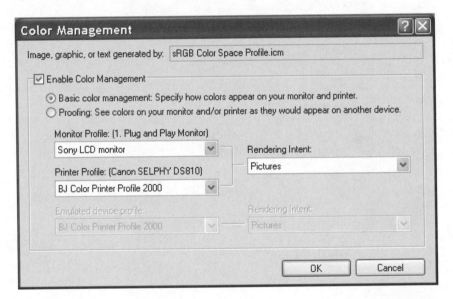

Additionally, every RGB image in Corel Paint Shop Pro has a profile associated with it. By default, these advanced color settings are enabled, allowing the application to make use of a consistent color working space. You can define advanced features for color working spaces and profiles. For example, you can set a CMYK profile that determines how CMYK images are processed when you split or combine CMYK channels, or when you output to a CMYK TIF file.

Color Working Space

This dialog box (shown next) is used to define what color working space Paint Shop Pro uses when working on an image. All consumer digital cameras use an sRGB color working space (also called a *color model*) which is why the default color working space for Paint Shop Pro is sRGB. If you are working with images that use a different color space (like Adobe RGB 1998), you can set the working space that Paint Shop Pro uses from this dialog box.

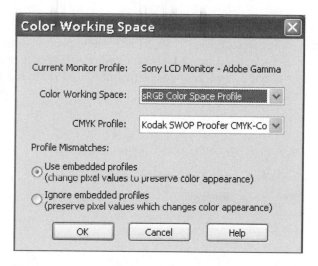

Monitor Calibration

Paint Shop Pro provides a wizard-style monitor calibration procedure. The accuracy that can be achieved with this approach depends on a lot of factors including your room lighting, your eyesight, and others. This calibration routine was designed for CRT monitors and its use with LCD (flat panel displays) may not produce the most accurate results.

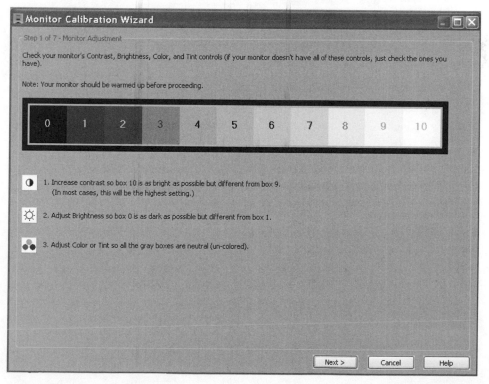

Creating the critically accurate monitor and printer profiles requires third-party color profiling tools that range in cost from \$150–\$1500. These professional tools include software or hardware for determining how your monitor and printer produce color.

Now that you have configured your copy of Paint Shop Pro, in the next chapter you will learn how to get images and photos into your computer.

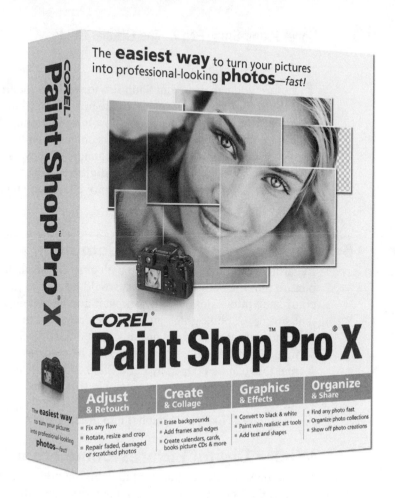

CHAPTER 3

Getting Pictures into Paint Shop Pro

Before you can use Paint Shop Pro to work on pictures you must first get the photos into the computer. Digital cameras are now more common than film cameras and with the advent of inexpensive scanners we now have the ability to digitize our existing treasured photos into digital form as well. In this chapter you will learn how to get pictures into the computer from digital cameras and scanners so they can be opened in Paint Shop Pro. First, you will discover how to set up your digital camera to speed up the transfer of pictures and how to use your scanner to obtain improved output and ultimately better pictures from Paint Shop Pro.

Bringing Images into Your Computer

Regardless of what you plan to do with or to an image, the first step requires that you get the picture into the computer. While it would be nice to just stick your favorite photograph or color slide into a slot on your computer and have it appear on the computer screen, it isn't that simple. A photograph must first be converted to a digital file before it can be opened in Paint Shop Pro. And not just any digital file—it must be in one of the many graphic file formats. Some images, like photographs taken using digital cameras, are already in a file format that can be opened by Paint Shop Pro, while photographs taken with traditional film cameras must be converted into graphic files using a scanner. In this section we will learn about available sources of digital images and what equipment is necessary to convert non-digital images (like photographs) into graphic files.

Where Digital Pictures Come From

Digital pictures that can be used in Paint Shop Pro are available from a variety of sources. Most of the images you will work on come from either a digital camera or a scanner.

Getting Pictures from Digital Cameras

In the span of a few short years digital cameras have changed the way we approach photography. Early digital cameras were expensive and produced poor quality photographs. Today, digital photography has almost completely replaced film photography. In fact, it has become such an important part of the digital experience that most computers sold today have a card reader built into the front panel allowing you to insert the digital camera memory card directly into the computer; other computers offer USB connectors in the front panel to allow the connection of a card reader.

Making Digital Pictures from Traditional Photographs

Scanners, like digital cameras, have also enjoyed a dramatic price drop over the past few years and as a result they have become a normal part of many home systems. In 1989, a scanner that could only scan black-and-white photographs sold for over $3,000. Today, there are a variety of good color scanners that sell for less than $100. A scanner can turn almost any photograph, printed image, or even 3D object (like a coin collection or flowers) into a graphic image file that can be brought into Paint Shop Pro for enhancement, correction, or restoration. Even if you own a digital camera, you may still need a scanner because most certainly you have old photo albums with photographs or negatives tucked away that should be scanned and converted into digital images if only to preserve them.

Connecting a Digital Camera to Your Computer

Digital cameras store pictures on internal removable memory devices. Whichever type of media you use, you need a way to get the pictures off of the camera's media into the computer. To do this you need a physical or possibly a wireless connection between the camera and the computer. This can be done using the following types of connections:

- Dedicated card reader
- USB connection to the camera/docking cradle
- Wireless (look for this type of connectivity to continue to gain in popularity)

Speeding Things Up with Card Readers

Card readers come in several different sizes, shapes, and interfaces. For desktop computers, the most popular dedicated readers use a USB interface. Dedicated USB readers offer the advantage of being *hot swappable* (meaning that they can be plugged into the computer or removed without the necessity of restarting the computer), which is an advantage that not many other interfaces can offer. The PC Card (PCMCIA) readers are quite popular with laptops due to their small size and low cost. The PC card adapter shown here is a 32-bit CompactFlash card reader. It is the fastest card reader available at the time of this writing.

Photo courtesy of Lexar Media

Regardless of the type of reader that is used, when a card reader is connected to the computer the camera's media appears in My Computer/Windows Explorer as a disk drive.

What Is the Fastest Way to Transfer Photos?

Most new digital cameras today can connect directly to your computer using a USB cable. At the moment there are two different speeds for USB interfaces. USB 2.0 is the newest and moves pictures at speeds 40 times faster than the original USB 1.0/1.1. Some digital cameras advertise that they have a USB 2.0 interface but if you read the fine print you discover that the transfer rate is actually at USB 1.0/1.1 speeds (approximately 12 million bits per second). This isn't false advertising, it's just that the USB 2.0 specification works at both speeds. Another interface is called FireWire or IEEE 1394 (Sony calls it iLink). This interface is as fast as USB 2.0 but was used almost exclusively for connecting video cameras and some professional digital SLR (D-SLR) cameras. FireWire's popularity with camcorders is fading and, with the exception of Mac FireWire, isn't being seen in newer computers.

With all of this talk about the USB and FireWire interfaces, it might surprise you to know that one of the fastest ways to get pictures from the digital camera into the computer is often using a card reader. Surprised? It's because the processor in the digital camera controls the speed of the transfer when using a USB connection and quite frankly it is relatively slow. When a card reader is used the transfer is controlled by your computer, which is many times faster than your camera. Still, as newer models of USB 2.0 cameras appear in the market they are getting faster all the time and someday may be faster than card readers.

Using wireless to transfer photos to your computer has been an expensive option in professional digital single lens reflex (D-SLR) cameras for years. At the time this book was written there was only one consumer camera that offered wireless communication using the popular IEEE 802.11B/G, but with the increasing popularity of wireless networking expect to see many cameras offering wireless in the immediate future.

Moving Digital Camera Pictures into the Computer

When you connect a digital camera or card reader to your computer it is the Windows XP operating system (not Paint Shop Pro) that detects it and responds. If it is the first time you connected your camera or card reader, the operating system may ask you for additional software drivers and your camera may need an additional action in the menu, such as accepting a PC setting.

If your digital camera software was installed before you installed Paint Shop Pro, its photo downloader may still appear when you connect your camera. If you have not installed Album, a Windows XP Action dialog box appears. The choices that appear in the dialog box will depend on how the USB connection on your camera is configured and what software you have installed on your computer.

Downloading with Corel Photo Downloader

Corel's preferred solution is to employ the Corel Photo Downloader of Album to bring the images from the camera into the computer. If you have installed Album the Photo Downloader (shown next) will automatically appear. It is a wizard-style interface that offers you the choices of downloading all of the files, downloading specific files, or taking no action at all. Its use is explained later in this chapter. You also have the option to always do a selected action without prompting by clicking the Always Do the Selected Action for This Device checkbox. If you have not installed Album there are several other ways to transfer the photos into your computer.

If you have not installed the software that came with your digital camera, it will appear in My Computer as a hard drive and not a camera. Use the following method to access images directly from your camera. Typically, your camera will be labeled Removable Drive, or possibly after the name of the camera (for example, Kodak DC40 Camera). If your camera appears in My Computer as a hard drive, then you can directly access the images on the camera from Paint Shop Pro just as if they were on a hard drive or CD-ROM. Here is how to do it.

Open Paint Shop Pro, choose File | Open, and browse to your camera just as you would a hard drive. You should see the images inside the camera. Now you can select the images and open them in Paint Shop Pro for editing. This technique may not work with every USB-equipped camera ever made but it should work for most. It is very slow to open images directly on a camera, so your first action after opening the image should be to save it onto the hard drive of your computer before you begin working on it.

USB Settings of Your Camera

Most digital camera owners are unaware that their camera has two different USB modes: Mass Storage (on some cameras it is called Normal) and PTP (Picture Transfer Protocol), which may be selectable through the camera's menu system like the one from Dave's Nikon camera shown in Figure 3-1. Many newer consumer cameras do not offer the option of selecting the USB modes. If your camera does not, it is probably set to Mass Storage.

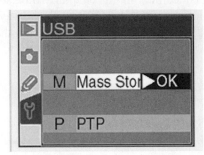

Photo courtesy of Nikon

FIGURE 3-1   USB settings in a camera are changed through the menu system.

Because PTP can only be used with Windows XP, by default most digital cameras are set to Mass Storage (MSC), which works with all operating systems. With the camera's USB setting set to MSC, when the USB cable of the camera is connected to the computer and the camera is switched on, the camera is recognized as a removable drive like a floppy or hard disk drive.

Moving Pictures Without Photo Downloader

If you are using a card reader or your digital camera appears to Windows XP as a hard drive, you have several choices you can make from the action dialog box (shown in Figure 3-2). While the actual choices that appear on your computer depend on which applications you have installed, and there are several that do not appear on the list until you scroll down, the following choices are available on all computers:

- ■ **Copy Pictures to a Folder on My Computer**   This choice launches the Microsoft Scanner and Camera Wizard, which is described in the next section. The wizard moves photos from your camera into a folder. Even though this option appears when you plug a card reader into the computer or use a camera set to MSC, don't use it because it stops when it fails to detect a camera and you must use the Cancel button to exit the wizard.

- ■ **View Pictures on Removable Media Using Paint Shop Pro**   Choosing this launches Paint Shop Pro with the Browser pointed to the card reader or camera. It doesn't transfer the photos, and trying to view images on a camera media card is never recommended because it is so slow.

- ■ **Open Folder to View Files Using Windows Explorer**   Choosing this one causes the contents of the camera or memory card to appear in a folder in Windows Explorer. From here you can drag the folder to another destination on your hard drive, as we'll learn later in the chapter.

FIGURE 3-2   The action list provides several choices for transferring photos.

■ **Launch Camera Software**   This may be the best choice depending on how good your camera's software is. Most software that comes with your digital camera provides a full range of features like image management, camera control, and the ability to rotate, flip, name, and move pictures to and from the camera.

NOTE   *When using the camera to transfer photos from your camera you should be aware that it can drain your battery pretty quickly. Consider attaching the AC adapter to your camera to prevent battery exhaustion in mid-transfer, which can damage the files being transferred at the time.*

Using the Microsoft Scanner and Camera Wizard (XP Only)

If your digital camera is recognized as a digital camera when it is connected to your computer, you have the option to move pictures from the camera into the computer using the Microsoft Scanner and Camera Wizard. It provides a very simple way to move pictures directly from your digital camera to the computer. Until recently, the Microsoft Scanner and Camera Wizard in XP did not support transfer of Raw format, but there is now a patch available from the Microsoft Web site that allows the wizard to transfer Raw files produced by cameras made by the major camera manufacturers.

Here is how to use the wizard to move pictures into your computer:

1. When you plug the camera into the computer, select the Microsoft Scanner and Camera Wizard option and an introductory splash screen opens. Click the Next button to start the wizard.

2. The wizard next reads the image card and displays thumbnails of the images that are contained on the card (shown next). From this box you can rotate the pictures using the two icons at the bottom-left corner of the dialog box. Just click on the thumbnail of the photo you want to rotate and click the appropriate icon. The next icon is clicked to display file information about the image and the last icon can be used to take a picture with the attached camera. That is one of those features that makes you scratch your head and wonder how you would ever use it.

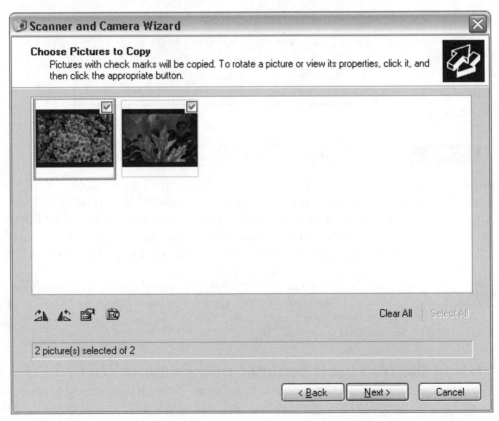

3. After you have all the photos in their correct orientation, just click the checkboxes of all the photos that you want to transfer and click the Next button. This opens the dialog box (shown next) used to select the name of the files and the location.

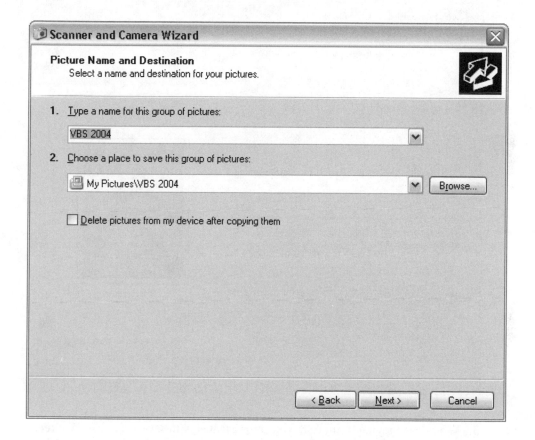

4. There are a few things to be aware of when using this dialog box. When using the wizard to transfer files from your camera, the original filenames assigned by the camera are replaced with the name you enter in step 1 on the screen followed by sequential numbers. For example, if you enter the name Vacation, the filenames will be Vacation001.JPG, Vacation002.JPG, and so on. Select where you want to put the files in step 2 on this screen. There is an option that, if checked, removes the images from the camera after they are transferred. We recommend not using this option. It is a simple matter to format the card with your camera after you are confident that the images have been safely stored in your computer. Click the Next button to begin copying the photos.

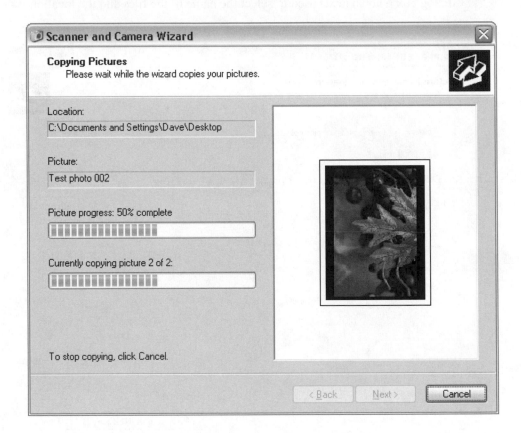

5. When the copying is finished, you are presented with several choices. We recommend that you keep the Nothing option checked since all of the options available to you can be better accomplished using Paint Shop Pro.

Moving Pictures Using a Card Reader

If you use a card reader attached to the computer, the operating system makes pictures appear in a folder in a hard drive. It has a drive letter and the name of the folder is usually the name and model of the camera. Every camera manufacturer has its own naming conventions but they all use the same file structures. When you open the drive (media card) you may find a folder named DCIM (Digital Camera Image) and inside that folder is another folder that will have either the name assigned by the camera or a custom name made by the photographer.

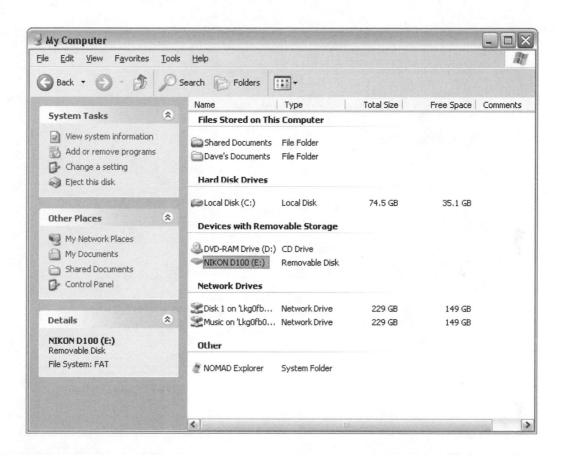

TIP	*If you have a USB 2.0 card reader but your computer only has USB 1.0/1.1 ports, the operating system will flash a message telling you this when you connect the reader. The card reader will work; it will just work at the slower USB 1.0/1.1 speed.*

Removing Your Card Reader

Whether you are using a USB or a PC Card (PCMCIA) card reader, when you are finished using the card reader there is a correct way to remove it from your computer that you should always use. Here is how to do it:

1. Locate the Safely Remove Hardware icon in the System Tray. Double-click it to open the dialog box shown in Figure 3-3.

2. Select the device and click the Stop button. If the operating system thinks that some application is still using the media card you may receive a message telling you that the device cannot be stopped. Check and make sure that an application isn't pointing

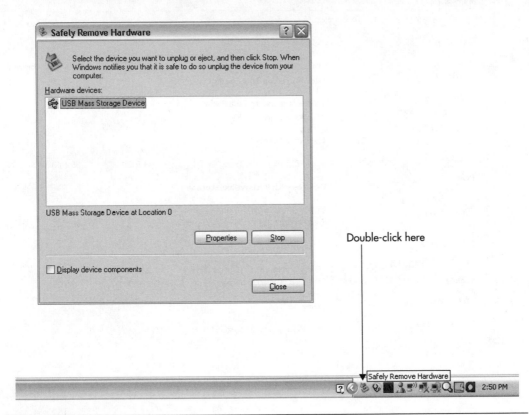

Double-click here

FIGURE 3-3   Using the Safely Remove Hardware feature is the best way to remove a card reader.

to the card reader. Most times you will see a message in a balloon in the Notification Area of the Taskbar telling you the card reader can be removed (as shown next).

When the card reader is disconnected from the computer the hard drive disappears from My Computer. The two most popular approaches for transferring photos when using a card reader are using Windows' My Computer or the software that came with your camera.

3

Transferring Pictures Using My Computer

Moving picture files from a card reader into your computer is done in the same manner as moving any computer file in Windows. You can either copy and paste or drag and drop.

Transferring Pictures Using Copy and Paste

1. Double-click the My Computer icon on the Windows Desktop.

2. We recommend creating a new folder for holding the photos being transferred from the card reader, even if only temporarily. To create a folder, right-click the Windows Desktop and when the secondary menu appears, choose New | Folder.

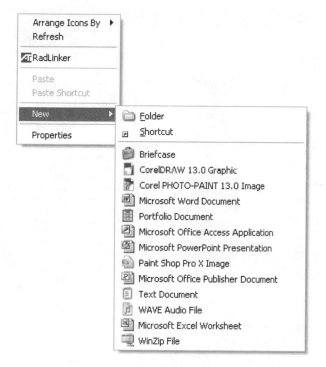

3. A new folder appears. Give the new folder a name that indicates what's inside. To rename the folder, right-click on the folder and select Rename. The folder name becomes highlighted and at that point you can change the name.

4. Locate the picture files you want to move from the card reader to the computer and either click on the individual picture or use CTRL-A to select them all.

5. After the files are selected copy them to the Windows Clipboard (CTRL-C) and then open the new folder you just created and use the Paste command (CTRL-V) to copy the files to their new location.

Transferring Pictures Using Drag and Drop

1. Do steps 1–3 as shown earlier in "Transferring Pictures Using Copy and Paste."

2. Click and hold down the left mouse button on any of the selected files while dragging the files to the desired destination folder on your desktop (as shown next). A copy of the picture files appears in the destination folder.

Click and drag from here to here

My Vacation

3

Lossy and Lossless Compression

All digital cameras apply JPEG compression to the photos so they can get the maximum number of pictures into the camera's storage media. While JPEG compression can really reduce the size of a picture file, it is a *lossy* compression, meaning it degrades the picture slightly when it compresses it. Increasing the amount of JPEG compression that is applied to the picture gives you a smaller picture file; therefore, more pictures fit into your camera's memory, but the quality of the picture is reduced. These are the facts.

There is an urban myth about JPEG compression that is not true so this seems like a good time to set the record straight. It is believed that JPEG images are degraded each time the image is moved to a new location, but it is not true. Simply copying a JPEG picture from the camera to the computer, or opening or displaying the picture, does not harm it in any way. You can copy a JPEG as many times as you want and it will not affect the quality. The exception is if photo editing is performed on the picture before it is saved—then more degradation happens to the image. This is why you should always save pictures you are working on in a losslcss format like TIF or PSP (Paint Shop Pro's native format.)

| TIP | *If you use the right mouse button to drag the files, you will have the option of moving the files to the new location (instead of just copying them), which means the files in the card reader are deleted after being copied.* |

Using the Browser Palette to Move Pictures

The Browser palette is a visual picture manager that provides an easy way to move, view, and manage images on your computer. The operation of the Browser couldn't be simpler.

1. With Paint Shop Pro open, launch Browser (CTRL-B) or click the Browser button. The Browser window, as shown next, opens and displays the currently selected folder on top and thumbnails of its contents on the right. Typically, the Browser is docked on the bottom of the screen. The Browser palette, shown next, is floating in the workspace. The size of the Browser palette can be changed like all other palettes—by dragging any edge of the palette. The size of the thumbnails is controlled by the slider on top

with the magnifying glass icon. Adjust the size of the palette and the thumbnails to make viewing your photos comfortable for your display.

Browser button

2. With the tools on the top of the palette, you can select the folder containing the pictures you want to work with. The first time you open a folder, Paint Shop Pro will take a few moments to generate the preview thumbnails in the area on the right side of the window. Once the Browser has created the thumbnails, it saves them in a special file in the same folder so that the next time you open it, the thumbnails appear instantly.

3. Select individual pictures by clicking on them one time, select multiple pictures by holding down CTRL while clicking the thumbnails, or select all of the pictures in the folder by pressing CTRL-A.

4. Once selected, you can also load the picture into Paint Shop Pro by dragging it into the Paint Shop Pro image window or just by double-clicking the thumbnail.

> **TIP**   *Place the cursor over a thumbnail in the Browser and after a moment a Tool Tip will open, displaying a lot of information about the picture.*

Customizing the Browser

You can customize several features in the Browser by right-clicking anywhere in the thumbnail area of the Browser palette and choosing Preferences from the drop-down list that appears. The Paint Shop Pro Preferences dialog box (shown next) opens on the Browser page with several features that you can customize.

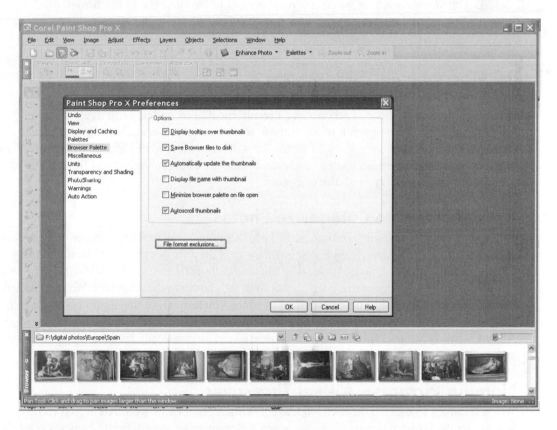

Most of the preference settings are self-explanatory, but a few are not.

■ **Save Browser Files to Disk**   When checked, this feature saves a copy of the generated thumbnails in the folder you are viewing so that the next time it is opened the thumbnails immediately appear.

■ **Minimize Browser Palette on File Open**   If this feature is enabled, any time an image in the Browser palette is opened the Browser palette is minimized to a single row of photos. This action only happens if the Browser is docked.

■ **Autoscroll Thumbnails** This feature controls the behavior of the Browser when you open a folder for the first time and generate thumbnails. If the checkbox is checked, the Browser scrolls as the thumbnails are generated so you can see the thumbnails as they are created. Leaving the checkbox empty does *not* scroll the Browser, so you will not see the thumbnails located past the bottom of the visible Browser area as they are created.

TIP	*When using the Browser to view the pictures that are still in your digital camera, you should uncheck the Save Browser Files to Disk feature in the Browser Preferences so it doesn't write a thumbnail file in the camera's storage media, which is often already full.*

Picture Management Suggestions

One of the big advantages of digital cameras is the ability to take an almost unlimited number of pictures at little to no cost. As a result, most of us end up with many photos on our computer. Keeping track of all of those pictures can be a real challenge, so here are some ideas to help you keep track of them. We will learn more about organizing photos later in the book; at this point we want to focus on the aspect of organization and file naming as it relates to moving photos into the computer.

Using Folders to Categorize Photos

When you transfer photos into the computer, keep them organized in folders named for the event, such as *Amanda's Wedding, Baby's first birthday,* or if they are not photos of events, then by subject matter with dates, for example, *Bluebonnets 03-04-2001* or *Clouds 12-15-2001*. The best time to do this is when transferring the photos from the camera to the computer. We recommend maintaining a master folder on a hard drive in which you keep all of the digital photo folders. This is also helpful when organizing the photos using a visual image manager like Paint Shop Album. Some organizers (like Portfolio by Extensis) can automatically read the file folder name and apply the name as a keyword to the image.

Naming Pictures—A Real Timesaver

When it comes to naming pictures, we have a few suggestions as well. All digital cameras automatically assign numbers to photos when the pictures are taken. Some cameras reset the numbers each time the media is removed from the camera. This can be a problem since the result is many photo files with identical names like *AGF0001.JPG*. If your camera works this way, look and see if this is an option that can be changed from a menu setting. If not, having photos categorized in individual folders keeps the duplicate names from being a problem. Most cameras make life a little easier in this regard by not resetting the picture number counter each time so each photo has a unique number (until it reaches 9999).

Regardless of how your camera works, you will want to give your pictures unique names that identify the picture. This brings up another potential headache. Let's say you have six pictures of Uncle Bob sitting in front of a fireplace. There are two possible solutions that prevent duplicate file names. You can use sequential numbers following the description, such as *Uncle Bob fireplace 01, Uncle Bob fireplace 02, Uncle*... Since we usually like to keep the original photo files under the original number assigned by the camera, we give the picture file a name by adding a descriptive name in front of the number. For example, Uncle Bob's photos would be *Uncle Bob fireplace DCN0001, Uncle Bob fireplace DCN0002*... We do this because we apply all changes, enhancements, or corrections to the named copy of the picture. Having the original photo number as part of the name allows us to locate the original picture file when necessary—and it is often necessary. Without the number, we would have to wade through dozens of images trying to see which original image is Uncle Bob fireplace 01.

So much for getting digital pictures into the computer. Now let's learn how to use a scanner to get photographs into the computer so you work on them with Paint Shop Pro.

Scanning with Paint Shop Pro

Through commands in the File menu, you can access any scanner installed on the computer and scan the images directly into Paint Shop Pro. There are dozens of different models of scanners that range in price from less than $40 to over $1 million.

Scanning Basics

The following paragraphs apply to most all scanners and represent thoughts and recommendations that are the result of our many years of scanning everything from photographs to cookies (no kidding). They are grouped into two general categories: scan preparation and scanner operation.

Preparing to Get the Best Scan

To ensure you get the best possible scan, there are a few simple steps you should do each time before scanning an image.

1. *Clean the scanner glass.*   We know this sounds really simple, but most users don't do it. Keep a small plastic bottle of glass cleaner and a lint-free paper wipe right by the scanner; otherwise, if you have to go somewhere else to find it, in most cases you won't clean the glass.

| TIP | *When cleaning the scanner glass, spray the wipe you use to clean the glass. Don't spray the glass directly in order to keep the liquid from getting under the glass.* |

   2. *Clean the photo.*   Use a soft hair brush and make sure that you remove any debris from the print before you scan. Even though you can always remove any scanned debris using Paint Shop Pro, it just makes good sense to make sure the photo is as clean as possible before you scan.

   3. *Align the picture on the scanner glass.*   Paint Shop Pro has an excellent Rotate command that can be used to correct any misalignment of an image on the scanner. However, any time a scanned image is rotated it suffers from mild deterioration that reduces the overall sharpness of the image. The exception to this rule is that images can be rotated in increments of 90° without any loss of sharpness. This is why aligning the photo properly on the scanner ensures the highest quality scanned image. If the image is crooked, lift the cover, reposition the photo, and try it again. You get better results when you reposition the photo than if you use the Rotate command.

> **TIP**   *When you are checking your glass for cleanliness, you may notice a faint fogging on the bottom side of the copy glass. This occurs sometimes and, as a rule, has little to no effect on the scanned image. Do not attempt to remove the glass unless the manufacturer has provided instructions to do so.*

Scanning a Picture into Paint Shop Pro

Scanning images into Paint Shop Pro is generally accomplished by doing the following:

   1. Launch the scanning software that came with your scanner.

   2. Preview the scan.

   3. Define the selection.

   4. Make the scan.

There are several ways to scan a picture using a scanner. Most scanners sold today have a button on the front of the scanner that automatically launches the scanning software that came with and controls your scanner. Paint Shop Pro does not need to be running, so if you use this method you will need to save the scanned image as a file—just don't forget where you saved the image file. After this you can then open the scanned image using Paint Shop Pro.

A quicker way is to start the scanning software from within Paint Shop Pro by choosing File | Import | TWAIN. That opens another drop-down list (shown next) with two choices: TWAIN Source and TWAIN Acquire. If this is the first time you have used the scanner or the scanner is the only TWAIN device installed, choose TWAIN Acquire and the user interface (UI) for the scanning software opens on top of Paint Shop Pro.

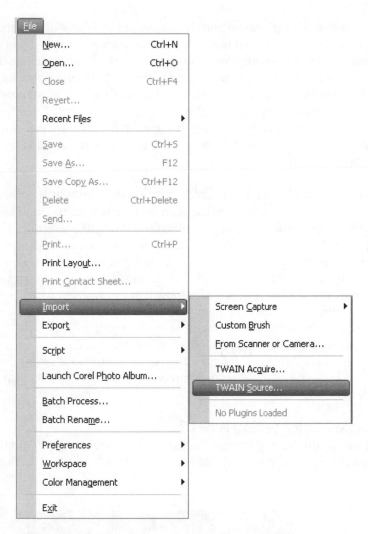

Regardless of how your scanner is physically connected to your computer, it uses an industry standard software method for programs like Paint Shop Pro to communicate with scanners that is called TWAIN. Before TWAIN was introduced, any program that wanted to communicate with a scanner had to write special software for each scanner. With TWAIN both the program and scanner speak the same language (so to speak).

When you first use the scanner and choose the Select Source option, the Select Source dialog appears, and you may find that it offers several choices, even if you only have one scanner installed. In the example shown in Figure 3-4 the choices include the scanner software provided by the scanner manufacturer and the WIA driver that was installed by Windows XP. Always choose the scanner software provided by the scanner manufacturer. The disadvantage of using the WIA is that it is a generic, "no frills" control interface and therefore not as full-featured as the controls found on the software that comes with the scanner. You won't need to select the scanner again unless you add additional scanners to your computer.

Using Preview to Define Your Color Mode and Selection

Most scanning software makes a preview scan as soon as it starts. Don't be concerned about the quality of the preview since it is only used for defining the selection. From this scan you can select the portion of the scanning area that you want to scan, as shown in Figure 3-5.

Make sure that the scanner is set to the correct color mode. For example, if you are scanning in a faded color photograph, the scanner's automatic detection sensor may think it is a grayscale image and set the color mode accordingly. An example of the color modes available on an HP scanner is shown at right.

Some scanner software doesn't automatically determine the color mode but leaves it set at a default setting or the color mode setting from the last time the scanner was used. Use the scanner controls in the software to change it to the correct color mode.

What Display Color Setting Is Best?

The best color quality setting that can be displayed on your computer monitor is 24-bit color. It goes by many names: *RGB (Red Green Blue), RGB 24-bit, 16.7 million colors,*

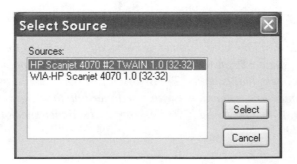

FIGURE 3-4 Even when there is only one scanner installed, there may be several scanners to choose from.

3

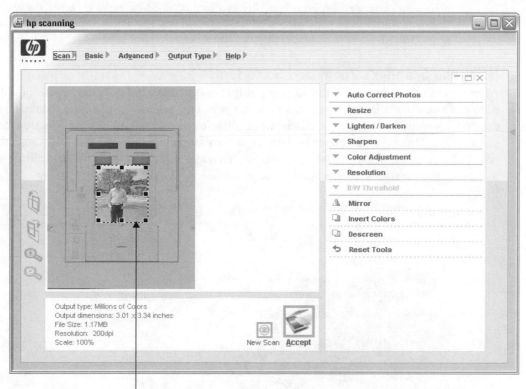

Selection determines the area to be scanned.

FIGURE 3-5   Make a selection of the preview.

Millions of colors, and *True Color,* to name a few. What confuses many Windows users is that beginning with Windows 98 one of the settings that began to appear was 32-bit color. In Windows XP, there isn't even a 24-bit color setting—it is called *Highest (32 bit)*. It seems logical that 32-bit color is superior to 24-bit color. Actually, they are the same. The additional 8 bits does not carry any color at all. It is called an *alpha channel* and reserved for special graphic information. So, always pick the highest color setting for your monitor and your scanner to display the best color information from your color photographs.

Some scanners also automatically detect the edges of the image area on the scanner; however, we recommend that you manually adjust the selection to remove parts of the image that you don't want (this is called cropping). This keeps the resulting file size as small as possible.

If the picture you are scanning will eventually need to be 256-color for use on the Web, you should still scan it in at RGB (also called 24-bit color). Only after the image is ready to be used on a Web page should you use Paint Shop Pro to convert it to 256-color.

Using the Scanner's Zoom and Scale Tools

After making the selection, if the scanning software supports a zoom feature, you should use it. When you do, the scanner will make another preview scan except this time the image in the preview window will appear much larger, allowing you to fine-tune your selection, as shown next. The zoom feature only changes the size of the preview and does not cause the physical size of the scanned picture to change. To make an image larger requires a different feature of the scanner software that is usually labeled *Resize* or *Scale*.

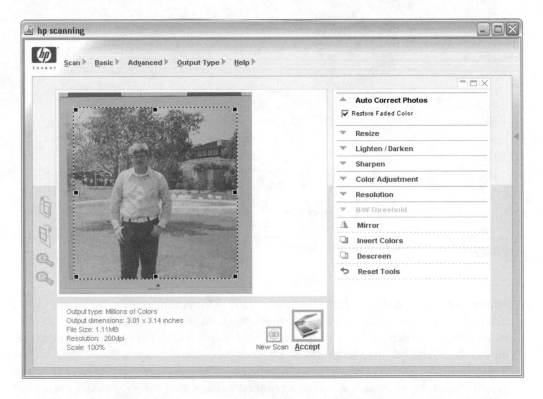

Scaling Pictures with Your Scanners   There are two fundamental reasons to enlarge an image during scanning. The most common reason is to produce a finished image that is larger than the original. For example, we all have seen at one time or another these tiny little school pictures that friends and relatives send around the holidays. By scaling the picture on the scanner you can make it larger than its original microscopic size. The other reason to scale an image is to make it easier to do restorative work on a photo. By increasing the size to 200% (shown next) it is easier to work with the picture and when you are finished you can resize it to the original size.

> **TIP**   *If you need to enlarge the size of a picture, you should do it using your scanner rather than Paint Shop Pro's Resize command whenever possible.*

Making the Scan

Depending on the scanning software, this can be confusing. If you are using the older Precision Scan software that comes with HP ScanJet scanners, it doesn't say anything about scanning, only "Return to Paint Shop Pro." The newest version says "Accept," which is an improvement. Other scanning applications are more direct with Scan Now or simply a Scan button (how original). When the scan is complete the scanning UI closes and the scanned image appears in an image window in the Paint Shop Pro workspace.

Scanning Printed Images

When you scan a printed image, like a picture in a magazine article, it usually develops a checkered pattern or something that looks like a plaid on it. Regardless of what it looks like, this pattern has a name: *moiré pattern.* When the pattern of the tiny dots that are used to print the picture (called *screens*) are scanned, it develops its own pattern for technical reasons that are beyond the scope of this book. There are two ways to reduce (not eliminate) these patterns. Your scanning software may have the ability to minimize the moiré effect. It may be called Descreen, or what has become increasingly popular is to have a preset for the subject you are scanning. For example, Dave's scanning software has a setting for *newspaper and magazines,* which means the descreening is accomplished automatically.

Be aware that regardless of how an image is descreened, the result is a softer picture, meaning it loses some of its sharpness. This is a small price to pay for the reduction of those annoying moiré patterns.

So much for scanning nondigital pictures to make them digital; now we'll discover a way to capture images directly from your computer display.

Capturing Pictures from Your Computer Screen

Paint Shop Pro includes a screen capture program that allows you to take still pictures of your favorite Web page, a game, movie video, or whatever else is currently displayed on your screen. Screen Capture works great, even though its operation seemed a little confusing at first. A screen capture (also called a *screen grab*) involves opening the Screen Capture Setup and answering three questions:

- What do you want to capture?

- How do you want to activate the screen grab?

- Do you want to make a single capture or multiple captures?

Setting Up Screen Captures

While using Setup isn't always necessary, many times you will need to use it to change what part of the screen is being captured or the key that is used to activate it. Here's how it is done:

1. Ensure Paint Shop Pro is running.

2. Choose File | Import | Screen Capture | Setup to open the dialog box shown in Figure 3-6.

3. Selecting the capture area determines what you are going to capture. Clicking the Help button opens a description of each choice. When in doubt select Full Screen.

4. To activate Screen Capture, you have three choices: Right Mouse Click (the default), Hot Key, or Delay Timer. Paint Shop Pro provides these different choices because some applications may already be using one or more of these. We recommend defining a hot key since Windows programs already use the right mouse button for a multitude of purposes and using delay activation can be tricky. If you click the down arrow next to the hot key name, a short list of keyboard combinations appears (shown

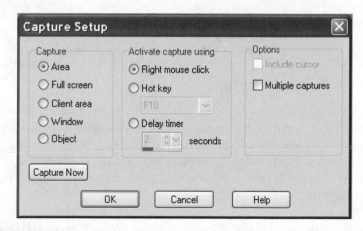

FIGURE 3-6   Screen Capture Setup dialog box

next). If you scroll down the list you will discover the list of available hot key combinations is actually quite long.

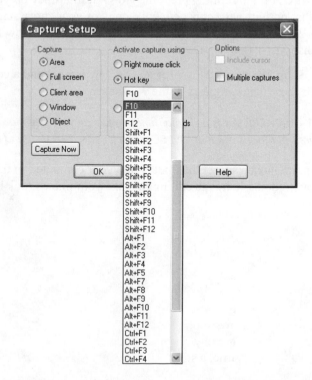

5. Leave the Multiple Captures checkbox unchecked if you only want to take one screen capture at a time.

6. Click OK to complete the setup and return to Paint Shop Pro or click the Capture Now button and Paint Shop Pro immediately minimizes (surprise!) and you are ready to capture something.

When capturing a still from a video, your best bet is to pause the video at the scene you want to capture and then do a full-screen capture. If you don't stop the video, most of the time the screen in the capture will be black. The exception to this rule is capturing a scene from a DVD movie. That is easy—no capture program can do it because of the way DVD players display video. The only workaround is to use the screen capture that is built into the better DVD players.

Using Windows' Own Screen Capture Capability

Every version of Windows has a built-in screen capture capability. While it isn't as versatile as Paint Shop Pro's Screen Capture, it does offer a fast and easy way to capture either the entire screen or a window on the desktop. Here is how it works:

1. With Paint Shop Pro running press the PRINT SCREEN key on your keyboard. It will appear that nothing has happened, but a copy of your entire screen has just been put into the Windows Clipboard. To capture only an open window instead of the full screen, use ALT-PRINT SCREEN.

2. In Paint Shop Pro press CTRL-V (paste as a new image) and a copy of either the full screen or the window appears in the workspace.

> **NOTE**   *The* PRINT SCREEN *key is a special function key on your keyboard and it can appear in many different forms, such as* PRT SC SYS, PRTSCN, PRNTSC, *and other abbreviations.*

Now that you know how to get the photos into your computer, in the next chapter you will discover how to do basic image editing to make your photos look better.

PART II

Photo Editing

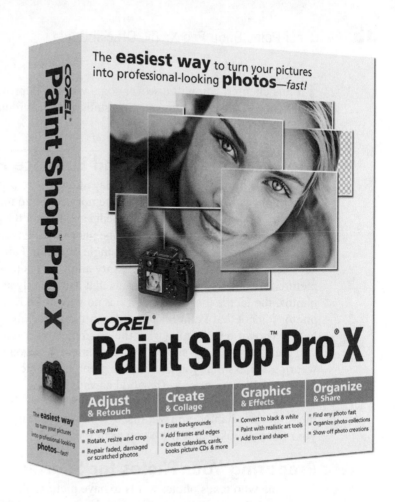

CHAPTER 4

Simple Image Editing and Printing

In this chapter, you will discover some ways to improve the composition of an image, enhance the overall photo quality, straighten out crooked photos, and set up and print photographs from Paint Shop Pro X.

Why You Need to Correct and Enhance Photos

Many photo printers on the market today allow you to print pictures without using a computer; you only need to insert the camera's memory card into the printer and you have a photograph. While the appeal of popping in the media and having the photograph appear is understandable, you'll probably want to fiddle with the photo a little (sometimes a lot) before you print it.

It would be nice if there were a single button in Paint Shop Pro that you could click to automatically make all of the necessary adjustments to your photo and turn it into a perfect picture. While there are a lot of tools that can quickly and automatically improve your photos, the fact is that a computer has no way of knowing what is right or wrong with your photo. It's not that Paint Shop Pro doesn't have the ability to fix the image. It's just that it has no way of determining what the original subject looked like or what parts of the image you consider to be the subject. For example, when you look at a photograph of someone wearing a dress that you know is sea green but in the photo it appears to be blue, you know that the colors are wrong. The good news is, if you can identify the parts of your photo that need improvement, Paint Shop Pro provides a large variety of tools to either enhance or fix them. In this chapter, you will discover how easy it is to make a few adjustments so that your photos look better when you print them.

Preparing Your Photos for Sharing

Everyone who takes photos wants to have pictures that look good, especially if you plan on sharing them with others. Conversely, very few people have the time to spend hours on photos making them look better. So, here is the quickest way to get pictures from your camera ready for sharing. It only involves four steps.

1. Rotate the picture (if necessary).

2. Crop the photo (if necessary—and it probably is).

3. Apply the One Step Photo Fix command.

4. Print the photo.

Rotating Your Photos in Paint Shop Pro

This is the first and most common correction you should make with Paint Shop Pro. Anytime you take a photograph with the camera in portrait orientation, it needs to be rotated. For the record, when we talk about the orientation of the camera, we are saying which part of the image is on top: if the wide part is on top, it's in landscape orientation; if the narrow part is on top, it's in portrait orientation. The choice of orientation is usually

FIGURE 4-1   Same subject photographed in landscape orientation (left) and portrait (right)

determined by the subject matter. The photo of the barn in Figure 4-1 was photographed in both portrait and landscape orientation.

Auto Rotation

You may discover when you view your photos the first time that they have already been rotated automatically. What happened? Many of the newer digital cameras can detect when the camera is not horizontal at the moment the photo is taken. These cameras include that information in the image data. When you open images with orientation information, Corel Paint Shop Pro automatically rotates photos to the correct orientation. For the record, the camera's orientation information works in 90-degree increments, so if your picture is crooked, it cannot automatically straighten the photo.

Manual Rotation

When you take a photograph in portrait orientation and bring it straight into Paint Shop Pro, as shown next, you will want to orient it to landscape for viewing on a display. For the record, if you only intended to print the photo, you could leave it as is.

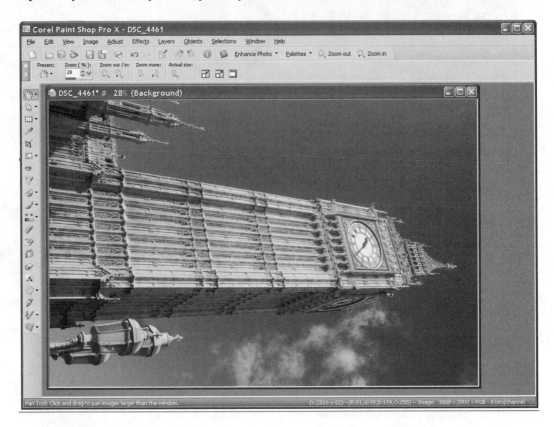

To rotate the photo to the correct orientation, from the Image menu, select the rotation that turns your photo so that the top of the photo is pointing up—in this case, 90 degrees counterclockwise—as shown in Figure 4-2.

Other Ways to Rotate Your Photo

There are several other ways to rotate images. The easiest way is to select the image and click the Rotate Right/Rotate Left buttons in the Standard toolbar. If the photo is a JPEG you can right-click on a thumbnail in the Browser palette and from the JPEG Lossless Rotation context menu choose one of several 90-degree rotations.

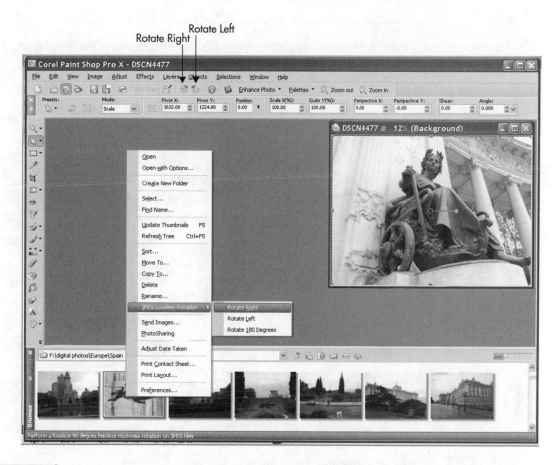

| NOTE | *You can only rotate JPEG images from the Browser.* |

You can also rotate your photo by using the Free Rotate command (CTRL-R), which opens the Free Rotate dialog box, shown next. From here, you can select one of the preset rotations or enter a custom value to rotate it at an unusual angle to create an effect (see "The Effects of Rotating a Bitmap Image," later in this chapter).

FIGURE 4-2   Select the desired rotation from the Image menu.

TIP   *Make sure the image is selected before pressing* CTRL-R. *If you have clicked on any thumbnail in the Browser palette, using the* CTRL-R *shortcut will open the File Rename dialog box.*

If your photo does not appear to be straight because it was placed crooked in a scanner, you should rescan the photo if possible rather than attempting to rotate it in Paint Shop Pro. If the photo is not a scanned image, you should use the Free Rotate command until it appears straight.

TIP   *Your photo doesn't always have to be level with the horizon. There are times when having the photo at an angle produces a desired effect, but as a general rule of composition, the horizon should be level.*

Straightening a Crooked Photo

No matter how hard you try to avoid it you will have times when your best photo is crooked. Even with the instant review capability of a digital camera you don't see subtle slants like the one shown in Figure 4-3. Dave was photographing the U.S. Capitol in Washington, D.C., as the sun was rising. He didn't notice his camera position on the tripod had a slight slant to it that makes the Capitol dome appear to be leaning slightly to the right. Fortunately, Paint Shop Pro has a tool to correct this type of problem. Here is how to do it. If you want to do the exercise yourself, you can download the sample file Capitol_sunrise.JPG from www.osborne.com.

4

> **TIP**   *To quickly find where the sample files are located on the Web site, use the Search feature and look for Paint Shop Pro. Be aware that the sample files that are available for download are found on a link labeled "Free Sample Code."*

Straightening a Photograph

This exercise uses the file Capitol_sunrise.JPG but you can use any photo that you want to straighten.

1. Open the photo Capitol_sunrise.JPG (select File | Open and then locate the image to be straightened).

FIGURE 4-3   Great sunrise shot but the camera wasn't level on the tripod.

2. On the Tools toolbar, click the Straighten tool. A straightening bar with end handles appears on the image. Because the photo is dark the straightening bar will be a little hard to see.

3. Click and drag each handle of the straightening bar to align it with the part of the image that you want to be straight. In this case we have made a straight line that follows the sloping grass lawn (which shouldn't be sloping), shown in Figure 4-4. The object is to level the base of the building as much as possible.

> **NOTE** *In case you were wondering why the dome of the Capitol was not selected, this photo was taken with a wide-angle lens and the Capitol dome is off center in the photo. Because of the natural barrel distortion in a wide-angle lens, if the columns of the dome were made perfectly vertical with the Straighten tool, the rest of the photo would have been a little crooked.*

On the Tool Options palette for the Straighten tool (shown next), set the Mode to Auto and select Crop Image. Auto is usually the best choice. It causes Paint Shop

FIGURE 4-4   The straightening bar (highlighted) is placed in line with the part of the image that should be straight.

Pro to automatically straighten the image based on the position of the straightening bar. The Crop Image option crops the edges of the image to make it rectangular after straightening. If you don't choose it PSP will fill blank areas around the edges with the background color—and then you'll have to crop it manually. Last point: look at the angle display in the example below. The rotation value is determined by the difference in position of the first and last points of the straightening bar from their default position.

4. Lastly, click the Apply button. The image is immediately straightened like the one shown in Figure 4-5 and the straightening bar jumps back to the middle of the screen.

FIGURE 4-5   The Straighten tool quickly took the slant out of our photo.

The Effects of Rotating a Bitmap Image

A bitmap (also called *raster*) image is made up of pixels. When you rotate a bitmap image such as a photograph either 90, 180, or 270 degrees, Paint Shop Pro rearranges the order of the pixels in the image. The image quality remains unaffected because only the order of the pixels changes and because pixels are square in shape, so rotating them does not change their aspect ratio or shape. However, when you rotate the same bitmap image at any angle other than a 90-degree increment, Paint Shop Pro must re-create all of the pixels to create the rotation effect. Any time you must re-create pixels in an image, it slightly degrades the image. The degradation usually produces a slight softening of the overall image, like the Capitol sunrise photo we rotated in the previous exercise. In most cases, depending on the subject matter, the deterioration may not even be noticeable. Still, you should be aware that the degradation occurs and avoid this type of rotation unless it is necessary. This is especially truc of applying multiple non-90-degree rotations. For example, if the first (non-90-degree) rotation doesn't straighten the image, undo the rotation (CTRL-Z) before trying a different value.

The Importance of Photo Composition

Now that your photos are all pointed the right way, the next step is to crop them. Many people don't like to crop their photos because they want to keep everything that's in the photo. The truth is that most photographs (like the one of a street band in Mexico shown in Figure 4-6) are greatly improved by removing parts of the scene that distract the viewer. There are several problems with the original photo in Figure 4-6.

FIGURE 4-6   This cluttered photo is a good candidate for cropping.

First, the photo is cluttered. When cropping a photo ask yourself this question: "What is the subject of the photo?" Next, the back of one of the musicians fills the right side of the photograph, and while we love the colorful serapes in the background we don't like the neon-green price tag. While we could use Paint Shop Pro to remove the tag, by simply cropping the photo (see Figure 4-7) we eliminate the brightly colored tag and direct the viewer to the subject, which is the brass players—who also sounded great.

> **NOTE** *In the previous example, we removed over 50 percent of the original photo. It is at times like this that having a large original image (the camera had a 5.0 megapixel sensor) allows you to aggressively crop an image and still have a photo large enough to produce a quality print.*

Cropping is done using the Crop tool (R) in the Tools toolbar (shown next), and its operation is pretty obvious. The part that requires judgment on your part is what to crop and what to leave.

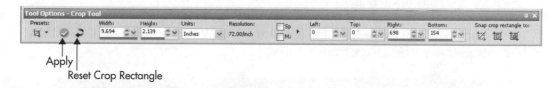

Apply

Reset Crop Rectangle

FIGURE 4-7   A simple crop of the image changes its appearance.

Why You Should Crop Before Doing Anything Else

Make it a rule to always crop before making any tonal or color correction. This is because the automatic correction features of Paint Shop Pro read the color and brightness information contained in the entire image to determine what and how much correction to apply. If you apply any of the automatic color or tonal corrections before cropping, a part of the photo that won't be in the final image may influence the results of the automatic tools. In most cases, the differences will be small but it is a good habit to get into when working with digital photos.

Setting the Zoom for Viewing

Before you can crop a photo you need to be able to see the entire image. How much of an image appears on your monitor depends on several factors—the display setting of your monitor (800 x 600 and 1024 x 780 are two of the most popular), which determines the document window size, and the dimensions of the image (in pixels), to name a few. Here are some fast facts to know about viewing images in Paint Shop Pro.

The Zoom tool is located in the Tools palette but if the Pan tool was the last of the two tools used, the Zoom tool will not be seen until you click on the tiny black diamond to open the submenu to see both tools, as shown next.

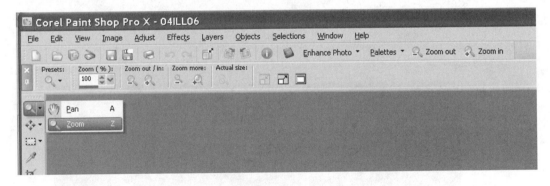

| TIP | *The fastest way to access the Zoom tool is to press the Z key.* |

If your mouse has a scroll wheel you can use it to zoom in and out of the image. As you zoom in and out, the current zoom settings appear on the title bar of the image window, as shown next. You will learn more about zoom settings throughout the book, but when cropping you always want to move your scroll wheel until the entire image fits on the display with no part hidden. If you don't have a scroll wheel mouse, go buy one—they're cheap and will make working with Paint Shop Pro much easier. If the store is closed at the moment, here are some shortcuts that you can use until you buy one.

- Click the Zoom Plus and Minus icons in the Zoom Option bar.
- **Zoom In**   Use the + key on the numeric pad on the right side of your keyboard.
- **Zoom Out**   Use the – key on the numeric pad on the right side of your keyboard.

When you need to quickly snap the image to predefined settings, use one of the three buttons in the Zoom Option bar, shown next.

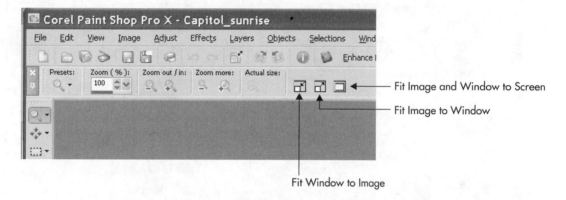

There are a lot of other Zoom settings, all of which are explained in both the online Help and the User's Guide. We will also be explaining uses for different Zoom settings as we cover topics that use them.

Cropping a Photo

Operating the Crop tool is pretty simple, but for the record the following exercise will give you some practice using it. If you want to use the same photo that we are using, download the file Civil_courts.JPG. Be advised that it is a large file. It is a photo of an old courthouse in St. Louis and we want to crop it so only the words "Civil Courts" appear along with the quote underneath.

1. Open the image Civil_courts.JPG or the photo you want to use. Zoom out until you can see the entire photo.

2. Select the Crop tool in the Tools toolbar and place the cursor inside the image. Click and drag a selection rectangle to surround the part of the photo to be kept and let go

of the mouse button. The area being removed appears darker (as shown next) to help you visualize what the cropped photo will look like.

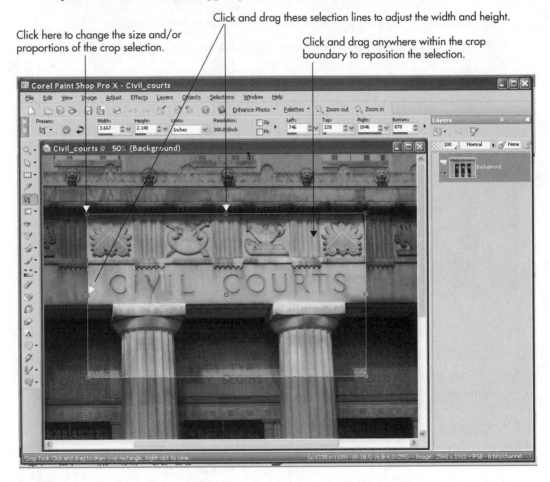

Click here to change the size and/or proportions of the crop selection.

Click and drag these selection lines to adjust the width and height.

Click and drag anywhere within the crop boundary to reposition the selection.

> **NOTE**   *To be able to click and drag the rectangle, the cursor must begin outside the rectangle that appears when you choose the Crop tool. The size and location of the rectangle is determined by the last crop made with the Crop tool.*

3. Adjust the rectangle by clicking and dragging either its sides or corners. You can move the entire selected rectangle around the image by placing the cursor inside it and dragging it around.

4. Double-click anywhere in the crop area or click the Apply button in the Tool Options palette to crop the photo. Zoom in (either with the mouse scroll wheel or keypad) on the cropped image until it reads 100% on the title bar. Don't worry if parts of the image are off of the screen.

5. Now comes the cool part. Select Full Screen Preview (CTRL-SHIFT-A). This is a great feature of Paint Shop Pro. The cropped image in Full Screen Preview is shown in Figure 4-8. By the way, clicking the mouse or pressing any key will cause Paint Shop Pro to exit Full Screen Preview.

Cropping Your Photos to a Specific Size

If you plan on printing a photograph you are working on, consider cropping it to one of the predefined photo sizes. This way your printed photograph will have the aspect ratio (ratio of width to height) necessary to fit into standard size picture frames and photo albums that can only accommodate certain sizes. Paint Shop Pro provides several ways to crop to a specific size using either the Crop tool or the Canvas Size command.

Using the Crop tool to create a specific size is similar to the steps in the previous section:

1. Select the Crop tool in the Tools toolbar.

2. In the Tool Options palette, you can enter a desired finished size or click the Presets button and pick a finished size from the list of preset sizes, as shown in Figure 4-9. Click the OK button to place a Crop rectangle on the photo.

3. Double-click inside the rectangle or click the Apply button in the Tool Options palette to complete the crop action.

FIGURE 4-8   The cropped image shown in Full Screen Preview

FIGURE 4-9 Using presets ensures the photo will fit the standard size photo paper when you print.

> **TIP** *If the requested crop size is larger than the selected photo, the Crop tool will change the resolution of the image so it fits. The resolution appears in the Tool Options palette.*

You can also change the size of the currently selected image with the Canvas Size command in the Image menu. This command either adds or subtracts pixels from the edge of the image, so entering a value that is smaller than the currently selected image will crop it. However, because you cannot visually control where the cropping occurs on the photo, as you can with the Crop tool, using the Canvas Size command for cropping is not recommended.

What to Crop

Here are some general cropping rules to consider and some examples. First, decide what the subject of the photo is and remove anything that distracts from the subject. The photograph we are going to use to demonstrate the importance of this was taken at the twenty-fifth anniversary and vow recommitment of some good friends—Brian and Debbie. The photo shown next doesn't appear to be anything special.

By cropping the photo, as shown next, the couple (and four of their eight children) becomes the focus of the photo. Don't be afraid to remove part of the photo to get in close. No one is going to look at the photo and ask what happened to the pastor or the exit sign.

Cropping the photo focuses the image and draws the viewer's attention to the youngest member of the wedding party who, like most kids, finds mom and dad smooching more than he can bear to watch.

Digital Pictures Have Their Limits

If you watch TV or go to the movies, at some point you will probably have seen the critical scene where someone asks a technician to zoom in on some part of a video or satellite photo, and then says our favorite line: "Now enhance it." Amazingly, the blurred license plate or face suddenly comes into crystal clear focus. Don't believe it. That only happens in the movies. When you crop out everything but a small part of your photo to emphasize it, be careful that you are not left with a photo the size of a postage stamp. If you only want to show the picture on the Web, you can make it pretty small, but if you want to print a photo, you should have enough size to print it at a resolution of 150 dots-per-inch (dpi) for most inkjet printers. For digital camera users, it is when you are cropping a photo and using only a small portion of the original that all of those extra megapixels the camera produces come in really handy because the remaining cropped image is still large enough to make an acceptable photo.

Our last cropping suggestion applies to taking the photograph. Whenever possible, avoid placing your subject in the center of the photo. Placing the subject in the dead center is what they do for passports and drivers licenses, and we all know how good those photos look.

Automatic Photo Correction

There are two overall photo correction tools in Paint Shop Pro X: One Step Photo Fix and Smart Photo Fix. One Step Photo Fix is totally automatic whereas Smart Photo Fix opens a dialog box that lets you choose what adjustments to make.

Applying One Step Photo Fix

The One Step Photo Fix command is a totally automatic feature that applies several tonal and color corrections to the selected photo. The majority of the time this feature does a very good job of getting the most out of the photo without having to open and use other correction tools.

You can try this one yourself by downloading the file Man in a hat.JPG. The original photo is shown at right. It is too dark and once the lighting issue is addressed, it may have some color correction issues.

The command is accessed by selecting Adjust | One Step Photo Fix. It will take a few moments for Paint Shop Pro to apply all of the filters. You can view the progress of each filter in the status bar that appears on the bottom of the screen. The corrected photo appears in Figure 4-10. In most cases, One Step Photo Fix makes all of the corrections that you need to do. This image was chosen because it demonstrates what can go wrong and how to fix it.

When you look at the results of applying the One Step Photo Fix to the image, there are two things that should be apparent. There is a definite shift in colors (color cast) toward magenta in his white shirt and the colors appear a little

FIGURE 4-10   Applying One Step Photo Fix may or may not provide all the enhancement many photos need.

oversaturated. To correct the problems, we need to undo the One Step Photo Fix and apply the Smart Photo Fix. Here is how it is done:

1. Undo (CTRL-Z) One Step Photo Fix.

2. Apply Smart Photo Fix by selecting Adjust | Smart Photo Fix. When the dialog box opens, check the Advanced Options checkbox, as shown next. This dialog box appears a little complicated but it is easier to use than it looks.

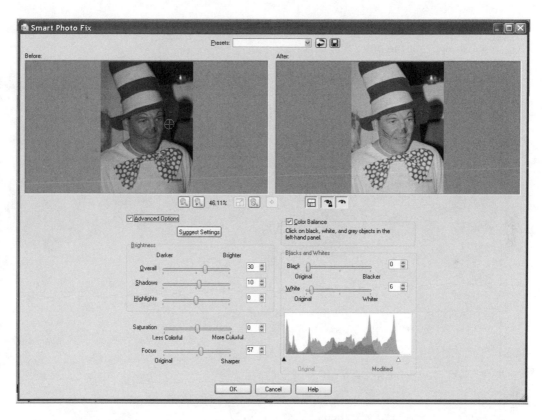

3. Make sure the Color Balance checkbox is checked. Place the cursor in the Before preview screen and it becomes a cursor. There should already be a marker (it looks like a crosshair) in the shadow to the right of the subject's face. This was Paint Shop Pro's best guess as to what was a neutral color. Remove the marker by putting the cursor over it (the cursor becomes a reject symbol) and click the left mouse button. There should be no markers in the Before preview pane.

4. Move the cursor around the white shirt. The three RGB values continually change as you move the cursor around. Find the area in which all three values are as close as possible to one another and click on it. The white dots on the bowtie should be the

best. Paint Shop Pro now uses that for the color reference. The After preview now shows that the color cast is gone.

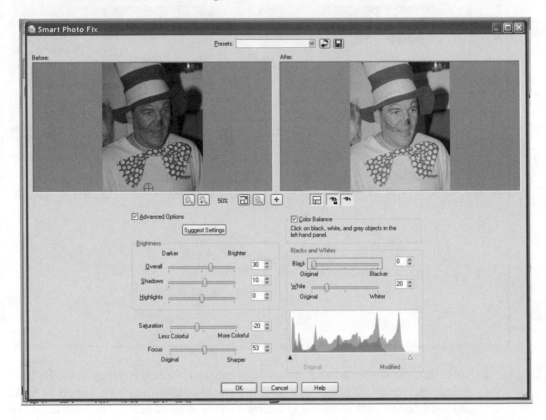

5. The face in the photo is still too saturated, so move the Saturation slider to –20 to reduce the oversaturation.

6. Finally, the whites don't seem very bright, so move the White slider in Black and Whites to the right until the marker moves just up to meet the red colored right edge of the histogram.

7. Click OK and the image correction is completed as shown in Figure 4-11.

Printing Photos

Now that you have cropped and otherwise adjusted your photo the way you want it, it's time to print it, maybe for putting in a frame on your desk or making copies to send to friends or family. A few years ago, it would have required a $10,000 printer to get a decent-looking color photograph. Now, with an inkjet printer (costing less than a few hundred dollars) and the new photo papers available, you can produce photographs that look like the real thing.

FIGURE 4-11   Smart Photo can be used when One Step isn't enough.

Sorting Out Today's Color Printers

With color inkjet printers being the dominant printer on the market today, you can walk into any office or computer store and see a long line of them on the shelves. Most printer manufacturers offer at least five different models of printers ranging in price from $100 to $800. If that isn't confusing enough, from the output produced by each printer, it appears that they all have roughly the same quality of output.

To help simplify the question of which printer to buy, you need to understand the different printer classifications and what they do. The following are the general categories of color printers available in the marketplace today:

- Color inkjet printers
- Photo inkjet printers using dye-based inks
- Photo inkjet printers using pigment-based inks
- Dye sublimation printers

Color Inkjet Printers

Most of the inkjet printers sold today are color inkjet printers. Most print their color using a black ink cartridge and a color cartridge that contains three different colored inks (called a tri-color cartridge). Black is always maintained as a separate color for two reasons: it allows the printing of standard text without wasting any color and, while it is theoretically possible to create black using the three different colored inks together, the black produced by the color cartridge would look more like dark mud than black. These color inkjet printers offer very fast print speeds (for text), and some can print on both sides of the paper (duplex). Hewlett-Packard (HP) even has a printer that can detect what kind of paper is in your printer and automatically select the correct media settings. In short, they are pretty amazing.

Sorting Out the Color Printers

Almost every inkjet printer that you can find uses dye-based inks to print. This is because the colors produced by dye-based inks are more vivid than pigment-based inks. On top of that, pigment-based printers cost roughly five times as much as dye-based printers. With these limitations, what is the advantage of pigment-based ink printers? Longevity. Prints produced using a pigment ink-based printer are certified to last over 100 years. How important is this? If you are a professional producing prints for a client, it is very important. If you are printing images for your own personal use and the photo begins to fade (after five to seven years), you can always print another one.

In the category of dye-based printers there is another question: What makes a color inkjet different from a photo inkjet printer?

Most color inkjet printers are described as four-color printers in that they use four inks to produce color output. The four inks used are black (K), Cyan, Magenta, and Yellow (CMY). There are still some three-color printers on the market that create their color output using CMY, and they have a separate black pigment-based ink cartridge that is only used for printing text. Three-color printers do not produce good color, especially for photos, and should be avoided.

What You Need to Know About Printer Ink and Media

It is a poorly kept secret that printer manufacturers make very little profit on the printers they sell. Instead, they look to the sales of the consumables (ink and paper) to make the profits that keep shareowners happy. Because these consumables are so expensive, many third-party companies provide their own ink cartridges and refill kits for existing cartridges while others make photo papers.

Should You Use Third-Party Ink Cartridges?

The important question is, are the inks used by the third-party ink cartridge vendors as good as those provided by the manufacturer? We have tested several of them and found their output quality ranges from poor to good. We recommend you use the printer manufacturer's cartridges if you only use a few cartridges each year. If your cartridge demands are heavier, you may want to consider one of the zillion vendors on the Internet.

The only way to find out how good third-party replacement cartridges are is to first print a sample photo using the printer manufacturer's cartridges, then buy a third-party set, print another sample, and compare the results you get. If you are not satisfied with the results, return the cartridges and ask for a refund. If you are satisfied with them, continue to use them and occasionally print another sample print, as the quality assurance of some of these houses varies.

What's at Stake If You Use Third-Party Inkjet Cartridges?

Most printer manufacturers state that using these third-party ink supplies voids the printer's warranty. Most users believe this. This is a common misperception by many printer owners. Manufacturers have threatened to void printer warranties when cartridges are refilled by third-party manufacturers, but the brand of supplies you purchase for your printer is your decision. You are not required by any machine manufacturer's warranty to use only its brand. The Magnuson-Moss Warranty Improvement Act prevents manufacturers from doing that.

Using the Media That Produces the Best Results for You

It used to be paper was just paper, but now it is a specialized media. Each type of paper is made for a specific purpose, such as inkjet paper, photo paper, photo glossy paper—and those are just the ones that you see at retail stores. There are many more unusual types of inkjet papers available on the Internet, such as papers that turn photos into puzzles, a coffee cup, or even canvases. You will be looking at a lot of specialty papers for different scanner projects throughout this book, but first, a few general facts about inkjet papers.

Printing color photos on cheap copy paper produces poor pictures even though it uses the same amount of ink as it would printing on photo paper. Printing a lousy-looking photo on very expensive paper won't make the photo look any better. The secret to getting the best printing results for your scanned images is to find a paper that has the texture and finish that you like and then to experiment with your printer settings to get the results that you want.

Adjusting Your Printer Settings for Best Results

Regardless of which printer you are using, you can access the software that controls your printer. To do this, click the Print button, and you will see the dialog box shown next. The name of the computer's default printer appears near the top of the dialog box.

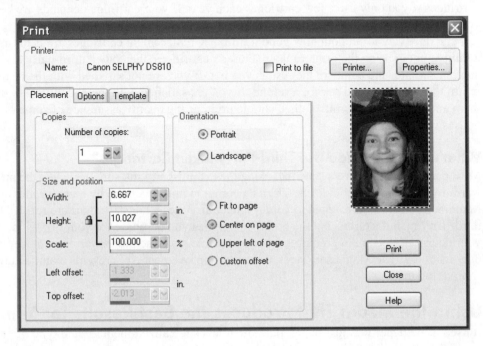

While the specific details will vary from printer to printer, the following procedure works for most situations:

- To change the selected printer, click the Printer button. This opens a list of all of the installed printers. To change the properties of a specific printer, click the Properties button alongside the printer name. This launches the printer-specific software that allows you to control many of the printer features.

- Within the Printer dialog box, you can select the media that is loaded in the printer, as well as the color management that the printer should use to print the scanned image. The choices of media (paper) are limited to the names and types offered by the printer manufacturer. This can cause a bit of head scratching when you are using a paper that is different from the choices shown. See "You Should Match Photo Papers with Printer Settings" at the end of the chapter for information about this.

- If this is your first time setting up the printer, you should experiment with several different settings. Print the scanned image and write on the back of the photo what settings you used. Once you are satisfied with the results, save the settings with a unique name and use these settings to print your photos.

Set Paint Shop Pro Print Settings

Once you have the printer set to print your photos, you can make any necessary adjustments in the Paint Shop Pro Print dialog box to control how the image is placed on the paper. There are tabs on the opening dialog box, which offer two types of settings: Placement and Options.

Most of the controls on this page are fairly obvious: number of copies, making the image placement portrait or landscape. The left side of the Size and Position section allows you to specify how much to scale the image. The right side contains several buttons that control how Paint Shop Pro places the image on the paper:

4

- **Fit to Page** Expands the existing photo so that it fills the page. This is not recommended in most cases, especially if the original image is very small, because the resulting print will be of poor quality.

- **Center on Page** Places the image (unaltered) smack in the center of the page.

- **Upper Left of Page** Places the image at the upper-left corner of the original. This is very handy if you are printing the photo on a page that is larger than the photo and it is going to need to be trimmed.

- **Custom Offset** Positions the photo on a specific part of the page.

The Options tab contains options that are primarily used for prepress work (images that are sent to printers). Check in the Paint Shop Pro User's Manual for details on these options.

NOTE   *Even if your inkjet printer is referred to as a CMYK printer (and many are), do not use the CMYK option. All of these printers expect the color information to be in RGB format.*

You Should Match Photo Papers with Printer Settings

What happens if you have an Epson photo printer loaded with Kodak photo paper? If you look at the Paper pop-up menu, you will not see anything but Epson papers listed, so how do you know which Epson paper matches the Kodak paper that you have installed? First, try looking at the printed information that came with the paper. Most of the paper vendors list the best paper settings for most major printer manufacturers. If your printer is too new to be listed, check the paper manufacturer's Web site to see if they give setting recommendations for your printer. If both of these don't pan out, try to match the type of paper (glossy, matte, and so on) with one that is closest on the printer's paper list.

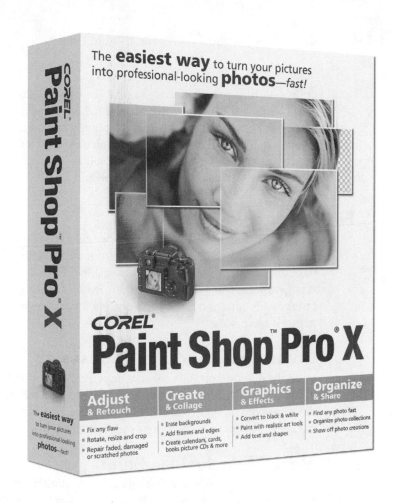

CHAPTER 5

Correcting Photographic Problems

With film photography, you take your photos during vacations or special events and hold your breath when you get the envelope of photographs back from the developer. Once the picture is taken there isn't much you can do. With digital photography and Paint Shop Pro, that's all changed. While you can still take bad photos with even the most expensive camera, now you have the ability to correct, enhance, and otherwise play with the photos on your computer before printing them.

Fine-Tuning Your Color

One of the biggest disappointments people experience with digital cameras is color that appears lifeless or seems a little off from what it should be. In this chapter, you will discover that adjusting the color isn't rocket science. In fact, with the tools built into Paint Shop Pro, it is pretty easy to get the color right. Because most of the discussion in this section involves color, we recommend that you put a bookmark in the color insert section so you can easily get to it from here.

Color Casts and Their Causes

Outdoor photographs taken with a digital camera often have a color cast, a subtle but dominant color that is introduced into the photo. The most common color cast produced by a sunny cloudless day is blue. This is because of the large amounts of light radiated by the blue sky. You don't notice it because your eyes automatically adjust to it.

More Than Just the Blues

If blue was the only color cast that affected digital cameras, everyone would be a lot happier. Unfortunately, there are several sources of light that affect the color balance of your photos. A photo taken in a windowless office lit entirely by fluorescent lights produces a sickly green color cast. Applying magenta (the opposite of green) using the Color Balance feature corrects the color cast.

Some light sources introduce a desirable color cast. When your subject is illuminated by incandescent light or a sunset, the resulting colors shift toward the warm colors, which are always more appealing. This is why colors in photos taken in the morning and the late afternoon are more appealing than those taken when the sun is high overhead.

Before You Begin Any Correction

There are some fundamental rules concerning digital photos and Paint Shop Pro that need to be made crystal clear before attempting any correction or enhancement.

The first rule is that nearly all of the adjustment and correction tools that are covered in this chapter will not work on 256-color (8-bit) images. If you attempt to do so, Paint Shop Pro will automatically convert the image to 24-bit (RGB). Earlier versions of Paint Shop Pro posted an Auto Action message box prompting you that the image color depth must be increased to RGB (24-bit) to apply the effect or filter. Clicking OK in the Auto Action box increased the color depth of the currently selected image. You need to be aware of how the Auto Actions work since they do not give any visual clues that the color depth of the image has been changed.

To define how an auto action works, choose File | Preferences | General Program Preferences and when the dialog box opens, select Auto Action, as shown next. Each Auto Action has three possible conditions: Never, Always, and Prompt. If Never is selected, no Auto Action occurs. If Always is selected, the selected Auto Action occurs without any indication to the user, while if Prompt is selected, a message box appears prompting you to approve the Auto Action about to be taken.

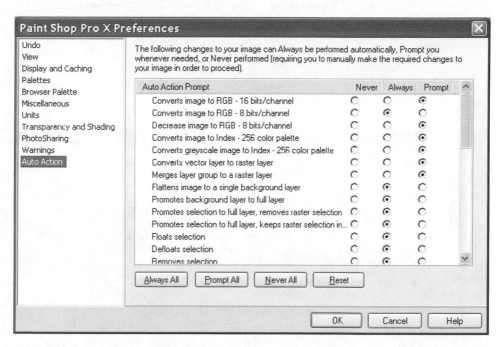

The second rule applies to images with layers (other than background). The tools and effects in Paint Shop Pro work only on the layer of the photo that is currently active. The exception to this is a few adjustment dialog boxes that have an option that allows the tool or effect to be applied to all layers.

Discover the Photo Toolbar

Most of the photo correction work you will do in this chapter will use a tool in the Photo toolbar; when enabled, as shown in Figure 5-1, it allows an effect or tool to be used with the click of a button rather than having to go through several levels of menus. To enable the Photo toolbar, choose View | Toolbars | Photo Toolbar.

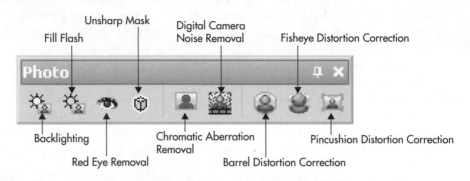

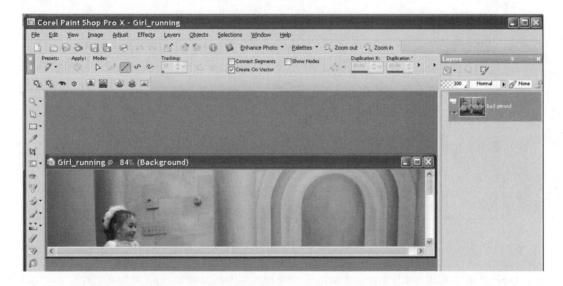

FIGURE 5-1   The Photo toolbar

The Photo toolbar in Figure 5-1 is undocked. You can drag the toolbar toward the top of the screen and dock it with the other toolbars, as shown next.

Using Adjustment Dialog Boxes

If you are an experienced Paint Shop Pro user, the Adjustment dialog boxes haven't changed. If you are new to Paint Shop Pro, there is a good chance that you might find the Adjustment dialog boxes confusing. While the Adjustment dialog boxes each have slightly different controls, overall the controls operate in a similar manner. We've used the Color Balance dialog box (see Figure 5-2) to demonstrate their different parts and operation.

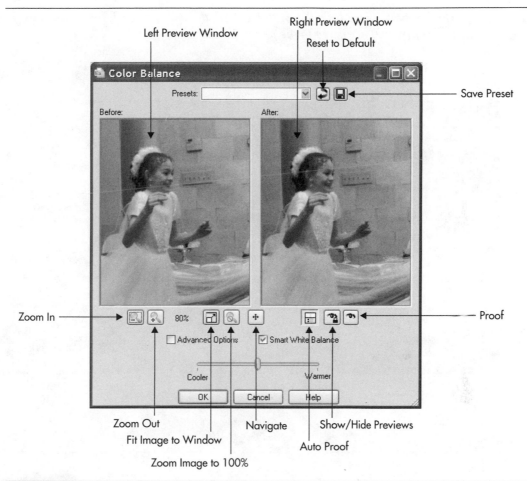

Left Preview Window
Right Preview Window
Reset to Default
Save Preset
Zoom In
Proof
Zoom Out
Fit Image to Window
Navigate
Show/Hide Previews
Zoom Image to 100%
Auto Proof

FIGURE 5-2   Color Balance dialog box

Dialog Box with a View

Six of the eight buttons under the current image and proof windows are used to control the windows above them. Obviously, the zoom buttons zoom in and out of the image in the windows. Clicking and holding the Navigate button opens another window containing a small version of the photo with the zoomed area indicated by a rectangle, as shown next. Drag the rectangle to a different part of the image you want to preview and release the mouse button. You can also drag directly in either of the preview areas to pan the image.

> **TIP**   *The Navigate button is only available when the image zoom level prevents the entire image from being viewed in the preview area.*

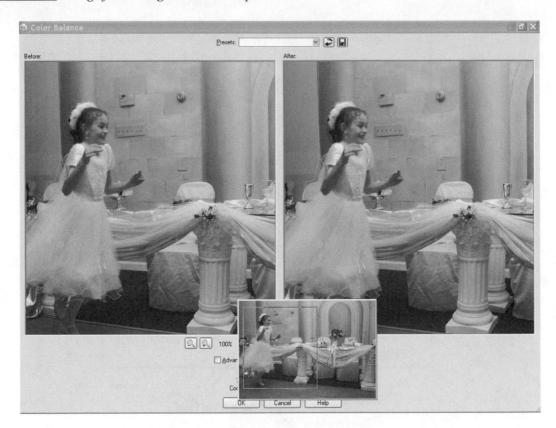

Changing How Your Preview Operates

If this is your first time working with Paint Shop Pro, you might be wondering how effective such a small preview window is. Often it is difficult to see the "big picture" in such a tiny window, and you may want to preview the effects on the actual image. To make the image bigger, you can click the Show/Hide Previews button to hide the preview windows, as shown next. Now any changes that you make are applied to the image on the screen and you must click the Proof button off and on to see a before and after comparison.

The Proof Is in the Preview

Whenever you make a change to one of the adjustments in the dialog box, the change always appears in the preview window. To preview the effect the adjustment is having on the image, press the Proof button. Depending on the size of the photo and the complexity of the effect, it may take a few moments for the change to appear. None of the changes that you see in the image are applied until you click the OK button. When the preview appears in the image, changing any of the settings will toggle the Preview button off. To continuously view the changes in the image, click the Auto Proof button on. This may sound like a good option, but when you are working with a large image or applying complex effects, Auto Proof can really slow things down.

Randomize

There is one additional button that appears on some of the dialog boxes—the Randomize button. That's the button that looks like a single dice, as shown next. Each time you click the Randomize button, it will randomly change all of the settings in the dialog box. This is one of those features that should not be used with standard photo adjustments. There are some effect filters that have a multitude of settings, and the Randomizer feature provides a quick way to discover some great and not so great settings for those.

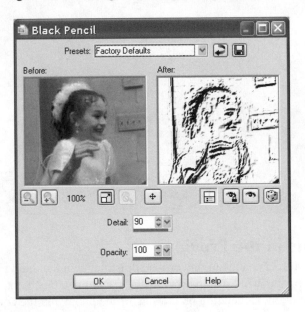

> **TIP**   *Toggling the Preview button on and off is one way to compare the before and after results of an effect on an image.*

Saving Your Settings

Once you have fine-tuned a setting for the dialog box it is possible to save it for use again on another image, and in fact, that is the purpose of the Save to Default (preset) and Save Preset buttons at the top of the dialog box. For example, if you were taking a lot of digital photos around the same time of day with the same camera, you could save the settings for the filter you used to correct the color cast and apply them to all of the other images. Doing this is quite simple. You can save, load, and delete the settings or restore to the factory defaults by clicking the appropriate button.

Color and Tonal Correction for Raw Format Files

If a Raw file is opened using the Paint Shop Pro Editor, the user cannot make any adjustments or corrections to the image before it appears in the Smart Photo Fix dialog box. Since the purpose of using the Raw format is to allow the photographer to make adjustments to the image before it is converted from the Raw format, it is recommended that any Raw photos be first opened and adjusted using the Raw Shooter application that has been included with Paint Shop Pro. Once you have made the necessary corrections the images can be saved in a standard graphic format that Paint Shop Pro can open. Now, let's move on and learn how Color Balance is used to correct color in an image.

The Automatic Adjustment Tools

In Chapter 4 you learned about One-Step Photo Fix, which does a great job of fixing an image by applying several of the automatic adjustment tools at the same time. However, if you just want to remove colors casts or make slight adjustments to the amount of lighting in a photo, then application of the individual automatic tools is the best choice. Let's begin with how to remove color casts using Color Balance.

> TIP   *In previous versions of Paint Shop Pro this feature was named Automatic Color Balance.*

Removing Color Casts with Color Balance

Digital photos taken on bright sunny days are the type of photos most likely to exhibit a bluish color cast. It isn't a result of the camera not working correctly but rather that the camera is capturing what your eyes and brain automatically filtered out when you were out on that bright sunny day. The blue sky naturally produces a blue color cast. How much color cast is produced is dependent on the time of year and shooting location in relation to the earth equator. Early digital cameras were not able to detect and compensate for these extremes in color temperature and that is why you may discover that your newest digital camera has less color cast problems than a previous camera that you owned.

Everyone seems to have a favorite method for removing unwanted color casts. Here is how to do it with the Color Balance feature. To do this exercise yourself, download the file bomber art.JPG from www.osborne.com. The photo shown in Figure 5-3 (and in the color insert) is a digital photograph taken of some art on a WWII aircraft. The background color should be a very light gray. The image has a bluish cast that is the result of photographing it on a bright sunny July day in Texas.

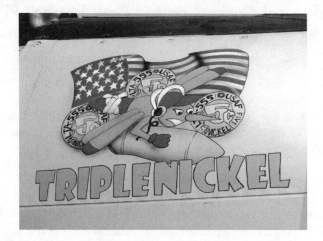

FIGURE 5-3 A bluish color cast detracts from an otherwise good photograph.

Open the image bomber art.JPG. From the menu, choose Adjust | Color Balance, which fills the screen with the Color Balance dialog box as shown next.

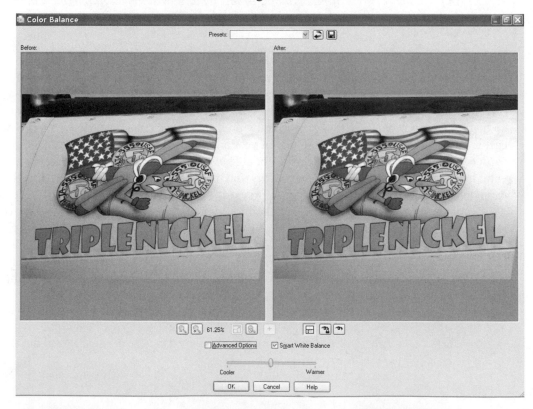

1. The color correction made in the default mode is accurate but it still is too cool so we need to open the Advanced Options mode of the dialog box. The dialog box has two modes. Check the Advanced Options checkbox and the dialog box will change as shown next. For more information about how these controls work, see the section, "How Color Balance Works."

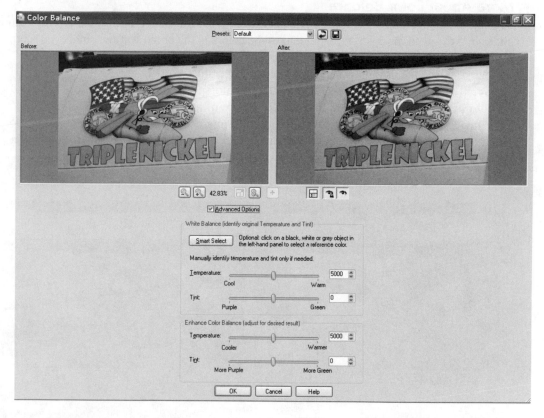

2. Click the Smart Select button. This causes Paint Shop Pro to evaluate the photo to find a white balance reference point (a neutral color that is either black, white, or gray). After you click the Smart Select button a marker appears in the Before preview image (left). This is a very small and faint marker. In the Bomber art.JPG image it will appear on the white headset bands of the dragonfly.

3. To change the color sample being used, move the cursor into the Before preview window and it will change into a eyedropper cursor with a floating box (shown in Figure 5-4) that displays the RGB values of the pixels under the eyedropper. Try clicking on different parts of the image to see how the different samples affect the image in the After preview window.

4. Click on the sample area in the Before window at a point near the one shown in Figure 5-4 and then click OK. To best evaluate the change in color cast, you should use the Undo and Redo buttons to jump back and forth between the corrected and uncorrected images.

More About Color Balance

Moving the Temperature slider in the Default mode (or the Enhance Color Balance Temperature slider in Advanced mode) to the right makes the colors in the photo warmer (more red) and moving it toward the left makes the colors cooler (bluish). For more information on color temperature, see the next section, "How Color Temperature Works."

What if the image doesn't have any neutral colors in it? There are a lot of them— a photo of a forest with a bright blue sky, a picture of a tropical beach, or a photo of your favorite UT Longhorn fan wearing burnt orange everything. At the top of the Color Balance dialog box is a Presets box. When it is opened (as shown next) you see a large

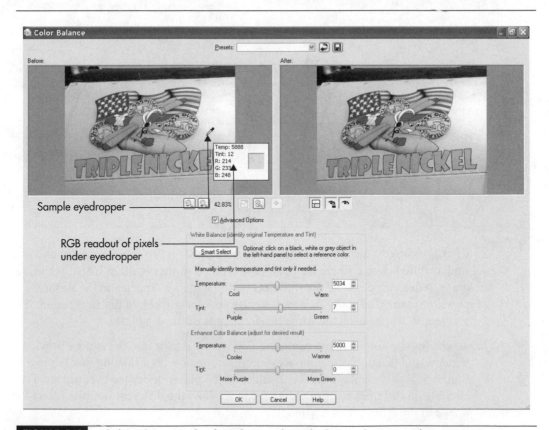

Select the neutral colors that produce the best color correction.

How Color Balance Works

The Color Balance dialog box's Default mode has the Advanced Options unchecked. In the Default mode the Smart White Balance checkbox is checked and makes Paint Shop Pro evaluate and make minor corrections to the image automatically—acting in the same way as the old Automatic Color Balance. If you are not satisfied with the color shift produced by the Smart White Balance you can drag the Temperature slider toward either the warmer or the cooler setting.

Checking the Advanced Options checkbox opens a more complex dialog box that has two pairs of sliders with a range from 2000 to 9500 Kelvin: White Balance and Enhance Color Balance. The White Balance sliders display the current white balance readings while Enhance Color Balance is used to change the white balance settings of the image. Dragging the Enhance Color Balance Temperature slider to the left adds cooler colors (more blue); dragging it to the right adds warmer colors (more orange).

list of different color temperatures including Tungsten, several Fluorescent settings, and Daylight.

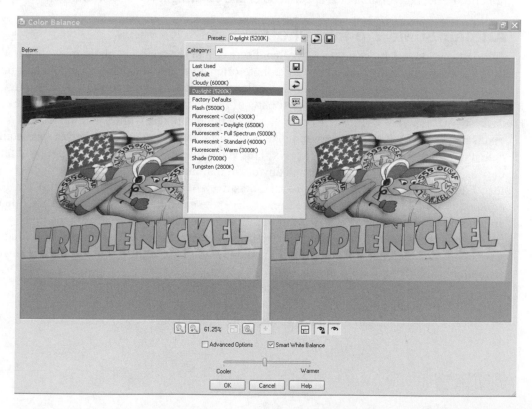

These presets are described as references to the general color temperatures of these light sources. Using these presets overrides any automatic settings. Using the preset changes the color temperature settings to a predefined value. Just because a photo is taken outdoors in the sunlight doesn't mean that selecting the Daylight preset will correct the color cast. In most cases for images that don't have a good neutral color for the automatic features to use as a reference, just move the color temperature slider until the result in the After preview window looks right to you.

How Color Temperature Works

To understand why the Color Balance works the way it does, it helps to understand some basics of color temperature. Even though the light from the sun or a light bulb looks white to us, it contains a mixture of all colors in varying proportions. The color of a light source is described by its color temperature. The color temperature scale is calibrated in degrees Kelvin, much like a thermometer that reads heat in degrees Fahrenheit. The color temperature scale operates in a manner opposite from what you might expect. That is, the lower color temperatures (reddish light) are considered warmer and the higher color temperatures (bluish light) are cooler. For example, daylight contains proportionately more light at the blue end of the spectrum, while incandescent light contains more light from the red end. Hence, daylight photos appear cooler and candlelight shots seem warmer.

Adding Some Zip to a Photo

After correcting a color cast you will often discover that the resulting photo may appear a little lifeless. Increasing the contrast of a photo often gives it some extra zip but it must be used with caution. Before using contrast it helps to understand what contrast is. In short, increasing contrast lightens the brightest parts of the image (highlights) and darkens the darkest parts (shadows). It does so by making the lightest pixels whiter, and the darkest pixels blacker. As the contrast between pixels increases, the image appears sharper but detail is lost in both the highlights and shadows. This is because as the lighter pixels get brighter they eventually become pure white and any detail that may have been in the highlights is lost. Figure 5-5 shows both the positive and negative effects of applying contrast. After contrast is applied to the photo of the London Eye, the capsules (that's what they are called) and the supporting structure really stand out. If you carefully compare the clouds in the before and after photos, you will notice that some of the detail in lighter area of the clouds has been lost. In this example, the subject is the London Eye so the photo has been improved without negatively impacting the photo.

Previous versions of Paint Shop Pro offered a separate tool called the Automatic Contrast Enhancement (ACE) effect. The Automatic Contrast feature is now part of the Advanced Options of Smart Photo Fix. If you apply Smart Photo Fix without the Advanced

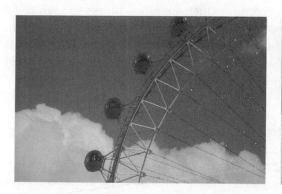

FIGURE 5-5 Applying contrast makes a dull photo (left) into a vivid one (right).

Options checked as shown, the photo is evaluated and several photo enhancements, including contrast, are applied.

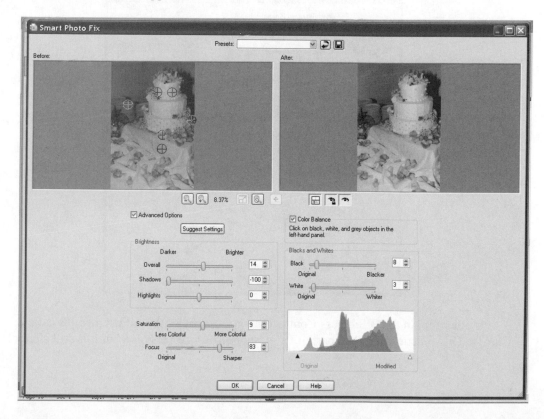

For more control over the amount of contrast that is applied, check the Advanced Options and you will discover the contrast controls (which are called Blacks and Whites). As you can see, the controls let you determine how dark the blacks are and how white the whites are. Where is the automatic part? Clicking the Suggest Settings button evaluates the photo and makes changes to the Blacks and Whites section as well as the others. If you only want to adjust the contrast, then uncheck the Color Balance checkbox and zero out the other settings.

More Ways to Control Image Contrast

There are several other ways to apply extra contrast to an image. The obvious one is the Brightness/Contrast command (SHIFT-B). From the Brightness/Contrast dialog box (shown next) you can manually apply both contrast and brightness settings. There are several presets for this dialog box and most of them are pretty heavy-handed so you should only consider using them as a starting point and adjust the image to suit your needs. Again, the Brightness/Contrast control does not evaluate your photo; it depends on you to adjust the settings manually until it appears the way you want it to look.

Another tool in the Brightness/Contrast menu category of the Adjust menu is called Clarify. This function has been part of Paint Shop Pro since version 6 but it is still a popular item. The only reference to the command in the documentation describes its use as a remedy for photos that appear foggy or hazy. In fact, it is a contrast enhancer that works best with photos that are lighter than average since part of the effect darkens the shadow region more than the typical contrast tool.

Making Colors Richer

One of the more common problems faced by photographers is photos with colors that appear dull, washed out, or both. The classic example of this problem is something most of us have experienced. You stand on the brink of some geological wonder like the Grand Canyon with your camera, taking photos with great expectations in the resulting photographs. But when the photos of the Grand Canyon come back, the colors don't look anything like what you remember. There is a reason for this. When you are on location, your eyes dynamically adjust and allow you to see a greater range of colors, but your camera records only a fixed amount of Red, Green, and Blue (RGB). Sometimes, when you correct the contrast of an image or apply other tonal corrections the colors appear to have become drab.

Color problems like these can often be corrected by increasing the saturation of the image. The term "saturation" may be new to you. If it is, it helps to think of saturation as the amount of color in an image. Technically, it is a lot more than that, but for practical purposes an image that has zero percent saturation appears to be a black-and-white photo. If you increase the saturation to its maximum setting the colors will appear to bleed together and any detail in the colored area will be lost.

There are several ways to enhance the color of an image with Paint Shop Pro. The easiest way is to use Smart Photo Fix with the Advanced Options selected. As you can see in the next illustration there is a Saturation slider from which you can control the amount of saturation that is applied. Be aware that applying too much saturation also changes the colors. Whenever you move the Saturation slider in the Smart Photo Fix it automatically enables the Color Balance feature. Often this automatic feature will over-saturate the image, especially if there are people in the photo. If it does, just drag the slider back to the left until the skin tone looks right and less like a tangerine. When using the slider in this dialog box on a large image (from a digital camera with more than six megapixels), after you move the slider give the program a few moments to update the After preview window before adjusting the slider again.

TIP   *When adjusting the saturation you should maximize the dialog box by clicking the Maximize icon in the upper-right corner so as to have the largest before and after previews possible.*

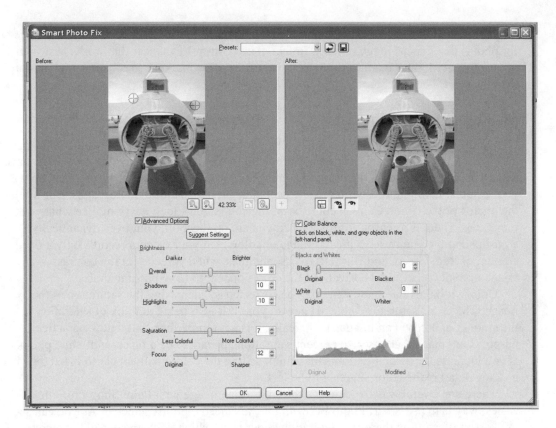

Another way to control the saturation in a photo is to use the Hue/Saturation/Lightness dialog box, shown next. It is found in the Adjustment menu in the Hue and Saturation category. The slider for saturation is just like the one in the Smart Photo Fix dialog box except that it is vertical instead of horizontal. There are two other sliders that control the other two color components, Hue and Lightness. Without getting into complicated color theory, and it really is complicated, it is possible to create any color using the three components Hue, Saturation, and Luminosity (lightness). This way of defining color is know as HSL. From the dialog box you can change the color by moving the Hue slider in one direction or the other. This works well—if all of the colors are off you can just move the Hue slider slightly to correct the colors in the image.

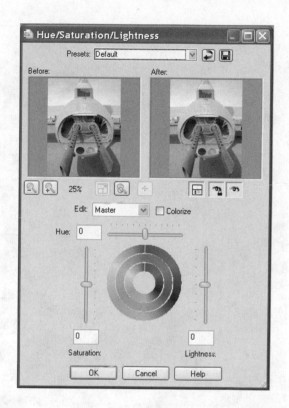

Fixing Red-Eye

Red-eye is a major problem for anyone who takes photos with a flash. Everyone has taken at least one photo that was ruined by red-eye rearing its ugly eyes—a problem that's even more frustrating when you use a camera with an anti-red-eye feature that rarely works as advertised. The red-eye effect is caused by the flash reflecting off of the retina of the person you are photographing. For the record, a couple things that help reduce red-eye are using an external flash or taking the photo in a well-lit room. Also, it helps if the subject is sober (no kidding!).

Some people are prone to red-eye, though, and no matter what you do, you get the "demon eye." However, you can get rid of red-eye like the one shown in Figure 5-6 with Paint Shop Pro's Red Eye Removal feature.

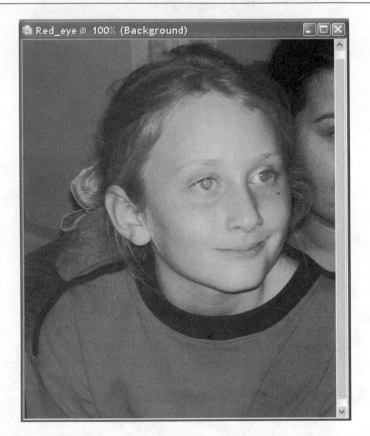

FIGURE 5-6 Red-eye gives photos a creepy appearance.

Here is how to get rid of red-eye. If you want to follow along with this exercise, download the image Red_eye.JPG from www.osborne.com.

1. Open the image Red_eye.JPG or a photo with red-eye. The sample photo is an example of extreme red-eye.

2. Choose Adjust | Red Eye Removal to open the dialog box shown next. Make sure the Method is set to Auto Human Eye. Use the Navigate button in the middle of the dialog box to position the red-eyes you want to remove in the Preview window on the left.

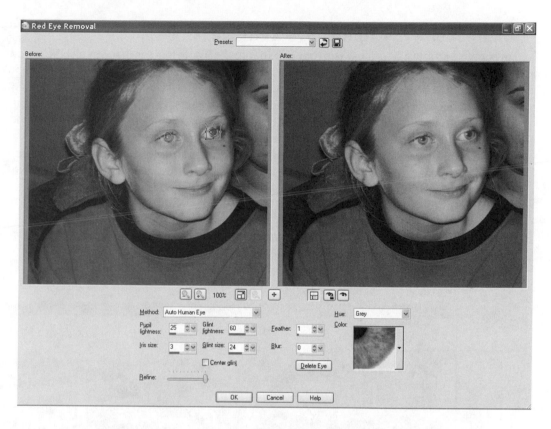

3. On the right side of the dialog box, select the general eye color from the drop-down list labeled Hue. The default setting is gray, which works almost every time. Try and pick the person's actual eye color. In most cases this is all you need to do. If you really want to get an exact color match (which no one will ever notice in the final print), click on the eye color in the Color box, and a large number of variations of that color appear.

4. Place the crosshair cursor in the left window directly over the red-eye reflection and click. After a moment, the preview window on the right will show the corrected eye.

TIP

This is not the time to change the subject's eye color. You should always do your best to match the eye color correctly. If you don't, viewers who know the subject will look at the photo and think (they never say) that something's not quite right about the photo, though they won't be able to tell you what it is.

A Quicker Way to Remove Red-Eye

As shown in Figure 5-7, there is a Red Eye tool in the Tools toolbar that can also be used to remove red-eye without opening the larger and more complex Red Eye Removal dialog box. The difference between this tool and the one discussed earlier is that it assumes all people have the same eye color (gray) and you must manually adjust the size of the tool so that it is large enough to capture all of the red. Once you have a size that is large enough to include the entire eye, you need only click on the red portion and the red-eye is immediately removed. In the case of the Red_eye.JPG image (which is an extreme case of red-eye), it is necessary to make the tool size quite large and even then it takes several clicks to get all of the red out. In extreme situations like this it takes less time to use the Red Eye Removal command and the Auto Human Eye option rather than the tool.

 TIP *When using this tool be careful not to get the tool effect on the eyelid. If you do it will appear that the subject's mascara has been smeared.*

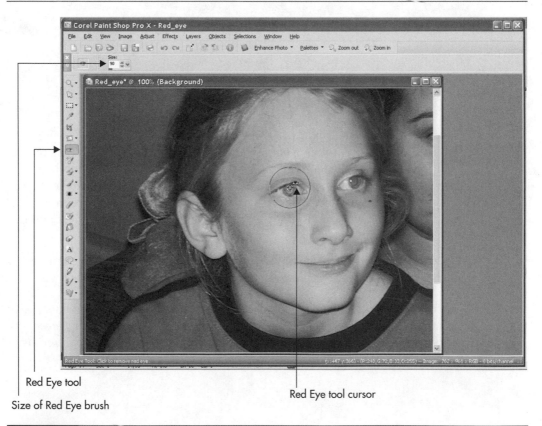

Red Eye tool

Size of Red Eye brush

Red Eye tool cursor

FIGURE 5-7   The Red Eye tool is a fast way to correct red-eye in a subject.

Other Touch-Ups You Can Do

Paint Shop Pro has added a tool in the Tools toolbar called the Makeover tool. This tool lets you fix blemishes, brighten teeth, and even add a suntan to improve the overall appearance of the subject. Before learning about that, let's learn how to brighten the whites of the eyes.

Making Eyes Brighter

You can use either the Lighten tool or the Dodge tool to slightly whiten the whites of the subject's eyes. Consider your subject when whitening eyes. Psychologically, the viewer expects babies, small children, and brides to have clear and bright eyes. If you apply the same amount of whitening to a destitute person on the street the subject may appear frightening. Here is how to whiten the eyes:

1. Select the Lighten/Darken tool from the Tool Options palette and change the Opacity to a low value (between 15 and 25).

2. Use a small brush size (only a few pixels) and lightly apply it to the white around the eyes. The result is shown in Figure 5-8.

The Makeover Tool

As mentioned earlier, the Makeover tool in the Tools toolbar has three different modes of operation. One of these is the Toothbrush, which correctly implies that it makes teeth whiter.

Making Teeth Their Whitest

With the current obsession with having glow-in-the-dark white teeth, this mode comes in very handy when enhancing photographs. Its use is simplicity itself. Select the tool in the Tools toolbar, change the mode in the Tools options to Toothbrush, and click on each tooth.

 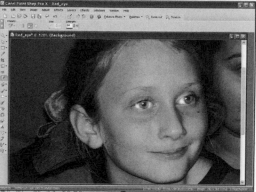

FIGURE 5-8   A little whitening of the eyes is an easy way to enhance a subject.

As you do, the tooth and other teeth that are contiguous to it will become whiter as shown in Figure 5-9. You can control the amount of whitening using the strength setting.

As with the whitening of the eyes discussed earlier, consider your subject before applying the Toothbrush. In an old episode of "Law and Order" the make-up and costume department had made a lot of effort to make an actor appear to be someone who had been living on the streets of New York for years. The effect was completely lost when he opened his mouth to speak and you saw rows of perfect teeth that were so bright you could have used them to light airport runways on foggy nights. The idea is to enhance the subject, not draw attention to any particular part of the body—that's why we have plastic surgeons.

Blemishes and Suntans

The other two Makeover tools, Blemish Remover and Suntan, are as simple to use as the Toothbrush. With Suntan all you need do is paint on a tan as shown on the young ladies in Figure 5-10. When applying Suntan, the strength is preset and to prevent overlapping, the tan always appears at the same level regardless of how many times you paint over the same spot. Be careful to only apply it to skin area as the Suntan brush has no idea what is skin and what is not. It will change hair color and darken clothes, backgrounds, and anything else that gets under the brush.

The Blemish Remover couldn't be simpler to use. The cursor looks like a bull's-eye. Click or drag the brush over a blemish and the tool uses the surrounding area to determine what colors to use to replace the blemish. This brings up an important point. If you look closely at the young lady on the left in Figure 5-10 you will see a minor imperfection just above her lip. If the Blemish Remover had been used to remove it, the brush would have

FIGURE 5-9   Brighter teeth are not necessary for this little girl but they add to the overall effect of the photo.

FIGURE 5-10 Use the Makeover tool to add suntans, remove blemishes, and whiten teeth.

detected the colors in her lips and tried to blend them into the other colors. The result would look a little like a deformed lip. If you wanted to remove it, you would need to use the Clone tool with a hard edge.

Perfection Isn't Always Perfect

Looking at the After photo in Figure 5-10, the teeth and eyes have been whitened and the small blemish between her eye and ear has been removed. If you look at the copy of this photo in the color insert you will see that she now has a tan. Notice that the blemish above the lip remains. The point is, it is not necessary to remove every imperfection from a photo. Some imperfections are associated with the individual. They are part of who they are. Can you imagine the actor Owen Wilson without his broken nose? This headlong pursuit of perfection will also confuse viewers generations from now. You may not be aware of this but even though Queen Elizabeth I ruled England (50 plus years) and was loved by all in the realm, we have few clues as to what she looked like because she was very concerned about her appearance as she got older and so portraits of her that were not flattering were destroyed. Make your photos somewhat honest and later generations will know what we really looked like—warts and all.

Why You Need Sharpening

No matter how crisp your original photograph is and how great your scanner is, you will always lose some sharpness when an image is digitized. An image also loses sharpness when it is sent to an output device or when it is compressed. As a result, most images will appear "soft" when printed unless some degree of sharpening is applied. Paint Shop Pro contains several sharpening filters that can help make your images as sharp as possible.

What Is Sharpening?

Sharpening adds edges. The human eye is influenced by the presence of edges in an image. Without edges, an image appears dull. By increasing the difference (contrast) between neighboring pixels, Paint Shop Pro enhances the edges, thus making the image appear sharper, whether it is or not. However, while sharpening filters help compensate for images or image elements that are out of focus, don't expect sharpening to bring a blurred photograph into sharp focus.

NOTE   *Sharpening is one of the last effects you should apply. Apply it after tonal and color correction, as it will affect the results of both.*

How Sharpening Affects Noise

All computer images include noise. *Noise* consists of pixels that may produce a grainy pattern or the odd dark or light spot. Images from photographs will always have noise. Actually, any image, including those captured with digital cameras, will have noise of some sort. Even the most pristine photo in your stock photo collection that was scanned on a ten-zillion dollar drum scanner will exhibit some noise.

What does noise have to do with the Sharpen filters? When you sharpen an image, you sharpen the noise as well. In fact, the noise generally sharpens up much better and faster than the rest of the image because noise pixels (like the tiny white specks in a black background) contain the one component that sharpening filters look for: the differences between adjoining pixels. Since the act of sharpening seeks out the differences (edges) and increases the contrast, the edges of the noise are enhanced and enlarged more than the rest of the pixels in the image.

This means that if you have an image containing a lot of noise, you should avoid applying any sharpening to it, as it will enhance the noise producing white or rainbow-speckled pixels over all of the image. Instead you should use one of the noise reduction filters to first reduce the noise. There is more about noise removal at the end of the chapter.

Chromatic Aberration

What is *chromatic aberration*? Technically speaking, it is color shifts and color artifacts in an image caused by faults in a lens, or by the camera's inability to register all three channels of color information. For reasons involving enough physics to make a "Nova" program on PBS, let's simplify this a little. First, digital cameras are prone to chromatic aberration. Second, it appears as a purple fringe on some pixels near the edges of a photo. Third, it doesn't occur all that often. If you see this phenomenon on any of your photos, your best solution is to apply the One-Step Purple Fringe Fix (that's really its name) found in the Adjust menu. In almost all cases this will resolve the problem.

For those of you who want a more sophisticated and professional solution, Paint Shop Pro has included a professional Chromatic Aberration Removal filter, which is also found in the Adjust menu. Unlike the One-Step Purple Fringe Fix, this command opens the dialog box shown next. Clicking on the Help button opens up an excellent explanation of how to use this tool. So which tool should you use? Again, this is a rare problem and the One-Step Purple Fringe Fix usually solves the problem. If it doesn't, then use the Removal filter. If you are seeing this problem in all of your photos, you either have a very cheap camera or something is wrong with your camera and you should speak to someone in a camera store (not the salesman at the super mega center where you bought it).

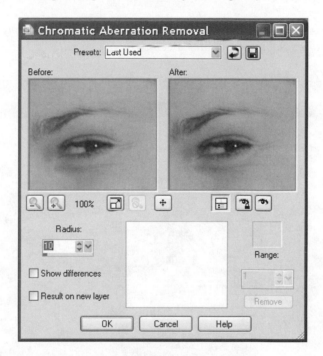

Lens Distortion and Correction

Since the sensors in a digital camera are physically smaller than a standard 35mm negative, digital camera lenses must be wider than their film counterparts to capture the same area. As a result, pictures taken with digital cameras can suffer from one of two forms of lens distortion: barrel (lines bowing out) and pincushion (lines bowing in).

Normally, wide-angle lenses exhibit barrel distortion. Barrel distortion is clearly shown near the edges of the photo. Pincushion distortion is a lens effect that causes images to be pinched at their center. Pincushion distortion is associated with zoom lenses or telephoto adapters and only occurs at the telephoto end of a zoom lens. The distortion is most noticeable when you have a very straight edge near the side of the image frame.

Correcting Barrel Distortion

Barrel distortion is a lens effect that causes images to appear sphere-like at their center. Barrel distortion is associated with wide-angle lenses and only occurs at the wide end of a zoom lens. This distortion is most noticeable when you have vertical or horizontal elements in the photo such as in the photograph of the Federal Reserve Bank door in St. Louis (see Figure 5-11). To do the barrel distortion exercise, download the file Fed_bank.JPG from www.osborne.com.

> **NOTE**   *If you attempt to make a panorama using images that have any lens distortion, it will make stitching the photos together more difficult.*

FIGURE 5-11   Barrel distortion is common in digital cameras.

To remove barrel distortion in an image:

1. With Fed_bank.JPG open, select Adjust | Barrel Distortion Correction to display the Barrel Distortion Correction dialog, shown next.

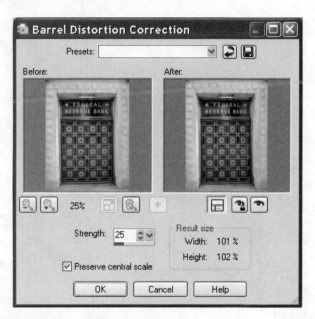

5

TIP *You can turn the Grid on (select View | Grid) to provide a point of reference when correcting distortion.*

2. Change the Strength setting until the horizontal or vertical elements no longer appear bent outward. Use the Proof button to see the effect on the image. Click OK. For the image Fed_bank.JPG, use the preset Pillow Corners. The corrected image is shown in Figure 5-12.

There are two other lens distortion correction tools, Pincushion Distortion and Fisheye Distortion. Both of these types of distortion are not seen as often as barrel distortion. Both of the tools work in the same fashion as the Barrel Distortion filter.

FIGURE 5-12   Correction of the barrel distortion is easy with Paint Shop Pro.

Dealing with the Noise

Noise is a fact of life with any digital image. Some noise isn't noticeable and some is. You can find noise in a bright blue sky or a night photo. Fortunately, Paint Shop Pro has some excellent tools to remove or at the very least reduce the noise in a photo.

Removing Digital Noise from Pictures

Photos taken with digital cameras under low-light conditions or high ISO settings (equivalent to exposure speed of film) have more than their fair share of noise appearing in the resulting image. Noise appears as a blotchy area on a solid blue sky or as multi-colored little dots, especially in darker regions of a photo, as shown next.

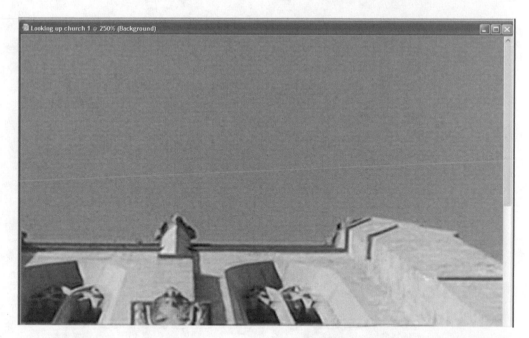

Up until now the only remedy was to buy one of the many third-party plug-in filters (some of which cost more than Paint Shop Pro). In Paint Shop Pro there is now a digital noise removal filter built right into the program. The new noise removal filter reduces both kinds of unwanted noise without causing the detail in the image to become soft or appear out of focus. The image shown in Figure 5-13 (original) is of a blue sky taken near sunset (low light) with an old digital camera. The noise is quite apparent. Applying the One-Step Noise Removal command from the Adjust menu removes the noise while preserving the details in the image.

Just as with Chromatic Aberration Removal there is a more complex and professional noise removal filter in Paint Shop Pro as shown next. It is accessed from the Adjustment menu under Digital Camera Noise Removal.

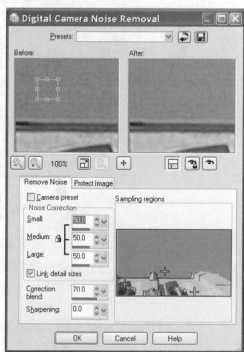

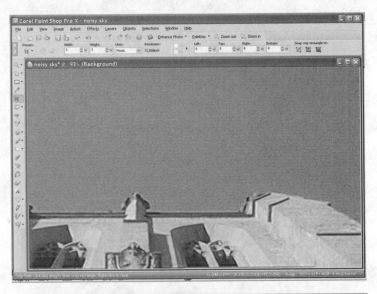

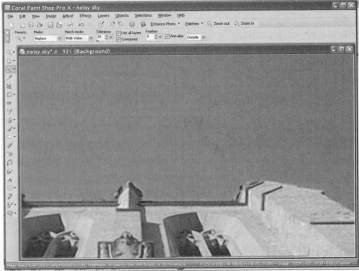

FIGURE 5-13 Before: a close-up of a noisy sky, and After: the same image with the noise removed

Like all digital noise filters, setting this filter up to work correctly is complicated, so if the One-Step Noise Removal provides satisfactory results, you should stay with it. For more information on using this filter, open the dialog box and you will discover an excellent description of how the tool works.

The **easiest way** to turn your pictures
into professional-looking **photos**—*fast!*

COREL®
Paint Shop Pro® X

Adjust & Retouch	**Create** & Collage	**Graphics** & Effects	**Organize** & Share
■ Fix any flaw	■ Erase backgrounds	■ Convert to black & white	■ Find any photo fast
■ Rotate, resize and crop	■ Add frames and edges	■ Paint with realistic art tools	■ Organize photo collections
■ Repair faded, damaged or scratched photos	■ Create calendars, cards, books picture CDs & more	■ Add text and shapes	■ Show off photo creations

CHAPTER 6
Repairing and Restoring Photographs

The increased interest in creating scrapbooks has caused many users to begin locating and preserving photos of their family's past. Many of these family treasures need restoration and many of those that need it the most are color photos taken in the '50s and '60s because the dyes used back then were not as stable as they are today and their colors are beginning to fade and shift. All of the features and power of Paint Shop Pro X make the job of converting old, torn, and otherwise damaged photos easy. In this chapter, you will discover how you can use Paint Shop Pro to reverse the damage done by time and mishandling. You will also learn the best ways to scan images for preservation and restoration.

Preparing Your Image or Document

Unlike digital camera photo goofs (leaving the flash off, putting a finger in front of the lens, and so on), older damaged images and other important documents must first be scanned before you can repair them. In most cases, you will need to remove the photo from its frame before scanning. If you cannot remove it from the frame without damaging it, then you will need to scan the entire photo or document (frame and all). Be aware that when you scan the entire photo, frame and all, there is a chance that the color of the frame will influence the scanner's auto exposure feature during the scan. To solve this problem, you should either select only the photo and try the automatic setting again, or manually adjust the tonal settings. Just remember to perform the evaluation of the scan with Paint Shop Pro and not from the preview window in the scanner software, which is a poor representation of the image.

Laying Image Flat on the Glass

It is difficult to scan a document or image that has been rolled up for a long time because it will curl up. If the image is not laying flat on the glass, it will create highlights and shadows, especially along the creases. Figure 6-1 is part of a photo panorama taken of a navy boot camp company over 35 years ago that was kept rolled up for most of that time. When placed on the scanner, the weight of the scanner lid wasn't enough to keep the photo flat to the glass and it lifted slightly, causing the white reflections.

When scanned the second time, the scanner lid was held down tightly (be careful: the scanner glass can break), and the resulting scan appears in Figure 6-2. While the crease remains, the bright reflections are now gone. There are still creases and tears and you will discover how to repair damage like this later in the chapter.

Preparing to Restore Photos

When you are scanning an image for the purpose of restoring it, you will need to make a few adjustments to your normal scanning routine. First, if the photo or image that you are scanning is really old (and most of the examples in this chapter are), they are fragile, and therefore you should exercise caution when handling and preparing them for scanning.

FIGURE 6-1   A photo not laying flat on the scanner glass creates highlights and shadows.

FIGURE 6-2   Flattening the image reduces reflections.

Scanning for Restoration

This section contains guidelines for scanning photographs and other documents specifically for restoration and preservation. In several ways they differ from normal scanning guidelines.

Enlarging the Original

When repairing or otherwise restoring, make it a general rule to scan images at 200 percent. By doubling the size of the original, you force the scanner to capture the maximum amount of detail in the original photo and give yourself more material to work with. One exception to this rule is when the original is really small. In such cases, you should consider using an even larger resize factor (such as 300 percent through 500 percent). If the original image is large enough to cover the entire scanner glass, don't enlarge it. The default setting of your scanner (100 percent) will probably be sufficient.

TIP	*If the photo is already scanned by someone else, do not enlarge the photo with Paint Shop Pro. The rule of making the image larger only applies during the scanning.*

Using the Highest Quality Scan Setting

When you are scanning for repair, restoration, or preservation you want to get as much image detail from the scanned image as possible without having to worry about how big the final file will be. For photos and memorabilia that you want to preserve, scan the original using RGB (24-bit) color. Black-and-white photos in most cases should be scanned in grayscale—the exception being if they have been hand-colored or have a colored stain on them. Preserving the color in such cases allows isolation of the stain using color-sensitive selection tools.

Some of the better scanners today offer the ability to scan at color depths that are greater than the 8-bit per color (24-bit) RGB, such as 16-bit per color channel (48-bit). If your scanner has that ability you should use that setting. If your scanner does not offer the ability to scan at 48-bit, it doesn't mean that if you purchase a 48-bit scanner the quality of scanning for restoration will noticeably improve. In most cases you will not notice a difference except that you will have a much larger image file size.

Scanning the Original, Warts and All

When scanning for preservation, you should not be selective and scan only part of the original. For example, Figure 6-3 is an old photo taken near the turn of the century that was glued to a stained paper frame. To preserve this image, you should scan the photo, the frame, and in most cases even include a little extra around the edges. When you get around to restoring the photo, you can crop out the frame from a copy of the scanned photo, but we recommend you preserve all of the original and how it appeared when it was photographed.

FIGURE 6-3   When preserving an image or document, scan the entire original.

Saving Photos Using a Lossless File Format

Do not save the original image as a JPEG file. For restoration work, you should save the images in either Paint Shop Pro native format (*.pspimage) or TIFF. Do not save the images you are working with using any file format that uses lossy file compression. This includes Wavelet, JPEG, and JPEG 2000. Lossy file compression degrades the image, and with 100+ GB drives selling for less than $100, file size is not as important today as it was in the early days of digital photo editing.

If your original will only be used by you, then saving in the Paint Shop Pro format is the recommended choice. If other people may be working on it, then you should save it as a TIFF file because it is the most popular lossless graphic format and all other photo editing applications support it. When you save it as a TIFF format you can choose one of several lossless compression options, meaning they do not degrade the image. Be careful not to choose the JPEG compression option that is now available as a choice for TIFF.

Repairing Tears and Creases

One of the more common problems with old photos is that they have not usually received museum quality care and storage. Unprotected, important images can easily become bent, folded, and otherwise damaged. Physically, there isn't anything that can be done for the original (with the exception of work done by a restoration specialist), but it's relatively easy to repair an electronic version and then to print a copy of it. If you are making a scrapbook, you can use the copy in the scrapbook and archive the original in acid-free paper in a safe place to prevent further damage.

How much damage was caused by folding a photograph depends on its age and the material it was printed on. Photos from the past 30 years are printed on a flexible Mylar that can stand almost any degree of contortion, while photos printed around the turn of the twentieth century through the late 1950s were printed on stiff material. In most cases, even a slight bend produces a hard, raised crease from which the image may flake off, as in the example shown in Figure 6-1. Ironically, the colors on the flexible Mylar are fading in many cases while the sepia tone images of 150 years ago are still crisp and sharp today.

Here is the step-by-step procedure to repair a crease from an old photograph; the example photo was taken in 1896. You can download the image Old Photo.JPG from the Corel Web site and follow along if you wish.

1. After ensuring the scanner glass is clean, position the original photo on the center of the scanner glass. Run a preview scan and change the output size so the resulting scan is twice as large (200 percent) as the original.

2. Save the original scan and then save a copy to work on using the Save As command. The original scanned photo (shown at right) doesn't appear to be in terrible shape.

3. When you open the copy, make sure that the Paint Shop Pro X view is set to 100 percent (see the sidebar titled "Zoom Settings," later in this chapter). Because of the large size of the image, only a portion of it will be visible in the image window. When doing retouching and restoration work, it is often necessary to

get in quite close—200 percent through 400 percent—to fix the image, but you must always return to 100 percent to accurately evaluate the changes made.

4. There are several tools that can be used to remove the diagonal crease on the photo: the Clone brush, the Scratch Remover, and the Object Remover. The Scratch Remover is best used on smaller scratches; if used on the crease it would result is a smeared line. The Clone tool and the Object Remover are both good choices, but since many Paint Shop Pro users are not familiar with the Object Remover that will be the one used first. Select the Object Remover from the Tools toolbar, as shown next.

5. Make sure the Selection Mode button is enabled in the Tool Options toolbar and draw a selection around the area to be repaired.

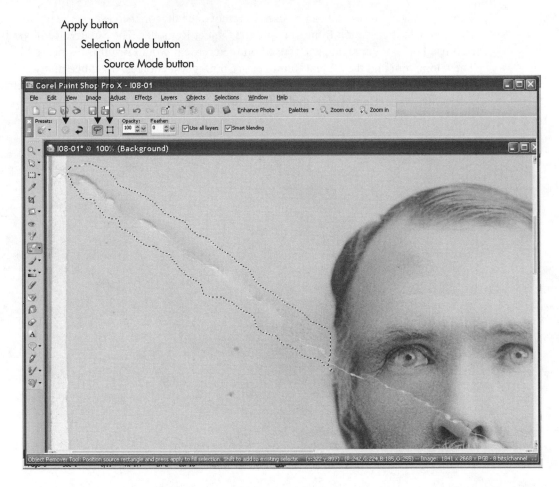

6. Click the Source Mode button and a rectangle appears. Position the rectangle over the part of the photo that will be used to replace the selected area—in this case, the crease. Drag the handles on the rectangle to resize it, or drag the rotation handle on the rectangle to rotate it. It is recommended that you make the rectangle as large as, or slightly larger than, the area you are removing. Once it is in place click the Apply button and the crease disappears.

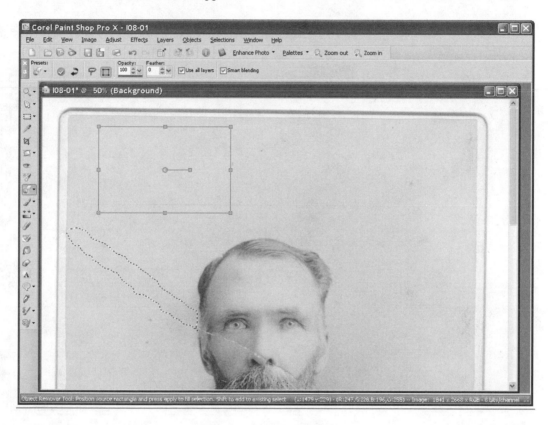

TIP *When you are zoomed in close the rectangle may appear on a part of the screen that is not displayed. If you don't see a rectangle after you select the Source mode, zoom out by using the scroll wheel on your mouse.*

7. Repeat the same procedure on the right side of the crease to remove that crease from the background as shown. You can use the same rectangle, but when you are finished using the Object Remover tool you must remove the selection (CTRL-D).

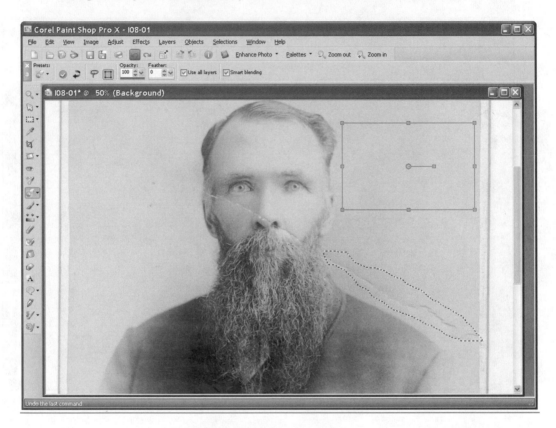

8. Select the Clone tool (C) and create a source point on his face that will be used to provide the pixels to paint over the crease. You create the source point by right-clicking the tool on the desired area. When you do this you will hear a thunk sound bite that is usually used when an improper action has occurred, but in this case it means it is working. When working on critical areas (like the crease across his face) zoom in as much as necessary so you can use the smallest, soft-edged Clone brush to get the small areas. In the image shown next, a magnification of 120 percent is used, allowing a smaller brush to get in and around the tear that went through the nostril.

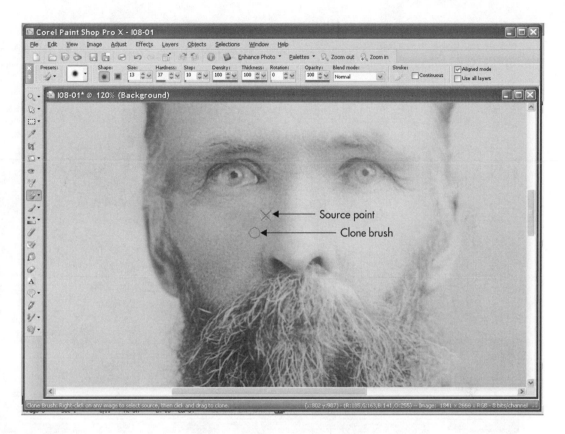

TIP	*To quickly move around an image (especially at high zoom levels), enable the Hand tool by holding down the* SPACEBAR. *When you let go of the* SPACEBAR *it reverts back to the previously selected tool.*

9. Use the Clone brush to remove the remaining parts of the crease and some of the dark spots on the background.

10. Return to either 100 percent or Fit to Window zoom level to see how the entire image looks.

11. This particular photo has lost some of its quality over the years. Using the One-Step Photo Fix feature makes the photo look even better by applying more than six different auto enhancements to the image. The finished image is shown in Figure 6-4.

12. To complete the work, resize the image to return it to its correct size. There is a natural softening of the image that is the result of making it smaller. This can sometimes make a harsh image look better. If it softens it too much, apply the Unsharp Mask filter at a low setting.

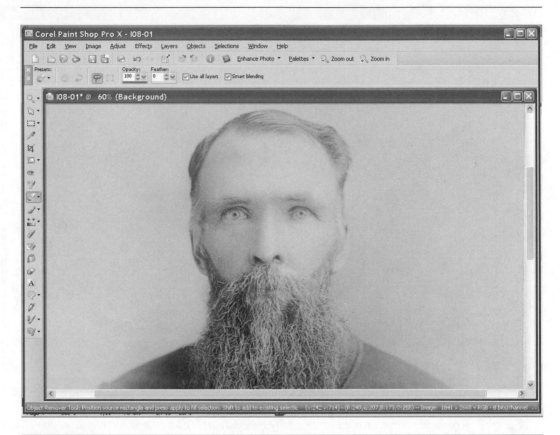

FIGURE 6-4 The finished restoration

Removing Large Stains

While the Clone tool and Clone brush are great tools, there are other solutions available for repairing and restoring a scanned image. When the area covered by a stain is too large, neither the Clone tool nor the Object Remover can effectively be used because the cloned area would be very apparent. In the example photo, the paper frame (shown here) in which the photo was mounted has seen more than its share of use and abuse.

6

Zoom Settings

Zoom settings are important when working on any bitmap image. To understand why, you must first understand how your display monitor works with your computer to display photos.

Pictures are made up of millions of units called pixels. These pixels have two characteristics: they are square and can only represent one color. Your computer display also has pixels and the number of pixels is determined by the display setting. Most displays (that are not widescreen) are 1024 pixels wide and 768 pixels in height. An application like Paint Shop Pro uses a portion of the display's pixels for menus, toolbars, and such. When you open an image that has more pixels than there are display pixels to show them, one of two things must happen. Either each image pixel is mapped to a display pixel and part of the image is off of the screen, or the program re-creates a smaller version of the image on the display, which is called zooming.

Regardless of how good the computer and the program are, the fact remains that when viewing at anything other than a 1:1 ratio (also called 100% zoom ratio) you cannot accurately view the image. Getting close to 100% doesn't improve the image being displayed. At zoom settings other than 100% many strange things happen to the photo's appearance: if the subject has a pattern it may display a checkerboard pattern (called a moiré pattern) or lines and text might appear to be rough or crude. It is important to know that the image is not affected in the least; it is only the display of the image that is being affected.

The image's zoom setting is always displayed in the upper-left corner of the image window. Paint Shop Pro calls the 100% setting by two different names. When the Zoom tool is selected, a button appears in the Tool Options toolbar called the Actual Size button. From the View menu it is called Zoom to 100% (CTRL-ALT-N). Different names, identical results.

In this restoration, you are going to use portions of one part of the frame to cover another part. With the image loaded in Paint Shop Pro, change the view to 100 percent (actual pixels). In the lower-left corner there are two serious stains, so that's where we'll start.

1. Select an area of the frame that is clean, create a rectangle selection, and put a feathered edge on the selection, like the one shown next. The feathering of the selection produces gradual transitions so your patch work isn't apparent. Because

this is a large image, the 6-pixel feather we chose will produce a very small transition area.

2. While holding down the ALT key, drag the selection to the left until it covers the bad spot on the corner, as shown in Figure 6-5. By ALT-dragging, you'll copy the pixels inside the selection marquee.

3. There are several ways to de-float the selection. The easiest is to right-click inside the selection or remove the selection (CTRL-D). Continue making more selections to repair all of the stains on the paper frame.

4. The final step is to make a hard-edged selection (no feather) of the dark-edged border to rebuild the worn corner of the print. The finished corner is shown in Figure 6-6.

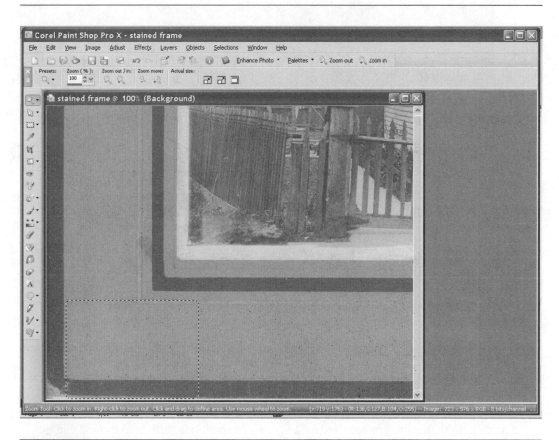

FIGURE 6-5   A floating selection covers the stain.

FIGURE 6-6 The paper frame looks brand new.

Cleaning Up Dirty Backgrounds

Just as with the frame you repaired in the previous section, a dirty background can be repaired with a Clone tool or brush, but it would take too much time. Instead, you'll learn how to clean up the debris in the background of an old photo—the example was taken way back in 1897 (see Figure 6-7).

Here is how to clean up the dirty sky in the sample photo:

1. Open the image. Using the Freehand Selection tool, select part or all of the background that you want to clean. Use the Smart Edge of the Freehand Selection tool to quickly create a rough selection composed of the background of the image, as shown in Figure 6-8.

FIGURE 6-7   This old photo has a lot of debris that needs to be removed.

2. With the background selected, there are several ways to remove the dust and debris. You could just press DELETE, and the background will become pure white (assuming your background color is set to white). However, this produces an artificial-looking backdrop that can be distracting. Instead, use the Salt and Pepper filter (Adjust | Add/Remove Noise | Salt and Pepper Filter) at the setting shown next to remove the debris and leave a background that appears to be part of the original print.

FIGURE 6-8 Select the sky with the debris.

NOTE

If you only see transparent checkerboard in the dialog box, you can click and drag in either panel to view the dirty sky in the panel. In this example, the transparent checkerboard does not appear because most of the image is already inside the selected area.

3. In this photo, the right side of the house is overexposed. Here is a fast and easy way to correct that. Invert the selection (CTRL-SHIFT-I). Now everything but the sky is selected. Select the Lighten/Darken brush (L) from the Tools toolbar. Set the opacity to about 50% and use the

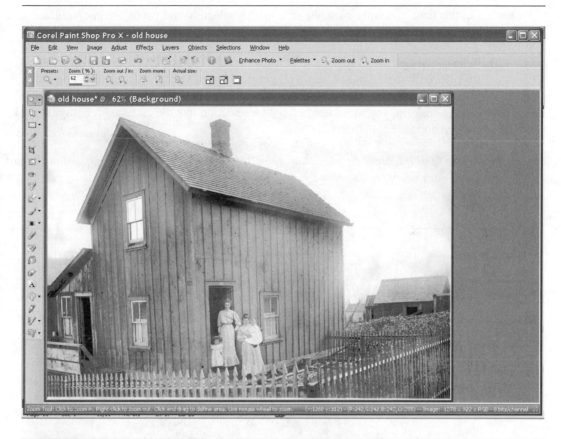

FIGURE 6-9   Dirty sky is removed and the exposure is balanced.

right mouse button to paint (Darken) the over-exposed parts of the photo to make the exposure appear more even. In this case, the left mouse button (Lighten) was also applied to the left side of the house, which was darker. The completed photo is shown in Figure 6-9.

Another Way to Remove Stains

The image shown in Figure 6-10 has a stain on it caused by a clear oil such as mineral oil or sewing machine oil. What makes this type of stain unique is that it darkens the color, but the stain is, for all intents and purposes, transparent. The placement of the stain on the oval paper frame pattern precludes placing a selection over it, as you did earlier in the chapter. In this case you will isolate the stain with a selection and tweak the hue, saturation, and lightness. Here is how it is done:

1. Use the Magic Wand tool set to a low tolerance and select the stain. You will need to play with the tolerance until you get the correct setting. If your selection includes areas isolated from the stain, check the settings for your Magic Wand tool. With a little tweaking, you should end up with a selection like the one shown in Figure 6-11, which accurately outlines the stain.

TIP *Don't put a feather on your stain selection; if you do, you will see a faint outline of the stain when you are done.*

FIGURE 6-10 Old oil stains are hard to cover up.

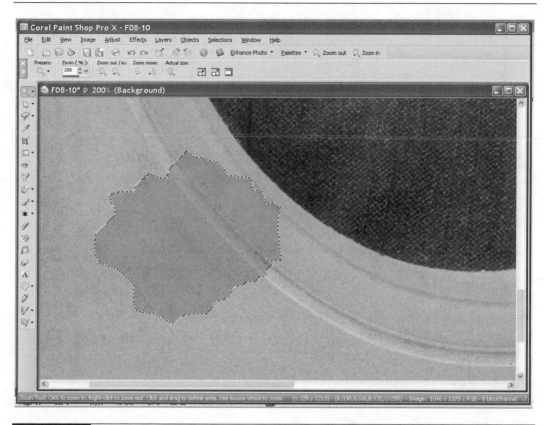

FIGURE 6-11   Select the stained area.

2. Once you have the selection the way you want it, hide the marquee (CTRL-SHIFT-M) and open the Hue/Saturation/Lightness dialog box (SHIFT-H), as shown here.

3. Adjust the Lightness first until it appears to be as light as the surrounding area. Note that the color inside the selection does not appear to be as vivid as the outside area. No problem: move the Saturation controls up slightly until the stain disappears. Click OK, and the big stain is gone.

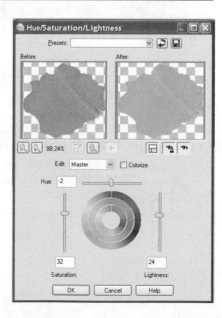

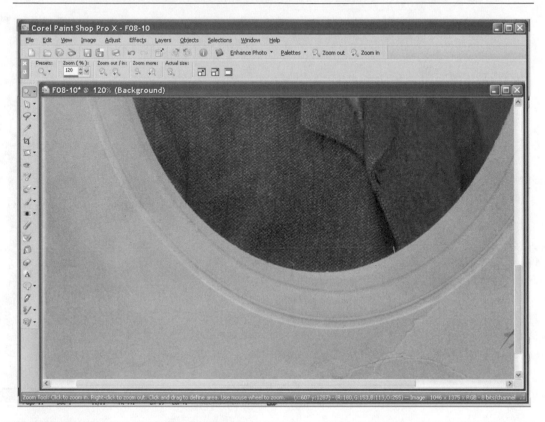

FIGURE 6-12   The stain is almost invisible.

4. Remove the selection (CTRL-D)—it's easy to forget it's there when it is hidden. Use the Clone tool to clean up any remaining dirt or stains. The cleaned-up paper frame is shown in Figure 6-12.

Recovering Old Color Photos

Not all photos that need to be restored were made at the turn of the last century. Color photography became a usable tool near the end of World War II (1944–1945), which explains why nearly all of the WWII combat footage is in black-and-white. Early color photographs were not great. The colors were not vivid and oftentimes not accurate. Did you know that some of the early color films (like *The Wizard of Oz*) had to employ a consultant who worked with the set and costume designers to ensure that the colors they picked would look correct when the film was developed. Color photos from the 1950s through the late 1960s used organic dyes that have a relatively short life. After 20 or so years, the dyes began to fade, the colors shifted toward magenta, or both. Even well-preserved color photos can suffer this deterioration. Even though the tools in Paint Shop Pro are not specifically designed to restore old color photos, they can do a pretty good job nonetheless.

Bringing Back the Color

The original photo shown in Figure 6-13 (as well as in the color insert) was a very small print measuring 3" x 2". This may seem like an odd size but it is not uncommon for picture packages and film developers to include wallet-size prints. The first step in the restoration

FIGURE 6-13   This photo (also shown in the color insert) has shifted its colors with age.

was to scan the image so it was the size that the final print would be printed. Since there was no damage to restore, it wasn't necessary to scan it in at a large size.

1. With the image open, apply One-Step Photo Fix from the Adjust menu. Using the default settings, the resulting image is a great improvement as shown.

2. Next, we evaluate the image. The overall contrast is soft so the next step is to use the Clarify tool (Adjust | Brightness and Contrast | Clarify). Using the default settings improves the overall contrast, as shown next. The only problem that was induced is that it was necessary to lose some detail in the shadows, but since nothing important was in the shadows, it is an acceptable loss to improve the overall appearance.

COREL PAINT SHOP PRO X:
THE OFFICIAL GUIDE

The Official Guide

▸ **One of the major** improvements in Paint Shop Pro X is the appearance of the desktop.

USE LAYERS TO CHANGE THE COMPOSITION OF PHOTOS

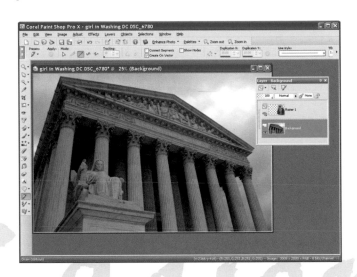

▸ **Using the Layers Palette** allows you to turn layers on and off to completely change the composition of a photo.

CROP PHOTOS

▸ *Learn how to* improve the composition of your photos through cropping.

MAKE QUICK FIXES

▸ *The flash* of a camera can produce an undesirable shift in colors.

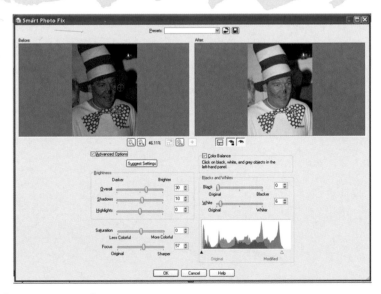

▸ *The Smart Photo Fix* feature provides a fast and easy way to see the changes to the photo as you are working on them.

▶ **While the change** is subtle, it makes the colors in the subject's face appear more vivid and lifelike.

COLOR CORRECT PHOTOS

▶ *This image* has a bluish cast that is the result of photographing it on a bright sunny July day in Texas. The background color should be a very light gray.

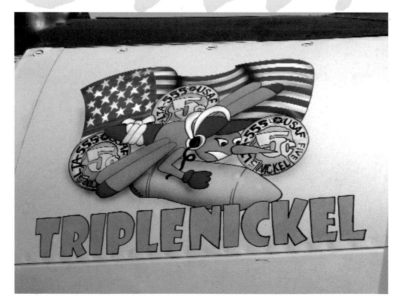

▶ *After applying* Color Correction with Paint Shop Pro, the offending color cast is gone.

GIVE YOUR SUBJECTS A MAKEOVER

▶ *These subjects* have cool colors produced by an overcast day, flat eyes, and dull teeth.

▶ *Using the Makeover tool* it was possible to add a suntan, remove blemishes and whiten both their eyes and their teeth.

RESTORE OLD PHOTOS

▶ **The dyes used** in this older original photo have shifted with age. Restoring the photo involves several steps.

▶ **First, applying** One Step Photo Fix brings out some detail.

▸ **The Clarify tool** is used next to bring up the contrast.

▸ **The restored image** isn't perfect but it is greatly improved over the original.

PLAY WITH REALITY

▶ *Before digital photo editing*, removing your ex from the photo was crudely resolved with a pair of scissors. Use the Clone tool to discover how to eliminate unwanted subjects from a photo.

▶ *This composition* demonstrates layers with selective transparency. Applying the Eraser tool allows the background to be seen through these objects, creating a greater sense of realism in this surrealistic scene.

ADD TRANSPARENT TEXT

▶ **Simply applying** the Outer Bevel effect to a text selection can add a great transparent text effect to a photo.

TRANSFORM AN IMAGE WITH TEXT

▶ *Adding a quote* turns a photo into an inspirational card or poster.

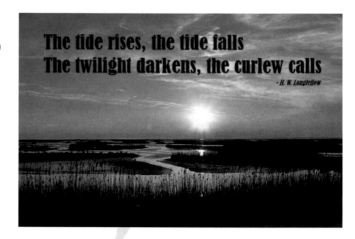

▶ *Use the Cutout* and Drop Shadow effects to carve a shape or text into a textured background.

ADD PAINTING OR POSTER EFFECTS

▶ **Applying blurs** or noise reduction adjustments can turn a photo into a digital painting.

▶ **Use the Posterize effect** to turn your photo into a piece of graphic art.

USE SCRAPBOOK TEMPLATES

▸ **Scrapbook templates** provide you with ready-made layout designs that include basic embellishments and one or more places for photos. In this case, the template includes a transparent area so that you can place your photo on a lower layer.

Template courtesy of Digital Scrapbook Place

Template courtesy of Digital Scrapbook Place

▸ **Here the template** has been copied and pasted as a new image. Then a photo was positioned on a lower layer so that it shows through the transparent area of the copied template. As a final touch, some text was added on a layer above the copied template.

CREATE EXCITING LAYOUTS WITH SCRAPBOOK KITS

Template courtesy of Digital Scrapbook Place

▸ **A scrapbook kit** contains individual image components, such as background paper, mats and frames, ribbons, brads and eyelets, staples, torn paper, and mesh or lace. Copy the components you want and paste them into your layout, along with your photos and maybe some text.

TRACE A PHOTO WITH ART MEDIA TOOLS

▸ **Besides enabling you** to draw and paint freehand, Art Media tools let you trace a photo to turn it into a digital painting. Begin by creating an outlined version of the photo on a raster layer with Edge Effects | Find All, then add rough brushstrokes on an Art Media layer sandwiched between the photo layer and outline layer.

▸ **Once you've added** all the rough brushstrokes, you can blend the strokes together with the Smear tool. Lower the opacity of the outline layer or delete it entirely to complete your painting.

3. Looking at the photo again, we can see the colors are not very vivid. In truth they probably never were when they were printed. Still, that doesn't mean we cannot add some color today. Using the Hue/Saturation/Lightness dialog box (SHIFT-H), we increase the saturation by 40 (which is a lot normally but in this case it is necessary) and after the colors look correct, we apply sharpening using the Unsharp Mask filter at its default setting. The completed image is shown in Figure 6-14.

FIGURE 6-14   The restored photo looks much better than the original (also shown in the color insert).

This chapter has shown some of the basics of how to use Paint Shop Pro for restoring and preserving photos. There is a lot more that can be done in this area, but with these fundamentals, you know the essential techniques that can help you through more than 90 percent of the photo correction challenges that you will face.

PART III

Creating Original Images Using Paint Shop Pro X

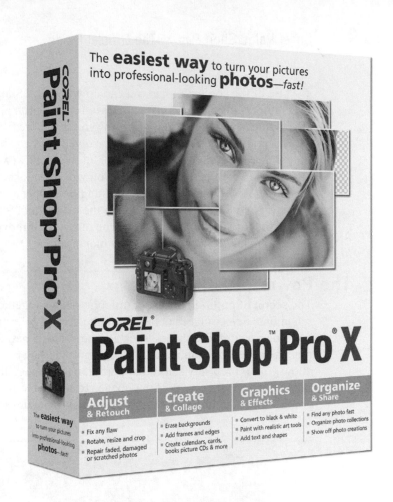

The **easiest way** to turn your pictures into professional-looking **photos**—fast!

COREL®
Paint Shop™ Pro® X

Adjust & Retouch	Create & Collage	Graphics & Effects	Organize & Share
• Fix any flaw • Rotate, resize and crop • Repair faded, damaged or scratched photos	• Erase backgrounds • Add frames and edges • Create calendars, cards, books picture CDs & more	• Convert to black & white • Paint with realistic art tools • Add text and shapes	• Find any photo fast • Organize photo collections • Show off photo creations

CHAPTER 7
Create a Photo Montage

One of the coolest things you can do with Paint Shop Pro is add or remove people or objects from a photo. We all have some favorite photo of ourselves or a loved one that also includes someone we wish wasn't in the picture. Before digital photo editing, removing the jerk from the photo was crudely resolved with a pair of scissors. Figure 7-1 is a classic example created, using the Clone tool, to seamlessly (well, almost seamlessly) eliminate the guy from the photo. Once you do it you will get hooked and will waste many an evening removing, adding, and generally rearranging people and objects in your photographs. In this chapter, you will discover how to use the many Paint Shop Pro selection tools to isolate the part of the photograph that needs to be removed or moved. You will also discover how to use layers to manage your photographic montages.

The Power of Selections

The secret of putting parts from different photos together in the same image is in creating selections. Selections can range from the very simple, such as the rectangular shapes of a building, to complex shapes, such as a person or a pet. Because these complex selections require more precision, Paint Shop Pro provides a large assortment of different tools that allow you to precisely select that portion of the image that you want to work on while still protecting the other parts of the image. To be able to use these tools effectively, you are going to spend a little time learning just how selections work and how to use them.

FIGURE 7-1   Breaking up isn't as hard to do with Paint Shop Pro.

Understanding Selections

Paint Shop Pro has a number of different tools whose only purpose is to define the part of the image you want to work on. The area that is defined is called a *selection*, and all of the tools that are used to make the selections are known as *selection tools*. If this is your first time using Paint Shop Pro, don't let the large number of selection tools with their strange-sounding names overwhelm you. You are going to learn this one step at a time, beginning with a look at what a selection is.

Isolating and protecting something using selections is a concept we all have used at one time or another in our lives. There are many analogies given to help people understand selections and their uses; here are a few of the more popular ones: If you have ever used a stencil, you have used a selection. The stencil allows you to apply paint to part of the material and it protects the rest. Another example of a selection that is closer to home (literally) is using masking tape to block off the parts of a room on which you don't want to get paint (which for us would be just about everything in the room!). Selections in Paint Shop Pro act just like a stencil or masking tape when it comes to either isolating or applying any effect to part of an image.

Rounding Up the Selection Tools

There are three different types of selection tools in the Tools toolbar that can be accessed by clicking the tiny black icon next to the Selection tool (S). These three tools are

- Selection
- Freehand Selection
- Magic Wand

While these tools have been mentioned and used in previous chapters, we are going to learn how selection tools can be used to create some cool stuff. First, let's look at the most basic of the tools: the Selection tool.

Expanding a Photograph Using Selection

Using the Selection tool you can create selections in the shapes of rectangles and ellipses. From the Tool Options palette, you can also choose unique selections in fixed shapes, shown in Figure 7-2.

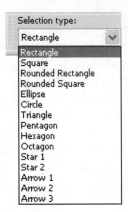

FIGURE 7-2 The Selection tool offers multiple predefined shapes to use.

Using a floating selection is a fast way to expand a photograph, such as the one shown in Figure 7-3, so it can be used in an ad. You can download the file used in this task (rock climber.jpg) from www.osborne.com and follow along.

1. Use the Canvas Size feature (Image | Canvas Size) to add additional area to the edge of the image. The arrow keys at the bottom determine which point on the image will be anchored. Because we want the left side to be expanded, the opposite side (right side) is anchored by pressing the right arrow button. Since the image aspect ratio (ratio of height to width) is being changed, it is necessary to uncheck the Lock Aspect Ratio box. For this exercise, we are adding four inches to the width on the left side.

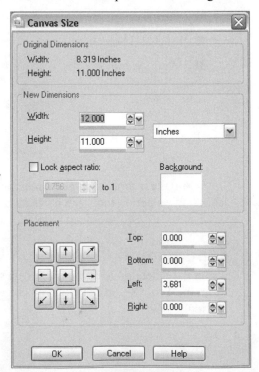

When the Canvas Size dialog box opens it retains its last settings. Make sure that you check all of the settings to ensure they are correct for the image you are currently working on.

FIGURE 7-3   This photo needs to be expanded to allow text to be added.

2. Choose the Selection tool (S) and choose Rectangle as your selection type in the Tool
    Options palette. Drag a selection over the part of the photo you want to duplicate to
    add on the edge of the photo. The edge of the selection is marked by a flashing black-
    and-white marquee that has come to be called "marching ants," as shown here:

3. After ensuring that the Selection tool is in Replace mode in the Tool Options palette, hold down the ALT key and drag the selection (it becomes a floating selection) over the new extension of the image shown next. Holding down the ALT key makes a copy of the current selection. If you don't hold it down, the contents of the selection are removed and replaced with the current background color.

4. Promote the floating selection to a layer (CTRL-SHIFT-P) and remove the selection (CTRL-D). In the next step we will be changing the shape of the newly created layer, and in order to see it better, you should zoom out as shown next using the Zoom tool.

| TIP | *If your mouse has a scroll wheel it provides the quickest way to zoom in and out of an image.* |

5. Use the Pick tool (K) to drag the promoted layer so it overlaps and the crevice in the rock aligns with the original as shown.

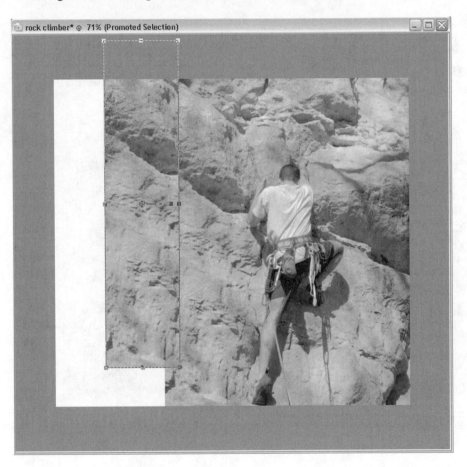

6. Use the Pick tool to drag the left handle of the promoted layer until it meets the left edge and then drag the bottom handle until the promoted layer slightly overlaps the bottom. Place the cursor in the center of the layer until the cursor becomes a four-headed arrow and realign the crevice in the rocks as shown before, double-clicking the selection to apply the transformation.

7. Select the Eraser tool (X) and erase along the overlapping parts of the promoted selection to blend the two parts as shown.

8. At this point you still have a layer that is much larger than the image floating above the background. Choose Layers | Merge | Merge All (flatten) to crop the layer to fit the image. Use the Clone brush (C) at Opacity: 74 and Hardness: 0 to apply small areas of the original rock to the new area to change the appearance even more. Enhance the image using the Clarify filter (Adjust | Brightness and Contrast | Clarify) with a medium preset. The final image of the new area is shown next and once the text has been added the ad is shown in Figure 7-4.

You should have noticed that as the added background material is distorted it becomes softer (less sharp) and the colors of the pixels begin to break down. When working with natural materials such as rocks, clouds, trees, and others, this distortion and pixel deterioration isn't all that apparent to the viewer because the viewer doesn't know what they looked like before you began changing them. The same cannot be said of man-made objects such as buildings and bridges, subjects with high contrast, or even people, so they should be avoided.

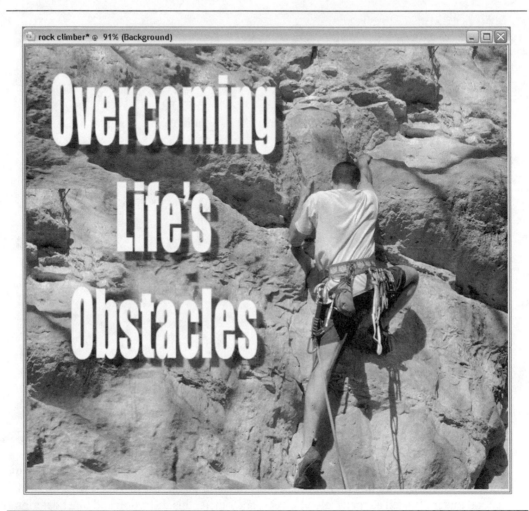

FIGURE 7-4 An ad made by expanding the background of the photo

The Selection Tool Options Palette

If this is the first time you have worked with Paint Shop Pro, the selection tools might seem quite limited. After all, how often will you need to select a rectangle? Corel has included many more shapes, which can be selected from the Tool Options palette. In fact, you can create about any shape imaginable using these tools if you learn how to use some of the features found in the Options bar.

Making Photo Shapes

Paint Shop Pro provides 15 different selection shapes, giving you a great way to create unusual photo shapes. Here is how to use the predefined selection shapes to create some fun photo shapes:

1. Pick the Selection tool (S) in the Tools toolbar and then choose the desired shape from the Tool Options palette. In this demonstration the shape Star 1 is used.

2. After selecting one of the shapes, click and drag over the image to select an area, like the star shape dragged over the photograph shown here. Copy the contents of the selection to the Clipboard (CTRL-C).

3. Open an image that you want to use as the background. In this demonstration a photo of a baseball is used. Paste the selection as a new layer (CTRL-L), as shown here:

4. After resizing and repositioning the star layer with the Pick tool, choose Effects | 3D Effects | Inner Bevel to add a 3D effect to the star and text describing the position the boy plays as shown in Figure 7-5.

There are three different ways that the selection tools interact with existing selections. The default setting for the selection tools is Replace. With this setting, any time you make a selection, it replaces the current selection (if one exists). The ones you will use most often are the Add To and Remove settings. (See the section "Adding Some and Taking Some" later in this chapter.) Their operation is obvious . By using the selection tools in combination with these modes, it is possible to make almost any irregular shape imaginable.

Feathering the Selections

Up until now we have been discussing selections that have a hard and defined edge. However, there are many times that you want to make a selection that has a soft edge, for example, when you are moving someone or something from one photograph into another.

FIGURE 7-5   Selection shapes allow you to produce professional results.

Using a feathered selection blends the subject being moved into the picture more smoothly. You need to be careful with the amount of feathering you apply to the selection, however. Usually, just a few pixels are sufficient. If you put in a large amount of feathering, the object looks like it has a glow or is furry.

There are two ways to feather a selection: you can enter a value in the Feather box of the Tool Options palette and the feathering will be applied to the selection as it is drawn. The value you enter is the distance from the selection (in pixels) that the feathering will be applied. You can also add feathering to an existing selection by using the keyboard shortcut (CTRL-H) and entering in a value.

Figure 7-6 is a photo of a young baseball player but the background is anything but baseball. After creating a selection around the boy and copying him to a photo with a baseball dugout in the background, a small amount of feathering was applied to the selection before adding a second copy of the boy to the new background scene. As shown next, the one on the left was not feathered and the one on the right had a moderate amount of feathering applied.

The feather effect produced by any particular setting is controlled by the size of the image. For example, the original photograph was taken with a 6-megapixel digital camera; as a result, the original photo is pretty large. On a larger image like this a 3-pixel feather will have less of an effect than the same feather setting would have on a much smaller image. The higher feathering setting in the image on the right allows part of the original darker background to be seen (as in his hat) but it is less noticeable where he covers darker parts of the background. So while feathering a selection helps it to blend seamlessly into a new background, too much feathering brings part of the old background with it.

While there are many things that can be done with the selection tools, they are essentially basic tools. When you need to create an irregular-shaped selection, it is time to consider the Lasso tools.

Rounding Up the Selection Tools

There are three different types of selection tools in the Tools toolbar that can be accessed by clicking on the tiny black icon next to the Selection tool (S). These three tools are

- Selection tool
- Freehand Selection tool
- Magic Wand

FIGURE 7-6   Potential baseball all star in a non-baseball setting

Unlike the Selection tool that we looked at previously, which only produces closed shapes, the Freehand Selection tool lets you draw a meandering path around a subject. When you are done you either let go of the mouse button or double-click it (depending on which tool you are using), and Paint Shop Pro will make a straight line back to the starting point to complete the selection.

The Freehand Selection Tool

The Freehand Selection tool has four methods (called types) for creating a selection: Freehand, Point to Point, Smart Edge, and Edge Seeker. Each type of selection mode is chosen from the Tool Options toolbar. While they all produce the same results, each uses a different method to produce a freehand selection.

Freehand Selection

The simplest selection type is Freehand. Using this method, you simply draw around the edge of the area you want to select or protect by clicking and dragging your mouse or stylus. As soon as you release the mouse button (or lift your stylus if you are using one), Paint Shop Pro completes the selection by closing the shape to the original starting point of the selection. This type of selection is a good choice for creating simple or rough shapes. This tool should not be used to draw complex or large freehand selections because you cannot rest your hand (by letting go of the mouse button or stylus) while creating a selection as you can with the other types of selection.

Point to Point Selection

The Point to Point method creates a selection made out of a lot of straight lines. A common misconception about this tool is that it is only for creating a selection containing straight lines. Nothing could be further from the truth. For those who doubt, here is a definition of a circle from a high school geometry book: a circle is a polygon composed of an infinite number of sides. As with the Freehand selection type, clicking once on the image produces the starting point of your selection, and clicking at points along the edge of the subject creates straight lines between each point. You continue adding these points to the selection as you continue clicking until your selection nears the starting point. To complete the selection, double-click the left mouse button or right-click. If you accidentally put a point in the wrong spot, you can delete the point by pressing the DELETE key. Each time you press the DELETE key, the last point of the selection is removed.

| TIP | *When making Point to Point selections, don't click your mouse button too fast when adding points to the selection. Paint Shop Pro might mistake it for a double-click and complete your selection.* |

Using Edge Seeker and Smart Edge

These selection types are similar to the Freehand tool except they have the ability to automatically detect the edge (in most cases) as you move either of them along the edge of the subject you want to isolate, which can save you a lot of work. Both of these tools work by examining the pixels surrounding the area being selected and attempting to detect an edge based on the difference between the color or brightness of adjacent pixels. What makes the two tools different is how they operate.

The Edge Seeker performs its edge detection beginning where you start the selection with your first click, and then you click around the edge of the area you want to select. In this manner it works similarly to Point to Point selection except Paint Shop Pro automatically detects the edge along a line between the points.

The Smart Edge detects the edge of a subject by creating a long rectangle as you drag the cursor over a portion of the edge you want to select. When you release the mouse button, the edge inside the rectangle is evaluated and the edge detected. With both types, you continue to do this until you get back to the starting point.

If you have ever worked with Adobe Photoshop or Photoshop Elements, the Edge Seeker Freehand tool in Paint Shop Pro is very similar to their Magnetic Lasso selection tool.

Magic Wand Tool Magic

The Magic Wand tool is a great tool for making selections of areas containing similar colors or levels of brightness. The problem with using this tool is the fact that many users have no idea how it works and are disappointed when the magic doesn't work. Here is a brief explanation of how it works.

The first fact about the Magic Wand tool: no magic (were you surprised?). Up until now, all of the selection tools you have used involved either closed shapes or lassos that surrounded the subject to be selected. The Magic Wand tool, however, acts a little like dropping a stone in a calm pool of water. The selection, like ripples of water, spreads outward from the starting point. It continues radiating outward, selecting similar (and adjacent) colored pixels until it reaches pixels whose color or shade is so different from the starting point that they can't be included.

Making Selections with Stylus or Mouse?

Most of you use selections to isolate a part of a photograph so you can copy it into another image. Because you are essentially drawing an outline, you may find that creating a complex outline using a mouse is a challenge. Why? Ask yourself this simple question: Can I sign my name with a mouse? If your answer is yes, you need to date more. Seriously, for most of us the answer is no; if you are going to be creating a lot of selections, you should consider getting a graphics tablet. The industry standard for graphic tablets is Wacom Technology (www.wacom.com). These tablets used to be quite expensive, but now some models like the one shown in Figure 7-7 can be purchased for less than $100. Does this mean you can't use

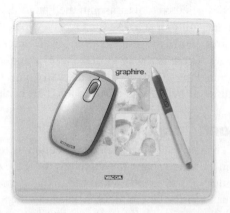

FIGURE 7-7   Pressure-sensitive tablets like this Wacom Graphire makes selection creation much easier.

selection tools without a graphics tablet? Of course not—it's just a lot easier if you have one. With that matter settled, let's consider some ideas on how to make better selections.

Getting the Best Selections (in the Least Amount of Time)

If you have tried to create a selection and been disappointed in the results, don't get discouraged. Isolating a subject from a background can be a challenging and time-consuming process. As you get more experience you will become aware of what tools work best with different subjects and backgrounds. Here is a short list of tips to help you make great selections.

Making a First Rough Cut Selection

If the image is so large that it does not fit on the screen when viewing at 100 percent (Actual Size), you should shift the zoom level to Fit on Screen in the Tool Options palette and make a rough selection. It doesn't matter which selection tool you use. You just want to get as close as you can without spending a lot of time doing it. This selection gets you in the ballpark.

> TIP: *You can quickly zoom in and out using the scroll wheel on your mouse (if your mouse has one).*

Zoom and Move

On some areas you may need to zoom in at levels even greater than 100 percent (Paint Shop Pro goes up to 5000 percent, which must allow you to select microbes and stray electrons). Now and again you should return to Fit to Screen just to keep a perspective on the whole image. This is done easily if your mouse has a scroll wheel that allows you to move in and out.

When you set the Zoom to Actual Size (CTRL-ALT-N), in most cases the image no longer fits inside the image window. Normally when you are zoomed in this close, you can press the A key and the currently selected tool turns into the Pan tool. Another way to move around an image without using the Pan tool is to use the Overview palette (F9). The problem with this approach is it requires you to move the cursor off the screen, thereby interrupting the selection you are creating. There is a way to make a selection at a high zoom level, however: While drawing a selection, Paint Shop Pro automatically pans the image as you approach the edge of the image window, allowing you to reach any part of the photo.

Adding Some and Taking Some

You can add or subtract parts from your rough cut selection using the Add to Selection and Subtract from Selection modes to shape the selection to fit the subject you are trying to isolate. Here is a trick that will save time when doing this part. First, rather than changing modes in the Options bar, use the key modifiers. Pressing the SHIFT key changes the selection mode to Add (for adding to the current selection), and the CTRL key changes it to Remove (to subtract from). Just remember that these modifier keys must be pressed before you click the mouse.

> **TIP** *You can change the mode to Add or Remove before you start. For example, if you select Add from the Mode drop-down list in the Tool Options palette as the Selection mode, you need to use the* CTRL *key only when you want to subtract from the selection.*

Fine-Tuning Your Selections

After you have created a selection and used the Add and Remove modes to make the marquee fit the area you want to select as much as possible, you can then use the Edit Selection mode to make the selection even more precise. By choosing Selections | Edit Selection, all of the selected area on the image will appear to be covered in a red tint, a carryover from the olden days when we did work like this using ruby lithe.

> **TIP** *If the Selection Marquee (marching ants) doesn't appear after you make a selection, make sure Hide Marquee (*CTRL-SHIFT-M*) isn't enabled.*

Keeping Your Final Objective in Mind

While you are fine-tuning and improving a selection, you should keep at the forefront of your mind the ultimate destination of the image you are selecting. Here are some questions that will help you decide on the degree of exactness you want to invest in your selection.

- *How close are the background colors of the image you are selecting and the current background colors?* If they are roughly the same colors, then investing a lot of time producing a detailed selection doesn't make much sense because a feathered edge will work just fine.

- *Will the final image be larger, smaller, or the same size as the original?* If you are going to be making the current image larger, every detail will stick out like the proverbial sore thumb, so any extra time you spend to make the selection as exact as possible will pay big benefits. If you are going to reduce the size of the subject, a lot of tiny details will become lost when it is resized, so don't invest a lot of time in the selection.

- *Is this a paid job (a priority) or a freebie?* Creating a complex selection is a time-consuming process. Dave once spent nearly half a day on a single selection for a project that wasn't as important as others he should have been working on. Don't let projects get away from you. Consider what you are going to do, keep your efforts within the allotted time, and don't get lost in the job.

Finding the Edge in the Dark

Before leaving the subject of selection options, there is one last situation that needs to be addressed. On some images, the edge and the background are in the shadows, which makes it difficult to see the edge you want to select. If it is difficult for you to see the edge, there is little chance of the Smart Edge or Edge Seeker selection modes detecting the edge either. The most common example of a darkened edge and background is in a portrait of someone in a dark business suit or with dark hair (or both) against a dark background, like the one shown in Figure 7-8. Because publications don't like to print dark images like this, it is often necessary to select the individual from the image and place him or her on a different background.

Here is a slick trick that will make it much easier to select such a difficult subject almost every time:

1. Choose Layers | New Adjustment Layer | Levels, which opens the Levels dialog box.

2. Drag the middle slider (gamma) of the Input Levels to the left until the edge becomes light enough to detect. The image may appear pretty ugly at this point but that doesn't matter because an adjustment layer doesn't make changes to the image. Click OK to close the dialog.

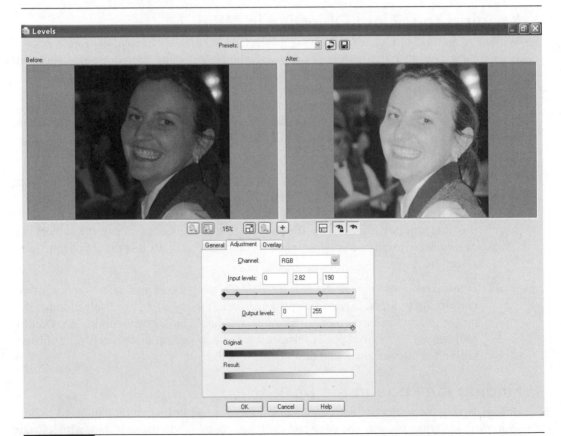

FIGURE 7-8   Use adjustment layers to lighten up the image enough to make a selection.

3. In the Layers palette (F8), select the Background, choose your favorite selection tool, and create the selection.

4. After the selection is complete, right-click the Levels adjustment layer in the Layers palette and from the pop-up menu select Delete. A message box will ask you if you want to delete this layer; click Yes. With the adjustment layer gone, the image returns to its former darkness, and the selection you created remains.

5. With only the subject selected you can use the One-Step Photo Fix to lighten only the image and not the background as shown below.

7

Let's Select Somebody

Let's make what is possibly your first freehand selection. This involves a groomsman named Jonathan in a cluttered church office wearing a ridiculously overpriced rental tuxedo. If his mother is going to frame this photograph, the background must be replaced with something a little less cluttered. If you want to give this exercise a try, you can download the files from the book's site at www.osborne.com.

1. Download and open the picture labeled TuxedoJon.pspimage. (The sample image was resized to be a lot smaller than the original so it wouldn't gag your system.)

2. Choose the Edge Seeker tool and, getting as close as you can to the edge of the tuxedo, click and drag a line around Jonathan until it looks like the one shown next. When you finish, you will have selected the subject, but because you really need to select the background, invert the selection using SHIFT-CTRL-I.

3. If you don't want to make the selection yourself, you can use the selection we made inside the PSP image. To load the selection embedded in the file, choose Selections | Load/Save Selections | Load Selection from Alpha Channel. When the dialog box appears, change the values to match those shown next, making sure to check the Invert Image checkbox.

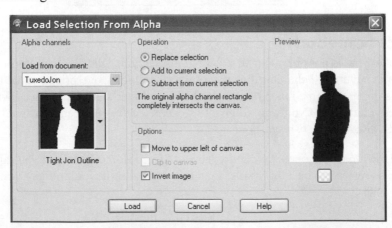

4. One way to emphasize the subject is to blur the background using Gaussian blur. The problem with this approach is that the background in this photo is so cluttered that by the time you get it blurred enough to do the job, it looks sort of surreal. On top of that, the subject and the couch on his right are the same distance from the camera, so it doesn't look right. Try replacing the background with a different one. Download and open the file background.jpg. When it is open, select the entire image (CTRL-A), copy the image to the Clipboard (CTRL-C), and close the image (don't save the changes).

5. With Jon's photo selected, choose Edit | Paste Into Selection (CTRL-SHIFT-L). Wow! A well-composed photograph has now replaced the previous cluttered one, as shown in Figure 7-9.

FIGURE 7-9   A new background adds a touch of class.

Saving and Loading Selections

After spending a lot of time creating a selection, you'll want to save it. If a selection is not saved as a Paint Shop Pro file, it will be lost as soon as the file is closed. There are two ways to save your selections. You can save it as a PspSelection file to your hard disk, or you can save it with the image in an alpha channel.

Saving a Selection to the Alpha Channel

Here is how to save your selection to the alpha channel:

1. Choose Selections | Load/Save Selection | Save Selection to Alpha Channel. This opens the dialog box shown in Figure 7-10.

2. If the image already has an existing channel, you can add your new selection to replace an existing one, but you will probably be saving to a new channel. If the selection already exists, you'll be prompted to see if you want to overwrite it. To check what selections already exist *before* entering a selection name, click the down arrow in the field just below the Add to Document field on the left side of the dialog box. This displays a list of the existing selections. Highlight the default name that appears and replace it with a descriptive name.

3. Click Save, and the selection will be safely tucked into the image, increasing its file size.

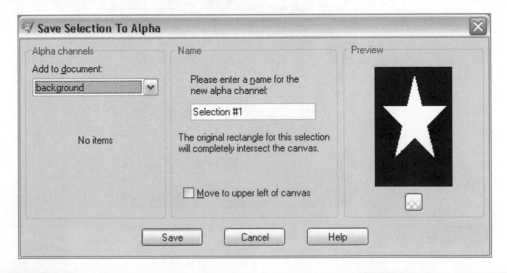

FIGURE 7-10   The Save Selection to Alpha dialog box allows you to manage selections saved in your images.

When you open a file containing a selection in the alpha channel, the selection won't appear on the image. To load the saved selection, choose Selections | Load/Save Selection | Open Selection to Alpha Channel and pick the name of the stored selection (if there is more than one) that you or someone else tucked away into the image.

You must save the image as a Paint Shop Pro (PSP, pspimage), TIFF (TIF), or Photoshop (PSD) file to preserve the selection you just saved.

Using Other Sources of Selections

It may surprise you, but many stock photography companies offer selections in their photos. Two different companies that offer photographs with selections are Photospin (www.photospin.com), which is a great online photo subscription service, and Hemera (www.hemera.com), which offers large collections of photo objects on CDs (lots and lots of CDs). The image shown in Figure 7-11 is a photograph of a diving mask that was downloaded from Photospin.com. Like many of their images, it contains a selection.

NOTE *Many stock photo agencies give you a choice of formats when downloading photos. If you are planning on using a selection saved in an image, remember that JPEG images cannot contain a selection.*

Photo courtesy of Photospin.

FIGURE 7-11 This photo from Photospin already contains a built-in selection.

Creating Photo Montages

Using a selection allows you to isolate an object in one photograph and place it in another. The following sections give you ideas on how to experiment to make different types of photo montages.

Making New Objects Appear Like They Belong

Sometimes the object being placed is not the right size. Fortunately, Paint Shop Pro allows you to resize the new object. If you have worked with previous versions of Paint Shop Pro you used the Deform tool to scale and transform objects. This feature has been moved to the Pick tool. Here is how to do it:

1. Select the object you want to copy into another photo and then copy it to the Clipboard (CTRL-C). To demonstrate this technique, the selection that was saved with the photograph of a diver's mask shown in Figure 7-11 is loaded and used to isolate the mask.

2. Open the image into which you want to place the diving mask and paste the contents of the Clipboard as a raster layer (CTRL-L). The result is the original photograph of a young woman in New Orleans (pre-flood) wearing a polyester wig and the diving mask (which is too large), shown here:

3. Select the raster layer containing the object (the diver's mask) in the Layers palette (F8) and use the Pick tool (K) to position the object where you want it placed on the image.

4. Control handles appear around the object. Use the different Mode settings in the Tool Options palette to change how the mask reacts to movement of the handles. Click and drag the handles to change both its size and shape, as shown next.

NOTE   *If you drag one of the object corner handles while in Scale mode, you can scale an object to a desired size and the aspect ratio is locked to prevent distortion. If you drag a corner with the right mouse button pressed, the aspect ratio lock is disabled.*

5. Flatten the image. Even with the mask resized, it appears to be floating above her face. That's because the mask isn't producing any shadows on her face. It is the little details that are missed that make a photo montage look fake. To resolve this, just select the Brush tool, set the Opacity to 40%, set Hardness to 10, and ensure the

Color is black. Now in the Layers palette select the Background and paint the shadows as shown next.

6. As long as she has a diving mask on, she might as well get wet. Here is how it is done. First, make a rectangle selection of the top half of the image, promote it to a layer, and then use the Pick tool to flip it vertically and then horizontally. Promoting the selection made the area under transparent but it is covered by the promoted layer. Now drag it down to the bottom of the image as shown next.

7. With the top (water) layer selected, apply the Ripple filter (Effects | Distortion Effects | Ripple…) at the default settings. The "water layer" now appears to have a slight ripple as shown.

8. The next detail we need to add is a soft, darker area where she stops and the water reflection begins. Since the top layer has a straight edge produced by the selection edge, it will appear fake when we darken the edge. To make the water appear to be following the contour of her neck, we need to modify the edge. In the Layers palette make the background invisible by clicking its eye icon. Next select the Eraser tool (X) and reshape the edge of the upper side of the layer as shown.

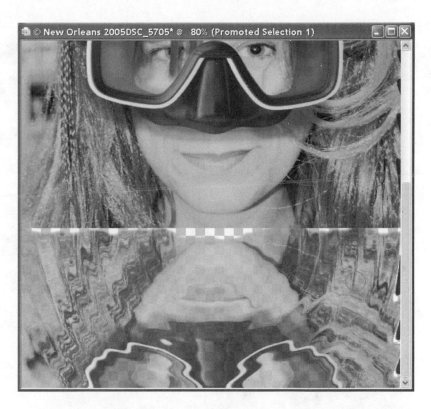

9. Turn the Background back on again and choose the Lighten/Darken brush (L). Painting with the left mouse button lightens while painting with the right mouse button darkens. The area near the woman will be darker at and near the waterline. So apply the Lighten/Darken brush to all of the layers and the background until it appears something like the image shown in Figure 7-12.

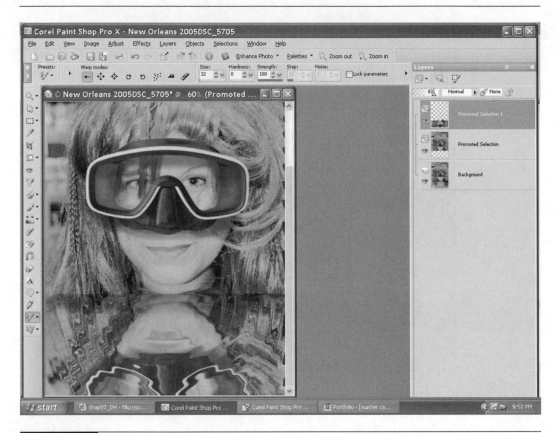

FIGURE 7-12   Now the figure has a diving mask and is in the water as well.

Recipes for Surrealism

The only limitation you will face with Paint Shop Pro when it comes to creating images both real and surreal is your imagination. In this section, you will discover tricks that will whet your appetite for making your own creations by including some examples that were made using selections.

The image in Figure 7-13 was created in parts. The background was created using a pattern made from a photograph of wooden shutters using the Kaleidoscope filter. Then the Planar filter (Kai Power Tools 3) made the pattern that appears to fade into the horizon. The glass ball was an object Dave made at another time, and he made it appear as if it were half sunk into the floor by erasing the lower half with the Eraser tool. The sky on the horizon came from another photograph that was pasted into the back. Then, using a photograph he took of an ornate wooden door in the Texas capitol, Dave created a selection around it and pasted it as a layer in the image.

FIGURE 7-13 A little simple surrealism

By using the Pick tool as shown earlier, it is possible to resize and reshape any object you place in a photo. Figure 7-14 shows what happens when the same Pick tool is used to twist and distort the door.

FIGURE 7-14 Distortion of the door adds a Salvador Dali look to the image.

With Paint Shop Pro you can create almost anything that you can imagine.

Figure 7-15 (also shown in the color insert) is a project that was made to demonstrate layers with selective transparency. The background is an actual photograph of a checkered tile floor. Applying the Eraser tool at a low opacity setting to the raster layer containing the glass ball and the capitol door glass allows the background to be seen through these objects, creating a greater sense of realism in this surrealistic scene.

Photo Montages Without Selections: Masks

Selections provide an excellent way to create photo montages, but in this section, you will learn that there are other ways to combine photos: You can use a mask to produce even cooler results. For starters, let's cover some basics about masks.

The concept of a mask is simple. It's a grayscale image that sits on its own layer. The mask controls the transparency of the layer below it. Masks act like regular layers in that their visibility can be turned on or off, and the opacity of the mask layer can be adjusted or linked to other layers. Masks can be created, edited, and saved in alpha channels just as selections can be. That was a lot of facts crammed into a few sentences. Corel has a wealth of details on the subject of masks in their help files and in the users manual. Now, let's discuss the incredible things you can do using masks.

Using a Mask to Make a Photo Montage

Here is a simple trick that allows you to quickly make a photo montage from two photos:

1. Open the first image. The example photo is the Texas capitol, as shown next. Select the entire image (CTRL-A), copy it to the Clipboard (CTRL-C), and close the photo.

7

2. Open the second image (the example is a photo of a glass door in the capitol, as shown next). Paste the contents of the Clipboard as a new layer (CTRL-L).

3. With the top layer selected, choose Layers | Load / Save Mask | Load Mask from Disk, which opens the dialog box shown next. Select the Mask and click Load. In this example, one of the sample masks (Edge Pattern) was loaded.

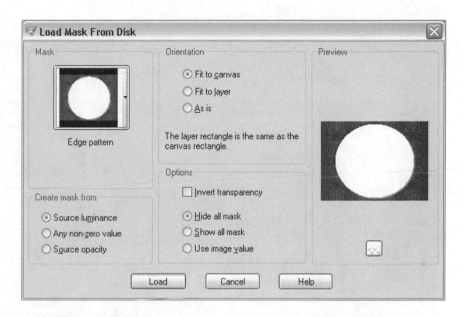

4. A new layer called Mask Raster 1 appears in the Layers palette and is grouped with the top raster layer, as shown next. Lastly, merge all layers and apply Texture (Effects | Texture Effects | Texture…). When the dialog box opens use the default settings and click OK. The photo montage that results is shown in Figure 7-16.

Using Masks Like Selections

In the previous technique, a sample mask was used to create an effect. Now you'll learn how to use a mask layer to selectively add and subtract areas of a layer from viewing. It is much easier to show how this works than to explain it.

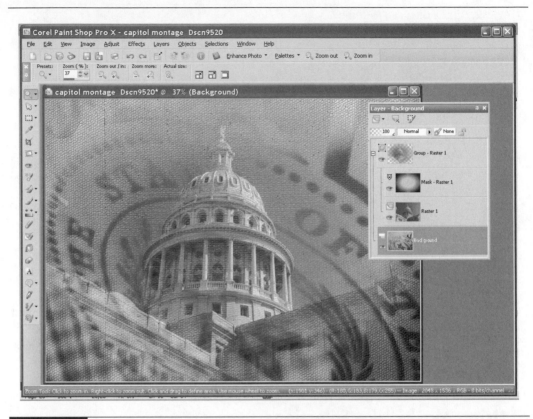

FIGURE 7-16   A montage of two photos

1. Open the image you want to put into another, select the part of the image you want to place in the other, and copy it to the Clipboard. You probably recognize the young lady in the photograph shown at right. If you think she is Dave's daughter's roommate, you're correct. If you thought she was a movie star, you aren't the first.

2. Open the second image (shown next).

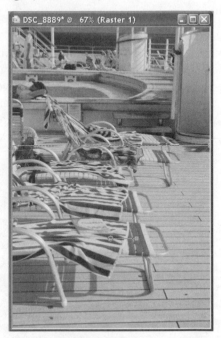

3. Paste the contents of the Clipboard containing the first photo as a new layer (CTRL-L), shown here.

4. Choose Layers | New Mask Layer | Show All. This creates a mask layer that is grouped with the raster layer that was pasted onto the image.

5. In the Layers palette, select the Mask layer. Choose the Brush tool and change the hardness of the brush to near 100% to achieve a definite edge. Ensure the foreground color is black and the background color is white. Paint away the areas that you want to become transparent using the left mouse button. Every place on the mask painted black becomes 100 percent transparent. If you accidentally remove too much, you need to paint only the area using the right mouse button; this paints it white and restores it to 100 percent opaque.

6. The finished result is a composite of a young woman who is no longer sitting on her couch but is now sitting on the deck of a cruise ship trying to figure out her bill as shown in Figure 7-17.

FIGURE 7-17   Getting off the couch and onto a cruise ship is a simple change with Paint Shop Pro.

Rearranging a Photo with the Clone Brush

The last way to add or subtract objects from your photos is to use the Clone brush (C). In Chapter 6, you learned how the Clone brush could be used to repair damaged images; in this section, you will look at how you can use the Clone brush to remove, replace, or rearrange objects from a photo.

Figure 7-18 shows a photograph that at first doesn't appear to be all that good. By using the Clone brush and other tools you learned about earlier in the chapter, however, you can remove and replace parts of it to make it a much better photo. Here is how it is done.

FIGURE 7-18   Nice photo that could use some improvement

1. First, you need to remove the clutter on the horizon. Use the Edge Seeker selection tool, to create the selection shown next, which preserves the foliage on the horizon but removes the buildings, signs, sky, and light poles.

2. Open a photo containing a replacement sky like the one shown here. Because you will only be using the top part of the photo, the bottom of the photo doesn't concern you. Select the entire cloud image (CTRL-A) and copy it to the Clipboard (CTRL-C). Close the cloud file and don't save any changes.

3. Select the flower photo and paste the cloud photo into the current selection (CTRL-SHIFT-L). Continue until it is finished and looks like the image shown at right.

4. The next step is to remove the sunflower that is pointing in the wrong direction. Change the size of the Clone brush so it is large enough to remove the sunflower in just a few passes. Right-click the area on either side of the part you want to remove, then clone it out. Change the source point several times while doing this to prevent a visual pattern from developing. Use the Clone brush to remove the plastic bag that was at the bottom of the photo. When you are finished it should look as shown next.

7

5. Lastly, use the Clone brush to replace the part of the lower sunflower that is covered by the leaf. The trick to doing this is to use a small soft brush (hardness 60) and to use as a source point a small spot on the yellow petal where the edges are clear and defined. Apply it in short strokes over the leaf (or the part of the image that you want to remove) and then go pick another source point. It is time-consuming to do it right. Figure 7-19 shows the down and dirty version Dave did in less than five minutes.

This chapter has introduced you to the essential elements needed to isolate and select portions of photos and make them into separate objects, or rearrange and combine them into new images. As powerful as these tools are, you need to practice using them to create the best selections. Don't get discouraged if your first attempts are something less than perfect. Keep working on it and soon you will be able to create seamless selections like a pro.

FIGURE 7-19   A fair photo becomes a work of art with a new sky and some minor repairs.

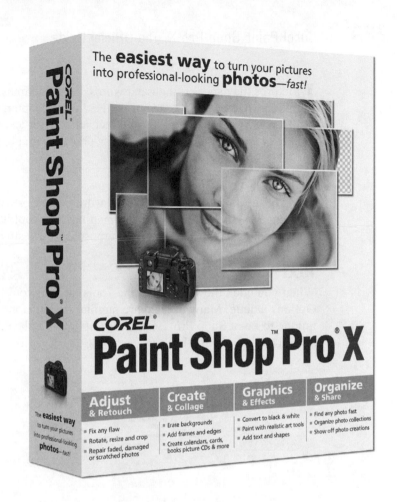

CHAPTER 8

Add Text to Your Images

Pictures may speak a thousand words, but sometimes there is no replacement for a clever phrase to add impact to your image. In this chapter, you'll discover how fun it is to add text to your images and create an effect suitable for an eye-catching poster or an elegant scrapbook page. So gather your favorite photos or graphics images, and let's have some fun.

Text, Plain and Simple

Think of the Text tool as a simplified word processor without all the fancy amenities such as spell check, tables, and complex formatting. This tool is not designed to help you write your next novel or magazine article; its purpose is to add small amounts of text to an image.

Text Tool Options

When you click the Text tool in the Tools toolbar, you'll see quite a few options in the Tool Options palette. Many of them are familiar options found in word processors but a few are unique to Paint Shop Pro. Here are the options displayed in the Tool Options palette, resized so you can see them all:

Choosing Text Properties

The Create As option enables you to define your text as one of three different types—Vector, Selection, or Floating.

- **Vector**   Creates the text on a vector layer as opposed to a raster layer. Unlike raster layers, vector layers can be edited, resized, and deformed without affecting image quality. With vector layers, however, you cannot apply any of the Paint Shop Pro effects. We'll be looking at vector text in Chapter 10.

- **Selection**   Creates an empty text selection that behaves very much like a stencil in the shape of the text you choose. The selection is made on the layer (or background) that is currently active. When you click the text selection with the Text tool and drag to move it, you get a cookie cutter effect: the pixels within the text selection move along with the selection marquee, leaving transparency or the current background color in the selection's place. There is a wealth of things that you can do with a text selection. For example, in Figure 8-1 the selection was left empty and the Outer Bevel effect (Effects | 3D Effects | Outer Bevel) was applied at the default settings.

FIGURE 8-1   Creating a text selection allows you to produce great text effects.

You can also paint with the raster tools within the selection. In Figure 8-2, the Picture Tube tool was used to insert a U.S. flag into the selection to create a patriotic image. We'll look at how to make these and other effects later in this chapter.

FIGURE 8-2   Filling a text selection with a Picture Tube is another way to create great text effects.

> **TIP** *If you want to move the text marquee but not the selected pixels, right-click inside the selection with the Text tool and drag the selection marquee to another location.*

■ **Floating**   Creates a floating selection that hovers over the layer. The text is added using whatever material is currently set in the Foreground/Stroke and Background/Fill swatches on the Materials palette. When you move a floating text selection, the layer underneath is not affected.

> **TIP** *You can readily convert a standard selection or a floating selection to a layer. With the selection active, choose Selections | Promote Selection to Layer or press* CTRL-SHIFT-P. *A floating selection can also be promoted to a layer by right-clicking its labeled button on the Layers palette and on the resulting context menu choosing Promote Selection to Layer.*

Now let's take a quick look at the other choices in the Tool Options palette. Some are common choices that you have undoubtedly encountered in other Windows applications, while others are unique to Paint Shop Pro X.

■ **Font**   Lists the available fonts installed on your system.

■ **Size**   Enables you to either choose a font size from the drop-list or enter a value in the textbox.

■ **Units**   Lets you choose the units (either points or pixels) to use for Size.

■ **Font Style**   Sets the way the font appears. Select B for bold, I for italic, U for underline, or A to insert a horizontal line through the text (commonly referred to as Strikethrough).

■ **Alignment**   Aligns the text to the left or right edge of the insertion point or centers the text around the insertion point.

■ **Direction**   Sets the direction of the text: Horizontal and Down, Vertical and Left, or Vertical and Right.

■ **Anti-alias**   Smoothes the jagged edges of letters by blending them with the background color. The available settings are Off, Sharp, and Smooth. Except in the case of very small text, it's usually best to choose either Sharp or Smooth. (Note that Anti-alias has no effect with 8-bit color images such as GIFs and paletted PNGs.)

■ **Stroke Width**   Applies an outline around the text when set to a value other than 0.0. The current foreground color in the Materials palette defines the color of the outline. Use the Stroke Width to create outlined text like the example shown next. Keep in mind, however, that although applying an outline works well on block-shaped text, it usually doesn't do well with fancy display text.

NOTE *No matter what the setting for Stroke Width, your text will be created with no stroke if Foreground/Stroke in the Materials palette is set to Transparent.*

- **Leading** Increases or decreases the space between text lines. When left at 0, the spacing is determined automatically based on the font type and size.

- **Auto Kern** Automatically defines the spacing between each adjacent character based on the font type and size.

- **Kerning** Increases or decreases the space between each adjacent character if Auto Kern is turned off. This is particularly handy when placing text along a path and you need to shorten or lengthen the text string without changing the font size. (We'll look at text on a path in Chapter 10.)

- **Tracking** If given a value other than 0, sets equal spacing between characters. Be care with Tracking, though: Very small values create very noticeable effects.

NOTE *You can make characters in a string of text overlap each other by assigning a negative value to either Kerning or Tracking.*

- **Line Style** If you have defined a Stroke Width greater than 0.0 and if Stroke/ Foreground is not set to Transparent, this setting enables you to select the type of line to use for the outline of the characters in your text. The color for the Line Style is determined by the current foreground color. Here's an example of outlined text with a fancy line style:

- **Join**   Defines the way the corners of each letter appear. Your choices are Miter, which forms a very square look; Round, which offers a smoother look; or Beveled, which creates a semi-round look. If you select Miter as a choice, it will produce mitered (pointed) corners if the width of the corner is within the value that you set in the Miter Limit box or produce beveled corners when the corner width exceeds the value of the limit.

- **Warp Text**   Available when text characters follow a path; enables you to warp the characters to best fit the specific shape of the path.

CAUTION   *When the curve of the path to which you are aligning the text is not gradual (that is, it's a sharp angle) the Warp Text option may cause the individual characters to overlap each other and may introduce severe distortion in the individual characters.*

- **Offset**   Determines how close or far away from the path to place text on a path. Values can be either positive or negative.

Using the Text Tool

Now that you are familiar with the settings of the Text tool, you need to understand a few things about how the Text tool works before you can use it well. Text is made up of two parts: Stroke and Fill. When you are adding text, for most situations, you want to have the Stroke set to Transparent and the Fill set to the desired color. The walk-through in the next section will show you how to set up the Materials palette for entering text.

Adding Plain Text to an Image

For this exercise, you can download the file Sunset.jpg from www.osborne.com or use your own photo and your own text.

To add text to an image, complete the following steps:

1. Open the photo Sunset.jpg or another photo to which you want to add text.

2. In the Tools toolbar, choose the Text tool (T).

3. In the Tool Options palette, make the following choices:

- ■ **Create As** Floating
- ■ **Font** Times New Roman
- ■ **Size** 28 (the size of the image will determine the font size that you actually use)
- ■ **Stroke Width** 0.0
- ■ **Anti-alias** Smooth
- ■ **Alignment** Right

4. On the Materials palette (shown next), click the Foreground and Stroke Properties color swatch and select Transparent so there isn't a stroke. Click the Background and Fill color swatch. From the Color dialog box that opens, select the color you want for your text (black is a good choice for this example), and then click OK.

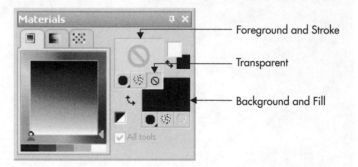

5. Click where you want to place your text in the image. (This sets the insertion point. Your text is aligned relative to the insertion point.)

6. In the Text Entry dialog, shown next, type your text. Press ENTER when you want to start another line. The Text tool does not automatically wrap. If you want this text to appear in the Text Entry box the next time it opens, select the Remember Text checkbox.

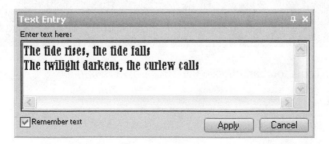

7. Click Apply.

8. If you need to reposition the text, position the Text tool inside the floating selection. The cursor changes to crossed double-headed arrows. You can then click and drag the text to the desired location.

9. If you like, promote the floating selection to a layer by pressing CTRL-SHIFT-P.

10. To preserve the layer structure of your image, save the image as a native Paint Shop Pro file using the Save As command. You can also save the image in another file format or export it as a Web-ready image by selecting File | Export | JPEG Optimizer.

Here's the completed image with its text:

NOTE

Once you click with the Text tool to define the insertion point for your text, you can change any of the settings in the Tool Options palette except Create As. Changes affect any text you enter after making the change. If you want to change text you've already typed into the Text Entry box, highlight the text by dragging across it and then change the Tool Options settings.

Adding a Cartoon Text Balloon to an Image

On those photos that simply scream for dialog, it is fun to add cartoon captions. Figure 8-3 is an example of what can be created.

To add a cartoon caption balloon, complete the following steps:

1. Open the photo to which you want to add text.

2. Add a new raster layer by selecting Layers | New Raster Layer or click the arrow for the New — Layer drop-list in the Layers palette and choose New Raster Layer.

3. In the Tools toolbar, click the Preset Shape tool. For this example, be sure that the Create As Vector checkbox is not checked and that Retain Style is selected.

FIGURE 8-3 A preset shape provides a quick way to add captions to photos.

4. Click to open the Shape List button in the Tool Options palette to view the available shapes.

5. Choose a shape for your balloon. You can pick from several cartoon caption balloons (which Corel calls Callouts). Callout 7 is the one used for the sample photo in Figure 8-3.

6. Click inside the image, then drag the cursor down from upper left to lower right to define the new balloon shape oriented as it appears in the shape list.

7. If you need to flip the balloon so that it faces the right direction, choose Image | Mirror or press CTRL-M.

> **TIP** *You can create a mirror image of a preset shape right when you draw it. To get a mirrored version, drag down from the upper right to the lower left (rather than from upper left to lower right).*

8. If you need to resize or reshape the balloon, choose the Pick tool. Click and drag a corner handle of the bounding box surrounding the shape to size the balloon proportionately, or click and drag one of the side, top, or bottom handles to stretch or shrink the balloon.

> **CAUTION** *Resizing or reshaping a raster figure can introduce distortion, degrading image quality. In Chapter 10, we'll examine vector text, which can be resized and reshaped without any degradation of image quality.*

9. To move the balloon shape with the Pick tool, position your cursor near the center of the shape. When the cursor changes to crossed double-headed arrows, click and drag the balloon to the desired location.

10. Add a new raster layer above the balloon layer.

11. Click the Text tool on the Tools toolbar. In the Tool Options palette make sure that Create As is set to Floating and select your favorite font. (Comic Sans is a nice choice for this example.) Adjust the font size so the caption fits in the balloon.

12. Change Background/Fill on the Materials palette to the color you want your text to be. Pick a color that offers good contrast to make the text easy to read.

13. Click in the image canvas inside the balloon you just created.

14. In the Text Entry box, type the text you want to place in the balloon and click Apply.

15. If you need to reposition the text, position the Text tool inside the text selection. When the cursor changes to crossed double-headed arrows, click and drag the text into position.

8

| TIP |
In the example here a caption was used to add a little humor to a photo. The use of balloon captions isn't limited to adding humorous comments, though; you can also use this technique to point out reference points on a photo or to provide instructions in a diagram or map.

Creating Special Text Effects

Creating special text effects gives your text a little attitude and offers a bit of a punch to your message. The following examples show only a snippet of what you can do with different fills and effects.

Transparent Text

If you have a photo with a lot of solid color in it or a graphic with a solid background you can use transparent text to create a professional-looking title. This is the effect used in Figure 8-1.

Follow these steps to create transparent text:

1. Open the image and select the Text tool (T).

2. Change the Create As setting to Selection in the Tool Options palette.

3. Enter the text you want to add. Adjust the text settings so the text fits your image. As you type, actual text appears in the image, but don't be concerned about that. When you're finished, click the Apply button and the text on the image is replaced by a selection marquee.

4. Choose Effects | 3D Effects | Outer Bevel and choose the default settings, then click OK.

5. Turn off the selection with Selections | Select None or press CTRL-D.

| NOTE |

This transparent text technique works well only on backgrounds that are not overly complex.

Adding Picture Tubes to Text

As you saw in Figure 8-2, you can really get creative using the Picture Tube tool to fill a text selection. To work through this example, go to www.corel.com, head over to the Picture Tube download page, and download the Summer picture tube set, which includes the Old Glory tube. Install the tube files and then let's begin!

1. Follow the first three steps in the previous technique. For this U.S. holiday example, "USA" is used as the text.

2. Select the Picture Tube tool in the Tools toolbar. Select the Old Glory picture tube. Click in the middle of the text selection to apply the Picture Tube to the selection, as shown next.

3. Choose Effects | 3D Effects | Inner Bevel and change the settings in the dialog box, as shown next:

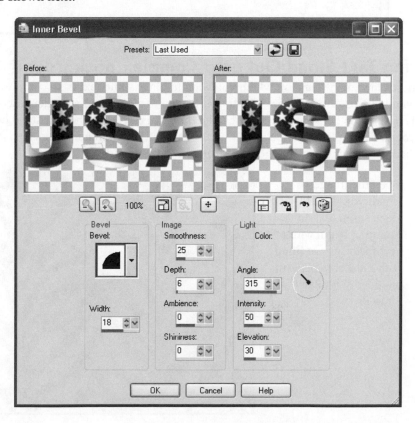

4. Click the OK button to apply the bevel, then turn off the selection (CTRL-D).

5. As an extra touch you can add a photo edge with Image | Picture Frames. (See Chapter 9 for information on using Picture Frames.)

Making Text Stand Out on a Complex Background

Sometimes the background on which you want to place some text is so complex that any text you add is just too hard to read. Or you'll want to add text of a particular color but that color is part of the background. In cases like this, you can make the text stand out from the background by employing a technique you've probably seen in numerous ads: Add a subtle drop shadow or two to separate the text from the background.

1. Open the image on which you want to place some text. In this example, begin with a new raster image filled with the Zebra pattern, included with Paint Shop Pro.

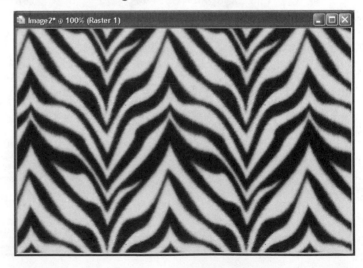

2. Choose the Text tool and set Create As to Floating. On the Materials palette, set Stroke to Transparent and Fill to a light color like the light part of the pattern. Enter your text, using whatever settings you like. At this point, the text isn't at all easy to read:

3. Now choose Effects | 3D Effects | Drop Shadow. Set both offsets to 0. Set the shadow color to a color that works well with your background but that is a shade that contrasts in brightness with your text: if the text is dark, use a light shadow; if the text is light, use a dark shadow. For the Blur, use whatever value gives you the result you want, but in most cases you'll want to keep the effect subtle.

4. Click OK when you have the effect you want.

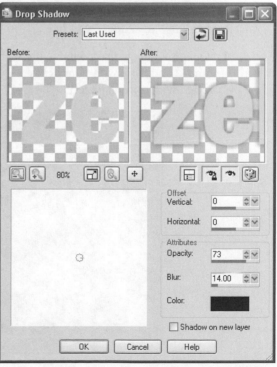

Here's the result for our example:

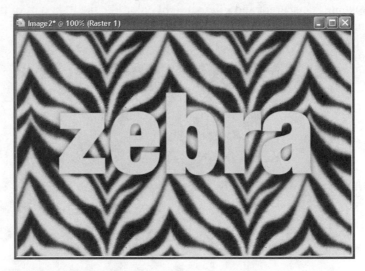

A whole lot easier to read, isn't it?

Creating Text Carved into a Background

Here's a popular text effect. You can use it to carve text into a sheet of metal, a stone block, a slab of wood—any surface you like.

1. Open the image that contains the surface you want to carve into, or open an empty image and fill it with your desired texture. For this example, we'll use a new image filled with a wood pattern.

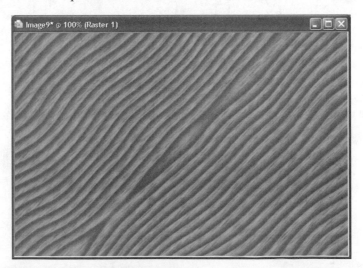

2. Choose the Text tool, set Create As to Selection, and enter the text that you want to carve into the surface.

3. If you're not working on a Background layer, then on the Layers palette, click the layer's Lock Tranparency toggle, whose icon looks like a padlock. If you're working on a Background layer, just go on to step 4.

4. Choose Effects | 3D Effects | Cutout. Use whatever settings give you the illusion of depth that you need. A dark color for the shadow is best. Be sure that the Fill Interior with Color checkbox is not selected. For the other settings, start with the defaults and make slight adjustments until you get the effect you want.

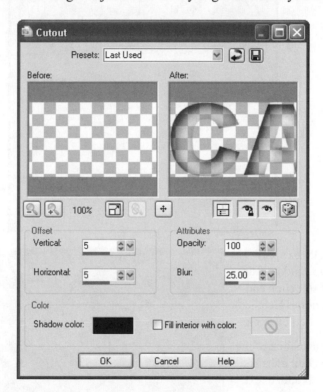

5. Click OK to apply the cutout, and leave the text selection active.

CAUTION *If you're working on a layer that supports transparency and you don't toggle on Lock Transparency before applying Cutout, the area within the text selection will be "cut out" (becoming transparent). Lock Transparency prevents any changes in transparency on a layer: Anything transparent remains transparent, anything opaque remains opaque, and anything semi-transparent remains semi-transparent.*

6. Choose Effects | 3D Effects | Drop Shadow. Set the color of the shadow to white. Use small positive values for the offsets, reduce Opacity to around 40, and set Blur to 0.

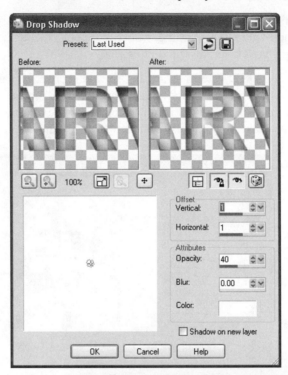

7. Click OK to apply the drop shadow. Turn off the selection and you're done. Here's the finished example:

These are just some of the many ways you can enhance your images with added text. You're sure to discover all sorts of other ways as well.

In the next chapter, you'll explore other ways to enhance your images, including adding Picture Frames and decorative borders, painting with Picture Tubes, and creating painting-like effects from photos.

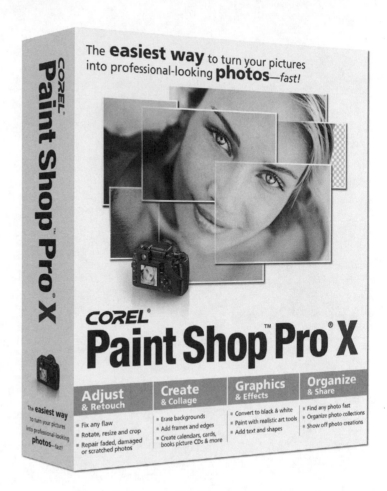

The **easiest way** to turn your pictures into professional-looking **photos**—fast!

COREL®
Paint Shop™ Pro® X

Adjust & Retouch	Create & Collage	Graphics & Effects	Organize & Share
▪ Fix any flaw	▪ Erase backgrounds	▪ Convert to black & white	▪ Find any photo fast
▪ Rotate, resize and crop	▪ Add frames and edges	▪ Paint with realistic art tools	▪ Organize photo collections
▪ Repair faded, damaged or scratched photos	▪ Create calendars, cards, books picture CDs & more	▪ Add text and shapes	▪ Show off photo creations

PART IV

Getting Creative with Paint Shop Pro X

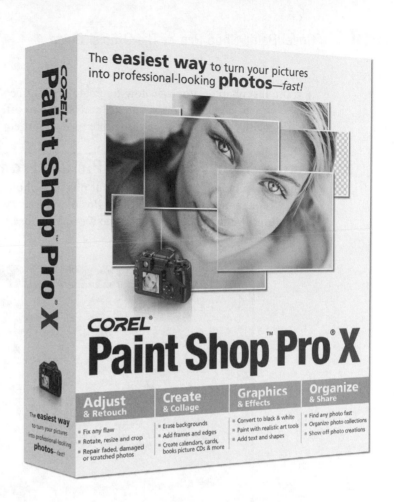

CHAPTER 9

Add Dazzling Effects to Your Images

In the last chapter, you saw how to create great effects with text. But adding text is only one way to enhance your images. Paint Shop Pro offers a number of other means for creating super effects, and we'll explore of few of them now.

Enhancing Your Photos with Picture Frames

A mat or a picture frame enhances your physical photos, and digital photos can also benefit from a nice mat or frame. Paint Shop Pro makes it easy to frame your digital image with its Picture Frame Wizard. To open the wizard, choose Image | Picture Frame. You'll see the Picture Frame dialog.

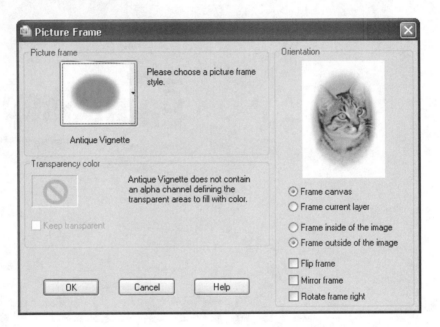

As the example here shows, a PSP Picture Frame can be other things besides what you probably think of as a picture frame. In this case, the "frame" creates a vignette. Of course, traditional frames like the one shown next are also available:

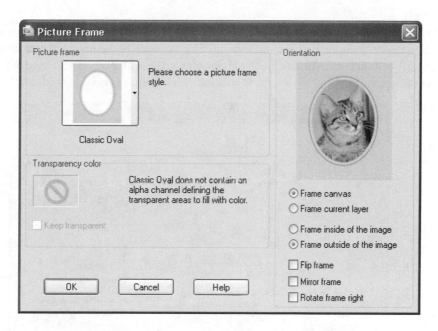

To select a picture frame, click the small arrow next to the preview on the drop-list, scroll through the list, and click the thumbnail of the frame you want:

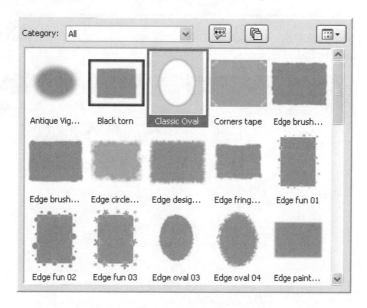

The two examples shown so far use the default settings for Picture Frame, with the frame applied to the entire image canvas and with the frame outside of the image (that is, with the inner opening of the frame revealing as much of your photo as possible). You also have the option of applying the frame inside of the image, in which case the frame covers up the edges of your photo:

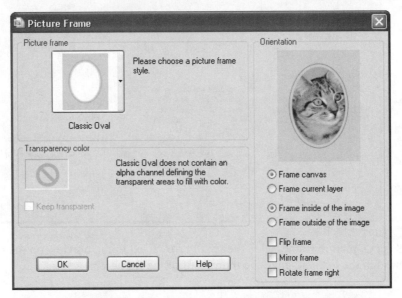

You can also manipulate the frame in several ways. Let's suppose you choose the Polka Dot Card frame included with PSP X:

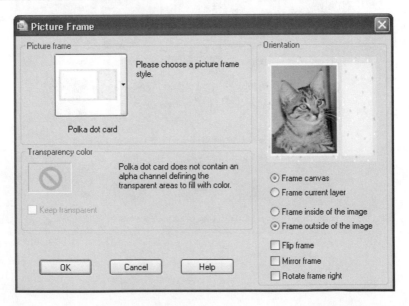

Now suppose that you'd rather have the patterned paper block that's to the right of the photo appear on the left instead. You can easily get just that by selecting the Mirror Frame checkbox:

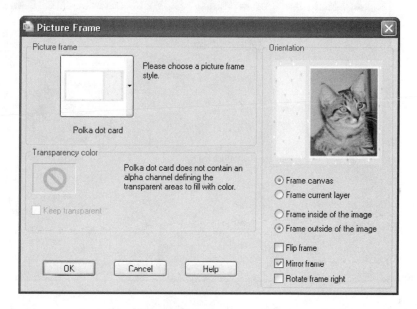

And how about if what you want is to have that block of patterned paper below the photo? In that case, don't select Mirror Frame but instead select Rotate Frame Right:

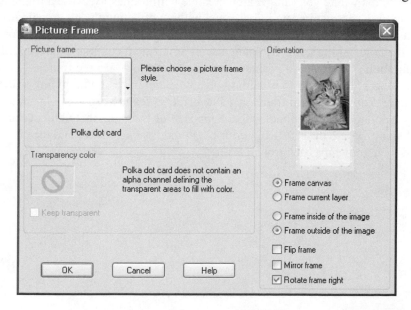

9

To get that block above the photo, select both Rotate Frame Right and Flip Frame:

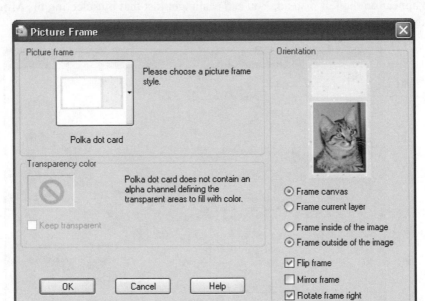

Once you've selected the frame and any settings that you want, click OK to add the frame. The frame is added as a new layer above your photo.

Now here's where you can get a bit creative with frames. Because a frame is added on its own layer, you can manipulate it easily and without affecting the photo below. For example, you can add a drop shadow to the frame by selecting Effects | 3D Effects | Drop Shadow or change the color of the frame by using a color adjustment command such as Adjust | Hue and Saturation | Colorize. You can even resize, distort, or warp the frame.

Speaking of layers and frames, did you notice that instead of applying a frame to an entire image canvas you can frame just a layer? This feature can come in handy when you're creating a collage or a scrapbook page. Suppose, for example, that you have an image like the following, where the solid-colored background is on one layer and the photo is on another layer above the background layer:

To apply a picture frame to the photo alone, make the photo's layer the current layer by clicking its layer button on the Layers palette. Then open the Picture Frame Wizard by selecting Image | Picture Frame. In the Picture Frame dialog, select the frame you want and choose Frame Current Layer. The result will be something like this:

Creating Your Own Picture Frames

Rectangular picture frames that include no transparency other than the opening in the middle are very easy to make. Simply open a new raster image with a transparent background, create your frame, then export the image as a Picture Frame:

1. Open a new raster image with a transparent background. Make the image about as large as you think you'll ever want the frame when applied to an image.

2. Choose Selections | Select All. This selects your entire image. Then decrease the size of the selection by the same number of pixels that you want for the width of the solid part of your frame, using Selections | Modify | Contract. The result will look something like this:

3. Invert the selection by choosing
Selections | Invert. Then use the
Flood Fill tool to fill the inverted
selection with whatever color or
pattern you want for your frame.
Here's an example with the selection
filled with a wood pattern:

4. Turn off the selection with Selections | Select None (or press CTRL-D). Apply any effects that you want. Here's our wood frame after choosing Effects | 3D Effects | Inner Bevel:

5. Export the image as a frame with File | Export | Picture Frame. In the Export Picture Frame dialog, enter a name for your frame and click Save:

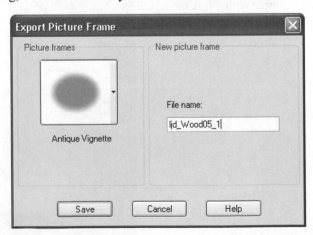

6. Unless you want to keep your image for editing later, you can close it now without saving it.

Frames can also include transparency outside the frame. Examples of such frames are Corners Tape and Lace, two of the frames included in PSP X. For frames like this, the transparent areas outside the frame can be maintained when the frame is applied (as in Figure 9-1) or those areas can be translated to a solid color (as in Figure 9-2).

Here's an example that shows how to create a picture frame that includes transparent areas other than the frame opening:

1. Open a new raster image with a transparent background. Make the image about as large as you think you'll ever want the frame when applied to an image.

2. Create any type of nonrectangular frame that you like. Here's an octagonal one, for example:

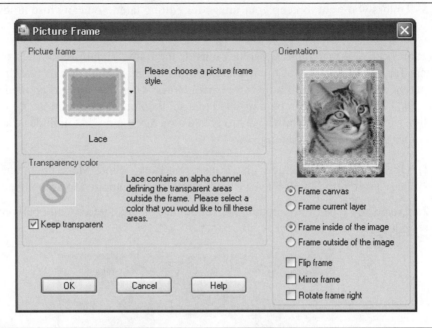

FIGURE 9-1   When a frame with transparent areas outside a frame is applied, the transparency can be maintained.

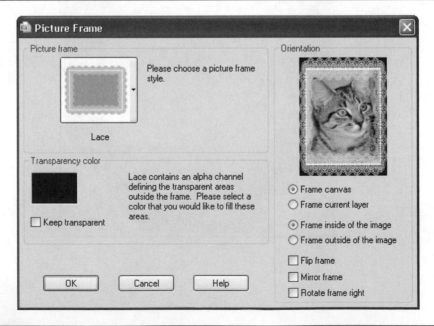

FIGURE 9-2   Alternatively, the transparent areas can be translated to a solid color.

3. With the Magic Wand set to Add, select all of the transparent areas outside the frame, but don't select the frame opening:

4. Invert the selection. Now the frame and the frame opening are selected:

5. Save the selection to an alpha channel by choosing Selections | Load/Save Selection | Save Selection to Alpha. Accept all the defaults in the Save Selection to Alpha dialog and click Save:

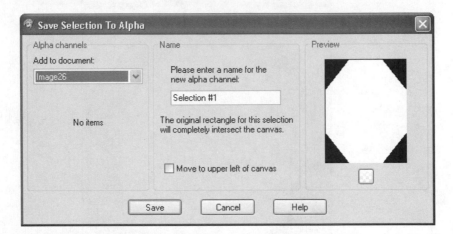

6. Deselect the selection by choosing Selections | Select None (or pressing CTRL-D). Then export the frame with File | Export | Picture Frame. You can then close your image without saving it. Your frame is ready for you to use the next time you choose Image | Picture Frame.

CAUTION *Be sure that the image you use for your picture frame doesn't have an alpha channel before you save the selection for your frame to an alpha channel. The Picture Frame Wizard always uses the first alpha channel it encounters in a frame file, so if you have multiple alpha channels you can get some pretty strange results. If there's a possibility that you've already added an alpha channel to your image, then before saving your selection to an alpha channel choose Image | Delete Alpha Channel, being sure to select Delete All Alpha Channels in the Delete Alpha Channel dialog. Then when you save your selections, you'll be certain that you have only one alpha channel saved.*

Adding Photo Borders with Masks

Picture Frames aren't the only means of enhancing your images. You can also add decorative edges with mask layers. Figure 9-3 shows an example.

A mask layer is a special kind of layer that is very similar to an adjustment layer. But while an adjustment layer is used to modify the color or brightness of lower layers without actually changing those layers, a mask layer is used to modify the opacity of lower layers without actually changing those layers.

FIGURE 9-1   A decorative edge can be added using a mask layer.

You can get a decorative edge effect with a mask in two ways. First, you can add a solid-colored layer below the photo layer, then apply a mask to the photo layer to let the solid color show through around the edges of the photo:

1. Open your image and duplicate it by choosing Window | Duplicate or by pressing SHIFT-D. Close your original image and continue work on the duplicate.

2. If the photo is on a Background layer, promote the layer to a true layer by right-clicking Background on the Layers palette and choosing Promote Background Layer in the resulting context menu.

3. Add a new layer and use the Flood Fill tool to fill the layer with the color you want for your solid background.

4. In the Layers palette, drag your photo layer up above the solid-colored layer in the layers stack. (If the photo layer is a Background layer, remember you'll first need to

promote it to a true layer. You can then drag the photo layer above the solid-colored layer.) The Layers palette then looks something like this:

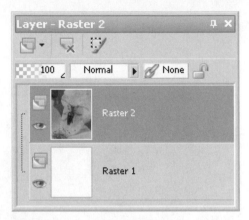

5. Make the photo layer the active layer by clicking its label in the Layers palette. Then choose Layers | Load/Save Mask | Load Mask From Disk. You then see the Load Mask from Disk dialog:

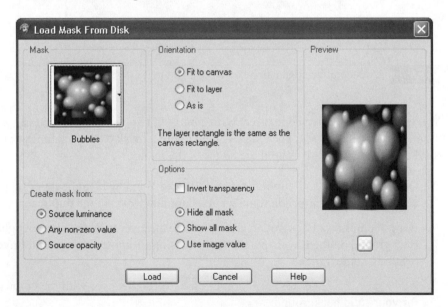

6. In the dialog, click the arrow or preview for the Mask drop-list and select the mask you want for your edge. Leave all the other controls at their default settings and click Load. Your photo now has its decorative edge, and the layer structure of your image looks like this:

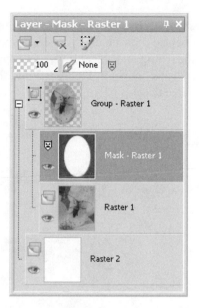

The other means of applying a decorative edge is to simply add a solid-colored layer above your photo layer, then apply the mask to the solid-colored layer. There's one twist, though. If you add the mask just as we did in the first method, with the default settings, the result will look like this:

9

Not quite what you wanted, right? But you can easily get the intended result: When the Load Mask from Disk dialog is displayed and you've selected the mask you want, go to the Options portion of the dialog and select Invert Transparency. When you load the mask, the result looks like what's shown in Figure 9-3 and the layer structure displayed in the Layers palette looks like this:

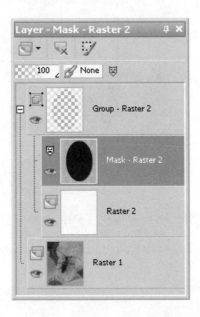

> **TIP** *If you try to use the second method but forget to invert transparency, there's no need to Undo and start over. Instead, just click the mask layer's button in the Layers palette to make the mask the active layer and then choose either Image | Negative Image or Layers | Invert Mask/Adjustment.*

Using Picture Tubes

Picture tubes are images that you paint with. A Picture Tube can contain either a single image, like the 3D Gold tube, or a collection of images, like the Autumn Leaves tube. The effect you get with a tube depends on how the images in the tube are applied. By default, 3D Gold is applied so that the single image overlaps itself. Clicking with 3D Gold creates a gold ball shape, but dragging with 3D Gold creates a solid snaking shape, as seen here:

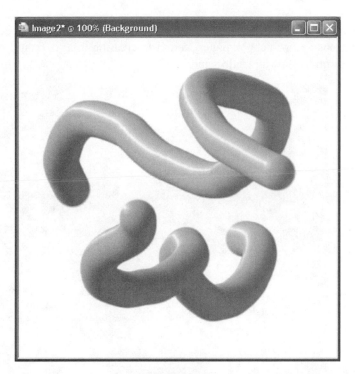

The Autumn Leaves tube is set by default to paint its many leaf images with random spacing as you drag, as seen here:

Picture tubes have many uses, including creating buttons and spacer bars for Web pages, enhancing photos and scrapbook pages, and even creating images completely from scratch, as this silly example shows:

To use picture tubes, open a raster image and choose the Picture Tube tool, whose Tool Options palette is shown in Figure 9-4. Select the tube that you want from the tube selection drop-list. Then paint on your image. Click to apply a single image from the tube, or drag to repeatedly apply the images from the tube.

If you want, you can also adjust the other settings available on the Tool Options palette:

- **Scale** Determines the size of the tube images, from 250 percent of the original size down to 10 percent.

- **Step** Determines the number of pixels between brush impressions for the tube. For example, if you have Placement Mode set to Continuous and you want the tube images to be 100 pixels apart from center to center when you drag with the Picture Tube tool, then set Step to 100.

- **Placement Mode**   Determines how your tube images are spaced when you drag with the Picture Tube tool. With Random spacing, your tube images are spaced randomly, anywhere from 0 pixels to the number of pixels set in Step. With Continuous spacing, the tube images are always spaced at the spacing set in Step.

- **Selection Mode**   Determines how the different tube images are selected when you drag with the Picture Tube tool:

  - **Random**   Selects the images randomly. This, the default, is probably the most commonly used selection mode.

  - **Incremental**   Selects the images in a fixed order. Once all the tube images have been selected, selection begins again at the first tube image.

  - **Angular**   Selects the tube images based on the direction in which you drag.

  - **Pressure**   Relevant only if you're using a pressure-sensitive graphics tablet. Selection here is based on stylus pressure as you draw with the Picture Tube tool.

  - **Velocity**   Selects the tube images based on the speed at which you drag.

For now, don't worry about the Settings control. We'll take a look at it near the end of the next section.

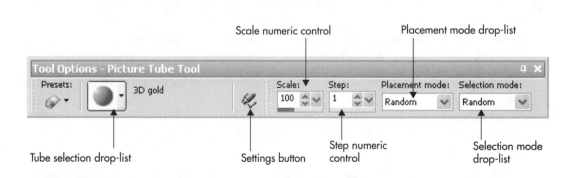

FIGURE 9-2   The Tool Options palette for the Picture Tube tool

Creating Your Own Picture Tubes

A Picture Tube is just a special sort of PspImage file with an extension of PspTube, and you can open a PspTube file in PSP just as you can any other image. For example, here's what the Autumn Leaves tube looks like when it's opened in PSP:

This example illustrates that a PspTube file has a single layer on which the various tube images are placed. The images are arranged as if each image occupies a cell in a grid, and the images are surrounded by transparency.

Let's make a picture tube of our own. We'll make our tube so that each of its component images is about 200 x 200 pixels in size, creating four images arranged in a grid with two cells across and two cells down.

1. Open a new raster image with a transparent background. Make the image 400 pixels wide and 400 pixels high.

2. To help make sure that each tube image is completely contained in its own grid cell, turn on PSP's grid by selecting View | Grid (or pressing CTRL-ALT-G). The grid is not actually part of your image, just gridlines temporarily superimposed over your image to help you position things correctly.

3. The default grid spacing is too fine for our purposes, so choose View | Change Grid, Guide & Snap Properties. You'll then see the Grid, Guide & Snap Properties dialog:

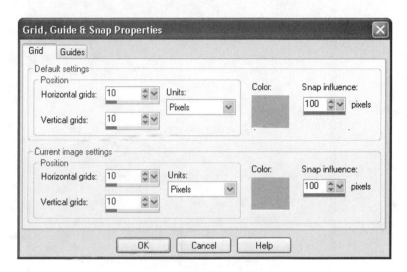

4. Now to change the dimensions of the grid to 200 x 200 pixels. In the Current Image Settings portion of the dialog, change Horizontal Grids and Vertical Grids to 200:

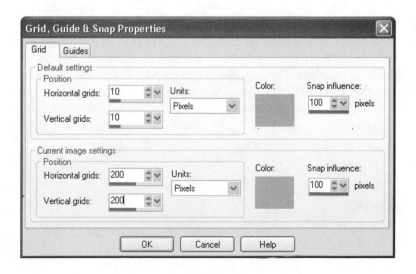

9

5. Click OK to close the dialog and superimpose the newly defined grid on your image:

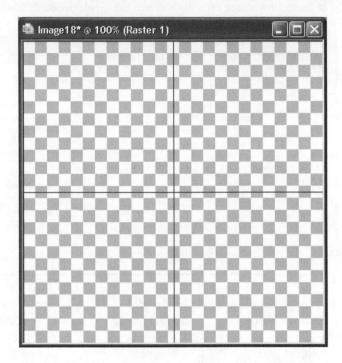

6. You're now ready to add some images. For this example, choose the Preset Shapes tool. On its Tool Options palette, choose Flower in the Shape drop-list, and uncheck both Retain Style and Create As Vector. On the Materials palette, set Foreground and Stroke to transparent and set Background and Fill to whatever color you want for your flower. Drag in the image canvas, filling the upper-left cell of the grid without touching any of the grid lines:

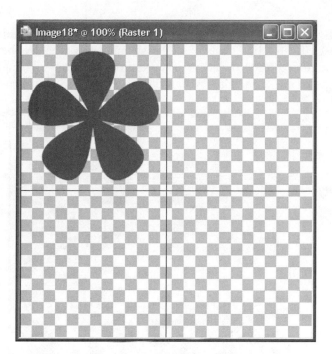

7. Choose Flower2 and fill the upper-right cell with this shape. Then choose Flower5 and fill the lower-left cell with it. Then choose Flower7 and fill the lower-right cell with it. The result should look like this:

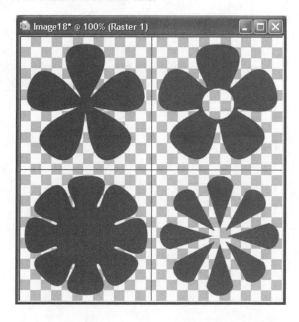

8. Before exporting the image as a tube, let's add a little dimension to those flowers. Choose Effects | 3D Effects | Inner Bevel and apply whatever bevel you like. Notice that you don't need to select the flowers first. PSP knows to apply the bevel to the shapes that are surrounded by transparency. The result will look something like this:

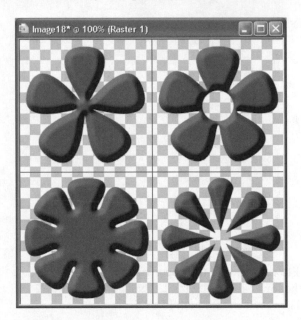

9. Almost finished! Choose File | Export | Picture Tube. You'll see the Export Picture Tube dialog:

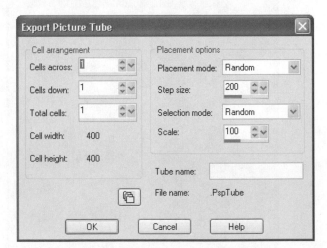

10. Set the Cell Arrangement properties. For the Cells Across option, enter 2, since your tube has two cells from left to right. For Cells Down, enter 2, since your tube has two cells from top to bottom. (Of course, if your tube had a different number of cells across and cells down, you'd enter the appropriate values.) Choose values for Placement Mode, Step Size, Selection Mode, and Scale. Whatever values you enter will be the defaults for your tube. Then enter a name for your tube and click OK. The next time you choose the Picture Tube tool, your tube will be ready to use!

11. Unless you want to keep your original image to edit later, close it now without saving it.

If it turns out that the defaults you chose for the various properties of your tube aren't really what you'd like, don't despair. Simply choose the Picture Tube tool and select your tube from the tube selection drop-list on the Tool Options palette. Then click the Settings button on Tool Options. You'll get the Picture Tube Settings dialog:

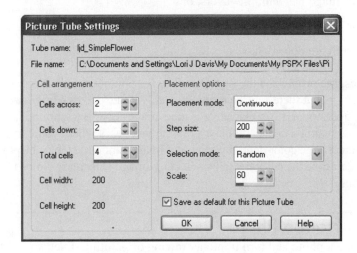

9

Looks familiar, doesn't it? It's almost identical to the Export Picture Tubes dialog. To change the default settings for your tube, choose the new settings, select the checkbox marked Save As Default for This Picture Tube, and click OK.

Before moving on, there's one other thing you need to keep in mind when creating your own picture tubes. At the beginning of this section, we mentioned that a Picture Tube file is single-layered. When you're creating your tube, you can create each individual tube image on its own layer. In fact, what you'll probably want to do if your tube is composed of several selected photo objects is to copy a selected object, paste it into your tube image canvas as a new layer, copy the next selected object, paste it into the tube image canvas as a new layer, and so on. Working this way makes it easy for you to position the pasted-in objects, since each is on its own layer. However, if you have multiple layers, you must merge those layers by selecting Layers | Merge | Merge Visible before exporting your image as a tube. If there are multiple layers when you try to export as a Picture Tube, you'll get this somewhat cryptic error message:

If you get this error, one of three things could be wrong:

1. Your image has multiple layers, or

2. Your image has a Background layer, whether or not there's also a transparent layer, or

3. Your image doesn't have a color depth of RGB – 8 bits/channel

In most cases, the problem is the first one and what you need to do is merge the visible layers. If the problem is that there's a Background layer, you need to delete it, assuming you have a transparent layer, too. (If you placed your tube images on a Background layer, you'll need to start over again using a transparent layer.) In the rare cases where you bump into the third problem, increase the color depth by selecting Image | Increase Color Depth | RGB – 8 bits/ channel, or decrease the color depth by selecting Image | Decrease Color Depth | RGB – 8 bits/channel.

Creating Art from a Photo

It's fun to take a photo and turn it into a drawing or painting. Even so-so photos can become digital art works. In fact, turning a very blurry photo into a painting can be a good way to save an otherwise hopeless photo.

The Brush Strokes Effect

First, Paint Shop Pro has a number of effects available under Effects | Art Media Effects. Most of these effects have been around since version 4 or earlier, however, and you may find the results rather primitive. One shining exception, though, is Brush Strokes.

With Brush Strokes, you can achieve a number of painterly effects. In fact, the variety of effects you can get with just a little tweaking may astound you. For example, the images in Figures 9-5 through 9-7 differ only in their settings for Softness and Color. All the other Brush Strokes settings for these are the same:

Bristles	256
Width	6
Opacity	0
Length	15
Density	26
Angle	131

FIGURE 9-3   Brush Strokes with Softness set to 20 and Color set to white

FIGURE 9-4   Brush Strokes with Softness set to 20 and Color set to black

Imagine the degree of variation you can achieve by adjusting the other settings as well. Experiment with Brush Strokes and see what sorts of painting-like effects you can create.

Posterize

Another group of effects you can use to create digital art is found under Effects | Artistic Effects. Quite a few of these—including Colored Edges, Contours, Glowing Edges, Halftone, Hot Wax Coating, Neon Glow, and Topography—produce interesting results when applied to photos.

FIGURE 9-5   Brush Strokes with Softness set to 0 and Color set to black

One particularly nifty effect is Posterize, which reduces the number of colors in your image in order to simulate a poster, as shown at right.

Posterize is easy to use. Its single control, Levels, determines the level of reduction. Values between 3 and 9 usually produce results most like actual posters.

Here's another way of producing a poster-like effect, this one using only two colors:

1. Begin by opening a copy of the photo you want to use for your poster.

2. Leave your photo image open and create another image that has the same dimensions as your photo. Give this image a dark-colored Background.

3. Add a new layer above the dark Background layer. Fill the new layer with your second color. This color should be much lighter than the color you used for the Background layer. Use either a lighter version of the background color or, for a bold pop-art effect, a color that contrasts with the background color.

4. Now the fun begins. Be sure the top layer is the active layer (with its label bolded in the Layers palette). If the top layer isn't the active layer, click its label in the Layers palette. Then choose Layers | New Mask Layer | From Image, which opens the Add Mask from Image dialog.

In the dialog, click the arrow for the Source Window drop-list and select the filename of your open photo image. Be sure that Source Luminance is selected and that Invert Mask Data is not selected. Then click OK. The Layers palette then shows a layer structure like this:

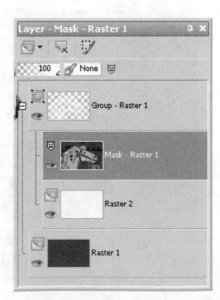

At this point, your new image resembles a duotone image, with the shadows of the original photo having the color of your dark background color, the highlights having the color of your light top layer, and the midtones a blending of these two colors.

5. To create the poster effect, make the mask layer the active layer, then apply Effects | Artistic Effects | Posterize to the mask. Your finished poster will look something like this:

The results of this method can be quite dramatic, especially if you use two contrasting colors. Give it a try and see what you think!

"Painting" with Noise Reduction

Sometimes you can get nice painting effects by applying extreme noise reduction to a photo. Try Adjust | Add/Remove Noise | Median Filter or Adjust | Add/Reduce Noise | Edge Preserving Smooth. In either case, use the adjustment's maximum setting. If you don't get enough smoothing with one application of the adjustment, try applying it one or two more times. Figure 9-8 shows an example made with Median Filter, and Figure 9-9 shows an example with Edge Preserving Smooth.

| TIP | *To reapply a command, press* CTRL-Y *right after applying the command. You can keep reapplying the command again and again by repeatedly pressing* CTRL-Y. |

FIGURE 9-6   Painting created with Median Filter

FIGURE 9-7   Painting created with Edge Preserving Smooth

"Sketching" with Find All

Many folks like to make line drawings from photos. The easiest way to do this is to apply
Effects | Edge Effects | Find All to your photo:

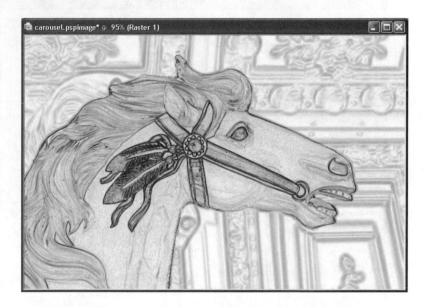

TIP   *You can simulate ink drawings by applying Find All followed by Adjust | Add/
Remove Noise | Edge Preserving Smooth or Adjust | Add/Remove Noise | Salt
and Pepper Filter. If you use Salt and Pepper Filter, select Include All Lower
Speck Sizes and Aggressive Action and then adjust the other settings to get
the effect you want.*

If you find that Find All creates too low-contrast an image with many gray areas, you
can darken the main outlines and brighten up the other areas of the image by selecting
Adjust | Brightness and Contrast | Levels. Set the Input sliders so that the left slider is

pulled to the right a bit and the right slider is pulled to the left a bit, setting the middle slider as needed:

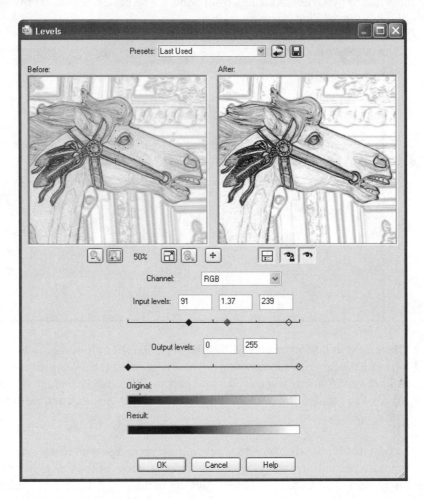

One other step you can take, if you like, is to create some pencil marks. Add a layer above your modified photo and fill the layer with white. Change the Blend Mode of the white layer to Multiply. Don't worry that the layer then appears completely transparent. Add some monochrome noise to the white layer by selecting Adjust | Add/Remove Noise | Add Noise, choosing Gaussian and Monochrome, and setting Noise to about 20. Gray spots appear on the layer. Then apply Motion Blur, using whatever settings give you the angle and length that you want for your pencil marks.

In this chapter, we've examined some of Paint Shop Pro's raster tools and adjustments. In the next chapter, you'll explore something quite different—vector graphics. With vectors, you can create precise shapes and editable text, tweaking the results without loss of image quality. With vectors, you acquire a whole new set of tools for working image magic.

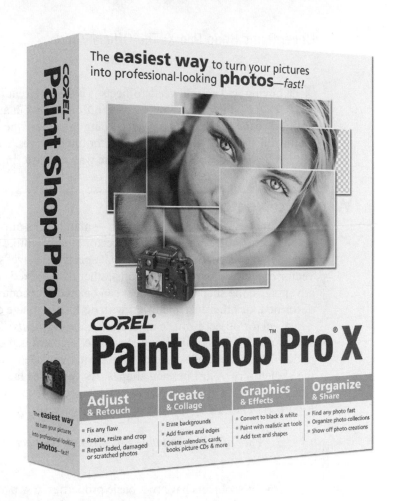

CHAPTER 10

Understanding the Vector Tools

Drawing and editing vector objects is quite different from working with pixels on raster layers. Many folks find vectors intimidating, but as you'll soon see there's really nothing scary about vectors. We're going to explore the vector tools and many of the features that enable you to modify vector lines, curves, and shapes. When you're finished with this chapter, you'll be well on the way to mastering vectors.

What's a Vector Object?

Raster images are made up of pixels—small blocks of color that are "painted" on a raster layer. Vector objects are drawn on vector layers. Unlike pixel-based objects, a vector object is made up of a set of instructions that specify the size, shape, and color of the object. That a vector object is a set of instructions rather than a fixed collection of pixels gives it two handy advantages: the shape of the object can be precisely controlled, and the object can be resized, deformed, or otherwise modified with no loss in image quality.

A vector object is made up of *nodes* and *segments*. The nodes are points that define the curves and corners of lines and shapes. A segment is the edge that lies between a pair of nodes. The nodes and segments aren't what you see in your finished image but rather are the skeleton of your lines and shapes. As you'll see later in this chapter, Paint Shop Pro lets you examine the nodes and segments, either superimposed on the actual object (as in Figure 10-1) or all by themselves (as in Figure 10-2).

| NOTE | *A set of nodes and the segments that connect them constitute a path.* |

All vector objects have two basic properties, a *stroke* and a *fill*. For a line, the stroke is what you think of as the line itself and the fill is material that lies "inside" a series of lines or within a curve. For a shape, the stroke is the shape's outline and the fill is the material inside the shape. Figure 10-3 shows some examples.

You set the stroke with the Foreground and Stroke swatch on the Materials palette, and you set the fill with the Background and Fill swatch. (For the rest of this chapter, we'll refer to Foreground and Stroke simply as "Stroke" and to Background and Fill simply as "Fill.") If you want a stroke but no fill, toggle on the Transparent button for Fill. If you want a fill but no stroke, toggle on the Transparent button for Stroke.

A First Look at the Vector Tools

Paint Shop Pro X includes three types of tools for vector drawing: the shape tools, the Pen tool, and the Pick tool. In addition to these, you can also use the Text tool to create vector text.

There are four different shape tools. The easiest of these to use is the Preset Shape tool. A preset shape is a ready-made vector object that you can use again and again. You can use a preset shape just as it was created or change its properties by setting your own stroke and fill for the shape. Figure 10-4 shows a few examples of preset shapes.

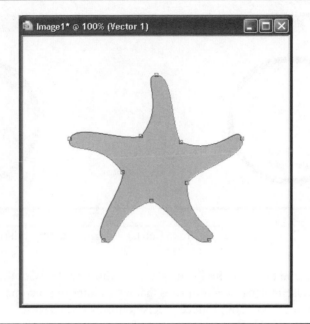

FIGURE 10-1   An object's nodes and segments can be superimposed on the object.

10

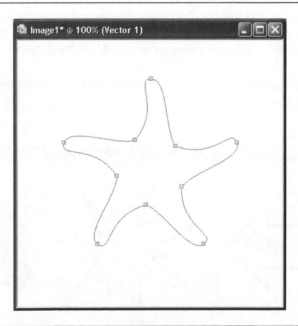

FIGURE 10-2   An object's nodes and segments can be shown alone, revealing the object's "skeleton."

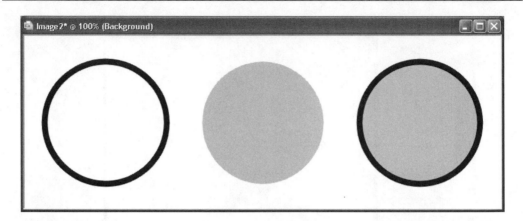

FIGURE 10-3   Objects can have a stroke (left), a fill (middle), or both (right).

Two other shape tools are the Rectangle and Ellipse tools. With the Rectangle tool, you can produce precise rectangles and squares that have either sharp corners or rounded corners. With the Ellipse tool, you can produce precise ellipses and circles.

The final shape tool is Symmetric Shape. This nifty tool enables you to create perfectly symmetrical polygons and star-like shapes. Figure 10-5 shows just a few of the possibilities.

The Pen tool is the workhorse of vector drawing. With the Pen tool, you draw your own lines and curves, either singly to create distinct lines and curves or in a connected series so you can produce your own shapes. The Pen tool can also be used in its Edit mode to modify lines, curves, and shapes, whether they were created with the Pen tool or with one of the shape tools.

The Pick tool is a multifunction tool. You can use it to select, move, resize, or deform an object or set of objects.

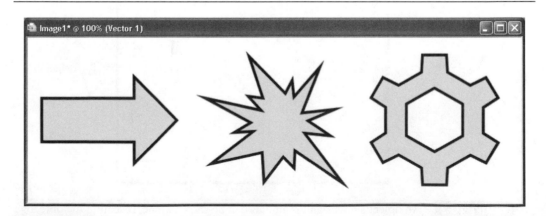

FIGURE 10-4   Examples of preset shapes

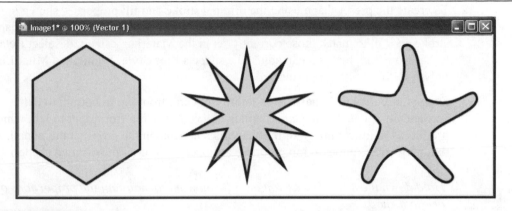

FIGURE 10-5 Examples of objects created with the Symmetric Shape tool

The Text tool can be used to create vector text. The advantage of vector text is that it's editable. You can change the color or size of the text, choose a different font, or even modify the content of the text string.

Working with Preset Shapes

Let's begin exploring vector drawing by using the Preset Shape tool. You'll find the Preset Shape tool in the Tools toolbar grouped together with the Rectangle, Ellipse, and Symmetric Shape tools.

Here's how to draw a preset shape:

1. Choose the Preset Shape tool, then click the Shape list in the Tool Options palette and select a preset shape from the list. Be sure that Create as Vector is selected.

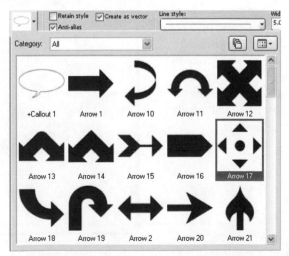

2. To create the preset shape using the original stroke and fill properties shown in the drop-list thumbnail, choose the Retain Style option. If instead you want the shape's stroke and fill to match those currently set in the Materials palette, deselect Retain Style. Note, too, that you can adjust the shape's Line Style, Width, and Miter Limit only if Retain Style is not selected.

3. Drag your cursor diagonally from left to right and from top to bottom to define the size and complete the shape. (Alternatively, you can drag from right to left, which produces the mirror image of the shape as it appears in the drop-list thumbnail. And dragging from bottom to top produces a flipped version of the original shape.)

TIP	*Hold down the* SHIFT *key as you drag if you want to maintain the proportions of the original shape.*

Mastering the Ellipse, Rectangle, and Symmetric Shape Tools

Now let's take a look at the other shape tools: Ellipse, Rectangle, and Symmetric Shape. All of these tools create shapes that can be tweaked to precisely modify the shape while maintaining symmetry.

Ellipses and Circles

The simplest of the new shape tools is Ellipse. With this tool, you can create precise circles and ovals in a snap.

Open a new image with a vector background. Choose the Ellipse tool. On the Tool Options palette, you have the option of setting the shape to either Ellipse or Circle. Let's try Circle. We'll create our circle with a fill but no stroke.

On the Tool Options palette, deselect Show Nodes but select Create on Vector. Set Width to 0 and check Anti-alias. On the Materials palette, set Stroke to Transparent and set Fill to any material you like. Click and drag in the image canvas to draw your circle. The result will look something like this:

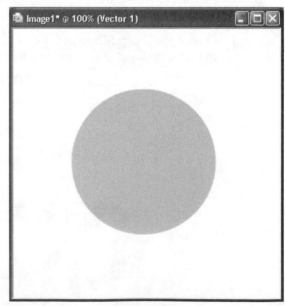

Next, with the Ellipse tool still the active tool, change the Mode on the Tool Options palette to Edit. You'll now see a rectangular bounding box around your circle, with handles in the middle of each side and in the center, like this:

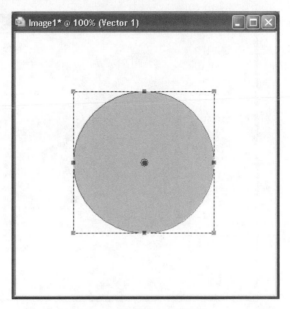

Try dragging the handle in the middle of one of the sides of the bounding box. Notice that if you drag either the top or the bottom handle toward the center, the circle is flattened horizontally, with both the top and bottom of the circle being flattened equally. Drag the top or bottom handle away from the center, and the circle expands to become a tall vertical oval, like this:

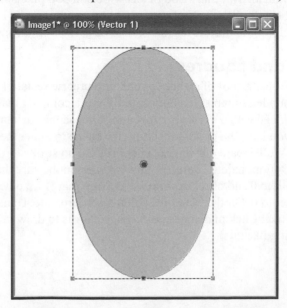

If you drag one of the side handles toward the center, the circle is flattened vertically, with both sides of the circle flattened equally. Drag one of the side handles away from the center, and the circle expands horizontally to become an oval, like this:

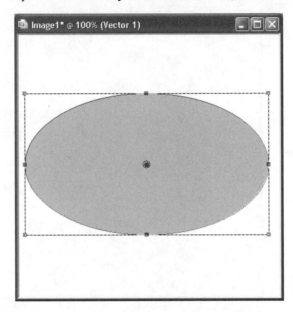

As you drag the handles, notice how the values of Radius X and Radius Y on the Tool Options palette change, too. Here's where the precision comes in. Instead of dragging the handles, you can enter values directly into the textboxes for Radius X and Radius Y. So, for example, if you want an oval that's 200 pixels wide and 350 pixels high, you can enter 100 for Radius X and 175 for Radius Y. (Remember that a radius is the length from the center of the ellipse to the edge, so the values to enter should be half the width and height that you want.)

Rectangles and Squares

The Rectangle tool is the tool of choice for creating precise rectangles, squares, rounded rectangles, and rounded squares. It's only slightly more complex than the Ellipse tool.

Open a new image with a vector background. Choose the Rectangle tool. On the Tool Options palette, you have the option of setting the shape to either Rectangle or Square. Let's try Square. We'll create our square with a fill but no stroke.

On the Tool Options palette, deselect Show Nodes but be sure that Create on Vector is selected. Set Width to 0 and check Anti-alias. Be sure that Horizontal Radius and Vertical Radius are both set to 0. On the Materials palette, set Stroke to Transparent and set Fill to any material you like. Click and drag in the image canvas to draw your square. The result will look something like this

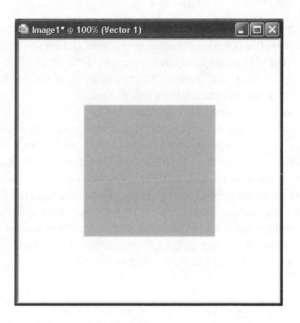

Next, with the Rectangle tool still the active tool, change the Mode on the Tool Options palette to Edit. You'll see a bounding box around your rectangle, like this:

10

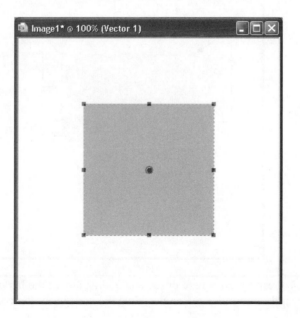

Notice that on the bounding box are four handles, one for each corner. You can drag the top or bottom edge of the bounding box up or down to flatten or expand the shape, and you can drag either of the side edges to squeeze or expand the shape. But those corner handles are a little bit different than what you might expect. Each of the corners actually includes a pair of special control nodes beneath the corner handle.

Position the cursor over one of the corner handles. When the shape of the cursor changes to a pair of crossed white double-arrows with a square next to it, click and drag to resize the shape. Click and drag when the cursor is shaped like a pair of crossed black double-arrows, though, and all four corners of the shape become rounded. You'll also see two new nodes near each corner, in addition to the corner handles, as shown in Figure 10-6.

Once those extra nodes appear, you can adjust one independently of its mate by dragging. Give it a try and see what happens. If you want both members of a pair of these nodes to move together, hold down the SHIFT key as you drag one of the nodes. In either case, changes made to one corner affect all four corners in the same way. All sorts of rounded squares and rectangles can be created in this way.

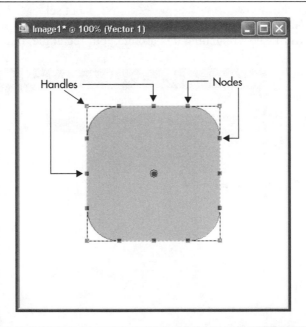

FIGURE 10-6   To resize your square or rectangle, drag any of the handles. To create various kinds of rounded rectangles, drag the nodes near the corners of the rectangle.

TIP	*Holding down a modifier key as you drag out with Rectangle or Ellipse constrains the shape in various ways:*

SHIFT	Hold down the SHIFT key as you drag if you want to make a square even when Rectangle is set to Rectangle or to make a circle even when Ellipse is set to Ellipse.
CTRL	To draw your shape with its center at the point at which you begin dragging, hold down the CTRL key as you drag.
SHIFT-CTRL	To constrain the shape's proportions *and* draw the shape with its center at the point at which you begin dragging, hold down both SHIFT and CTRL together as you drag.

Symmetric Shapes

The Symmetric Shape tool is the most complex of the new shape tools but also the most fun!

Open a new image with a vector background. Choose the Symmetric Shape tool. On the Tool Options palette, you have the option of setting the shape to either Polygon (for drawing regular polygons, such as pentagons, hexagons, and octagons) or Stellated (for drawing star-like or flower-like shapes). Let's try Stellated to explore star-like shapes.

On the Tool Options palette, deselect Show Nodes but select Create on Vector. Set Width to 0 and check Anti-alias. For now, keep Round Inner and Round Outer unchecked. Set Number of Sides to the number of points you want in your star, and set Radius to 30 or so. We'll create our star with a fill but no stroke, so on the Materials palette, set Stroke to Transparent and set Fill to any material you like. Drag in the image canvas to draw your star. The result will look something like this:

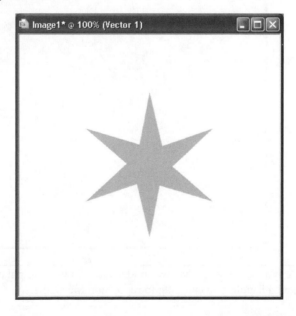

10

> **TIP** *To draw a symmetric shape with its center at the point at which you begin dragging, hold down the* CTRL *key as you drag.*

Next, with the Symmetric Shape tool still the active tool, change the Mode on the Tool Options palette to Edit. You'll see segment lines along the edges of the shape, and on the upper-right segment you'll see two nodes—one at the upper end and one at the other end of the segment, as shown in Figure 10-7.

Drag either of the two nodes and all the points of the star change shape symmetrically. Experiment to see what you get. Figure 10-8 shows you just some of the possible shapes that can be made starting with the example star.

For flower-like shapes, start out with Stellated but check Round Inner, Round Outer, or both. Figure 10-9 shows some of the possibilities.

> **TIP** *Depending on node type, some symmetric shape nodes have a set of control handles, which appear when you click the node. You can drag the control handles to change the shape or angle of the curve around the node. Any changes you make affect all the analogous areas of the shape symmetrically.*

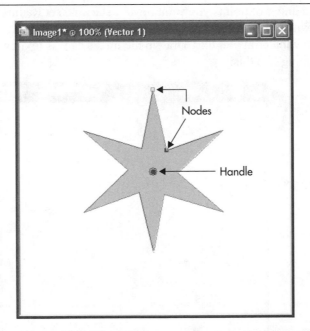

FIGURE 10-7   A symmetric shape has two nodes that can be manipulated to alter the shape and a handle you can drag to reposition the shape.

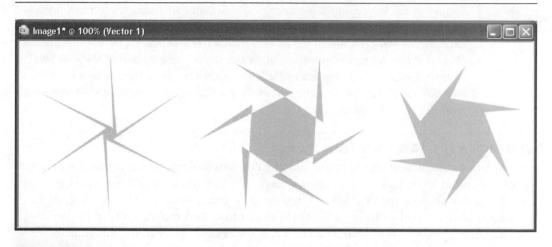

FIGURE 10-8 Some variations of Stellated shapes with Round Inner and Round Outer deselected

TIP *You can add additional nodes between the two shape-defining nodes of a symmetric shape. These additional nodes can then be manipulated to make further symmetric changes to your shape. To add a new node, hold down the CTRL key and click on the upper-right segment of the symmetric shape.*

10

FIGURE 10-9 Some variations of Stellated shapes with various settings for Round Inner and Round Outer: Round Inner only (left), Round Outer only (middle), and both Round Inner and Round Outer (right)

> **NOTE**   *Shapes made with Ellipse, Rectangle, and Symmetric Shape are special objects that are not made up of vector paths. To convert a shape to a path, select the shape by clicking its object button in the Layers palette. Then choose Objects | Convert to Path or right-click the object button on the Layers palette and in the resulting context menu choose Convert to Path. Once a shape is converted to a path, it will have standard nodes rather than the special nodes used to make symmetric modifications to the shape.*

Drawing with the Pen Tool

You draw straight and curved lines using the Pen tool in Draw mode. If you draw a series of connected lines, you create your own shapes. In Edit mode, which we'll look at in detail later in this chapter, the Pen tool can be used to edit your lines and shapes—even if the shapes were created with one of the shape tools or the Text tool rather than the Pen tool. The editing that you do with the Pen tool is at the node level, enabling you to make very fine changes to your lines and shapes.

With the Pen tool, the stroke is what you think of as the line itself and the fill is placed within the shape defined by the lines or curves that you draw. To draw a line, choose the Pen tool and on the Tool Options palette select one of the drawing modes: Draw Lines and Polylines, Draw Point to Point – Bezier Curves, or Draw Freehand.

Drawing Straight Lines

Let's begin with the simplest use of the Pen tool: drawing straight lines.

1. Choose the Pen tool from the Tools toolbar.

2. Specify the Stroke material for your line in the Materials palette. Be sure that Stroke is not set to Transparent, and in the Tool Options palette be sure that Width is set higher than 0. Set Fill to Transparent.

3. In the Pen tool's Tool Options palette, shown next, select Draw Lines and Polylines.

4. Click where you want your line to begin. This sets the start point of your line.

5. Click where you want your line to end. This sets the end point of your line.

6. If you want to add more lines, repeat steps 4 and 5. If Connect Segments in the Tool Options palette is selected, your lines will be connected, with the end point of the last line that you draw becoming the new end point for the series of connected lines. If Connect Segments is not selected, each of the lines will be separate and each will have its own start point and end point.

7. When you're done, click the Apply button near the left end of the Tool Options palette. It's as simple as that.

| TIP | *To draw straight lines that are perfectly vertical, horizontal, or at precise 45-degree angles, hold down the* SHIFT *key while you drag with the Pen tool to define your line with Draw Lines and Polylines.* |

| NOTE | *Discontinuous lines or shapes that make up a single vector object are called* contours. *A path is composed of one or more contours.* |

| TIP | *When you're creating a path with the Pen tool and Connect Segments is checked, you can end a contour by double-clicking instead of clicking. If you continue creating the path by then clicking anywhere in the image canvas, you'll begin a new contour, unconnected to the one just completed.* |

10

Drawing Precise Curves

With Draw Point to Point – Bezier Curves, you can click to define the start point, then click to define the next node in a series of line segments, and so on until you have all the line segments for a shape. If you want nodes that are connected not by a straight line segment but by a curve, click and drag. You'll see control handles radiating from any node you define in this way. You can change the size of the curve by dragging one end of a control handle either toward the relevant node or away from it. You can also change the shape of the curve by swiveling the handle around the node.

Examples of lines drawn with Draw Point to Point – Bezier Curves are shown in Figure 10-10.

To draw precise curves, choose the Pen tool and set it to Point to Point – Bezier Curves. Then click to make straight lines or click-drag to make curves.

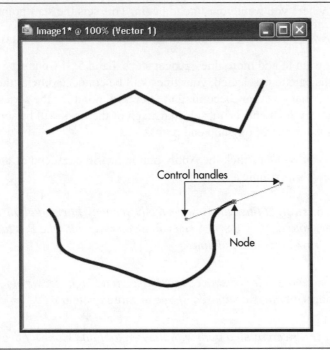

Image1* @ 100% (Vector 1)

Control handles

Node

FIGURE 10-10 The Pen tool's Draw Point to Point – Bezier Curves mode enables you to create straight lines by clicking (top) and curves by click-dragging (bottom).

Drawing Freehand

You can sketch a vector object freehand-style by choosing the Pen tool's Draw Freehand mode.

With Freehand mode selected, the Tracking option becomes available in the Tool Options palette. Tracking controls the number of nodes that are created as you sketch, which in turn determines how smooth your curve is and how precisely the curve conforms to your movement as you drag. A relatively small setting produces many nodes, which gives you precise tracking of your drag but also produces a rather bumpy curve. A relatively large setting produces fewer nodes, which gives less precise tracking of your drag but yields a smoother curve. Next is an example where two curves are shown (with their paths shown below them). The curve on the left has Tracking set to 1, and the curve on the right has Tracking set to 100:

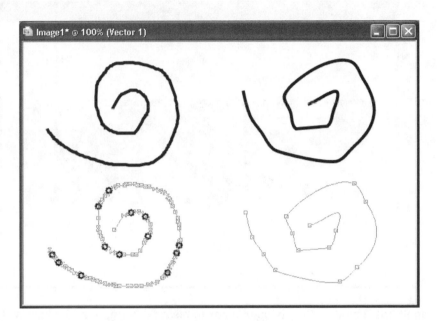

To draw freehand vector lines, choose the Pen tool; go to the Tool Options palette and select Create on Vector, Draw Freehand, and set Tracking to the value you want; then drag in your image to create your curve.

Getting Creative with Vector Text

Text can be added in vector mode. Choose the Text tool and set Create As on the Tool Options palette to Vector. Select any other options that you want for your text and click in your image where you want your text to be inserted. When the Text Entry box appears, enter your text there and then click Apply. Your vector text is added to the current vector layer (or to a new vector layer if the current layer is not a vector layer). There is a bounding box around the text:

You can use the handles of the bounding box to resize, deform, or rotate your text.

To edit vector text, choose the Text tool, then click inside one of the characters in the text string. The Text Entry box is redisplayed. You can then modify the text in the Text Entry box. You can also highlight some or all of the text in the Text Entry box and change the font or other characteristics in the Tool Options palette, or change the stroke or fill in the Materials palette.

Creating Vector Objects from Text

Vector text is a special sort of object. It isn't made up of a vector path. You can easily convert vector text to a path, however.

Vector text can be converted to either a single path or a group of individual paths (one for each character in the text string). In both cases, once the conversion is made the text can no longer be edited with the Text tool. Properties of the converted text can be changed like any other vector object, though, and the converted text can be edited with the Pen tool (as discussed later in this chapter).

To convert text to a single path, select the text by clicking its object button in the Layers palette and choose Objects | Convert Text to Curves | As Single Shape. The result is a single path showing up on the Layers palette as a single object. If you click the converted text's object button on the Layers palette and then choose the Pen tool set to Edit mode, what you see is shown at right.

To convert text so that each character becomes a separate object, select the text by clicking its object button and choose Objects | Convert Text to Curves | As Character Shapes. The result is a group of individual objects, each with its own object button on the Layers palette and with a group button dominating the group of character objects. To see the object buttons, click the + sign near the vector layer button to reveal the group button; if the group button isn't already showing, then click the + sign near the group button to reveal each of the object buttons within the group. The layer structure shown in the Layers palette will look something like the illustration at right. If you click one of the character objects and choose the Pen tool set to Edit mode, only that one character is ready for editing, as shown next.

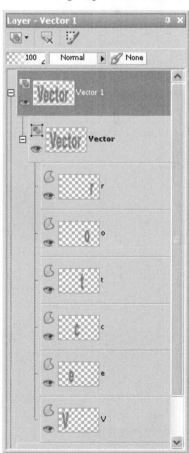

10

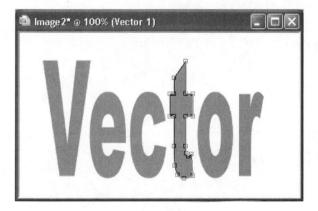

Text on a Path

It's very easy in Paint Shop Pro to make text conform to a path. Figure 10-11 shows an example of text on a path added to a photo. And Figure 10-12 shows how text on a path can be used in a graphics project.

Here's how to create text on a path:

1. Define a vector curve or shape with the Pen tool, one of the shape tools, or even the Text tool. (If you use a shape or text, you'll need to convert the shape or text to a path before going on to step 2.)

2. Choose the Text tool. Choose whatever you want for Create As: vector text, floating text, or a text selection can all conform to a path. Position the cursor over the path. When the cursor is in the proper position, a curve appears under the "A" label of the Text tool's cursor, like this:

When the cursor is in the right position, click and then enter your text in the Text Entry box. In the image, you'll see that the text is placed on the curve.

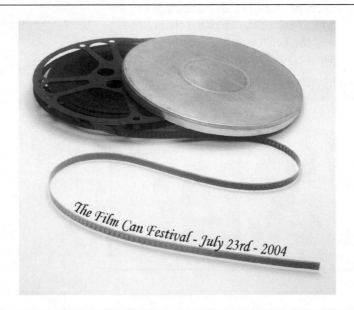

FIGURE 10-11   Text on a path can be used to enhance a photo.

FIGURE 10-12   Text on a path can be used in a graphics project.

3. Click Apply. The result looks something like this:

4. You probably don't want the path itself to be visible. To hide the path, click its Visibility toggle on the Layers palette. You'll then see only the text, which still conforms to the invisible path.

TIP   *If you want to add text over a vector object but you don't want the text to follow the object's path, hold down the* ALT *key when you click with the Text tool to set the insertion point for your text.*

TIP   *If you already have a string of vector text in your image, you can make that text conform to a path. Define your path, then on the Layers palette select both the vector text and the vector shape or curve that defines the path. (To select them, click the object button of one, then* SHIFT-*click the object button of the other.) Right-click the object button of the text or path and in the resulting context menu choose Fit to Path.*

Using the Pick Tool

Once you've created a vector object, you can modify its position, size, aspect ratio, and perspective with the Pick tool. You can also use the Pick tool to select an object so you can change its properties.

Selecting an Object with the Pick Tool

One way to select an object is to click the object's button on the Layers palette. There are also a couple of ways to select an object using the Pick tool:

■ With the Pick tool, click on the object within the image canvas. If you want to select multiple objects, click the first object, then SHIFT-click on each of the other objects that you want to select.

■ With the Pick tool, drag around any object or set of objects that you want to select.

No matter which method you use to select an object, a bounding box appears around the selected object, like the one at right.

Resizing and Repositioning with the Pick Tool

A selected object can be resized or repositioned. To resize an object while maintaining its original aspect ratio, drag with the Pick tool on any of the bounding box's corner handles. To adjust only the height, drag the top-middle handle or the bottom-middle handle. To adjust only the width, drag either of the side-middle handles.

To reposition a selected object with the Pick tool, hover the cursor anywhere within the object. When the cursor's shape changes to a pair of crossed double arrows, click and drag your object into position.

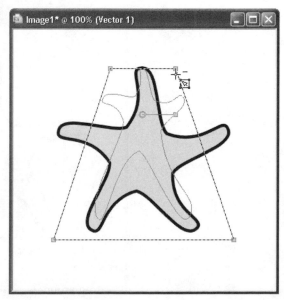

| NOTE | *You can rotate a selected object with the Pick tool by dragging on the handle at the end of the bar radiating from the center of the bounding box.* |

Deforming with the Pick Tool

There are several kinds of deformations you can apply to a selected object with the Pick tool.

Hold down the CTRL key while dragging on a corner handle to modify the perspective of a selected object:

Hold down the SHIFT key and drag on a corner handle to skew one side of a selected object:

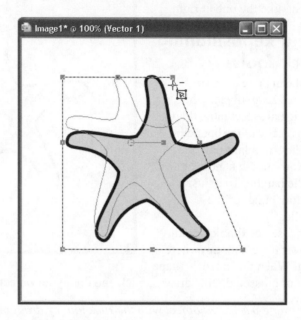

With the SHIFT key held down, drag on a middle handle on the top, bottom, or side to symmetrically skew a selected object:

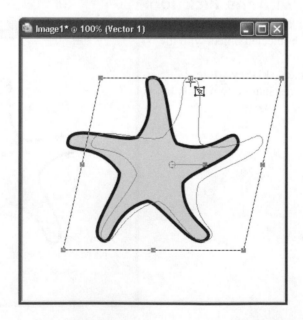

To freely deform a selected object, hold down both the CTRL and SHIFT keys while dragging on a corner handle:

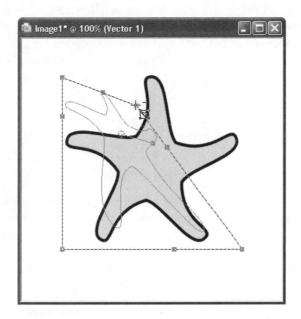

Changing an Object's Properties

You can change an object's properties using the Vector Property dialog:

In this dialog, you can change the vector object's name, add or remove a stroke or fill, change the material used for the stroke or fill, adjust the width and other properties of the stroke, turn anti-aliasing on or off, or toggle the object's visibility on or off.

You can access the Vector Property dialog for a selected object from the Objects menu (Objects | Properties) or by right-clicking the object's button on the Layers palette and selecting Properties on the resulting context menu. (Be sure to right-click the object button for the individual object, not the vector layer button. Choosing Properties displays the Vector Property dialog for an object but the Layer Properties dialog for a layer.)

You can also access the Vector Property dialog using the Pick tool. First, select the object whose properties you want to change. Then on the Pick tool's Tool Options palette, click the Properties button:

 If you have a set of objects all of which need to have the same properties, select all of the objects, access the Vector Property dialog, then set the properties. When you click OK, all of the selected objects will have the properties you selected.

Editing Vector Objects with the Pen Tool

For more fundamental changes than those you can achieve with the Pick tool, use the Pen tool in Edit mode. The Pen tool allows you to reposition individual nodes, add or delete nodes, and change the nodes' properties to create straight lines where you now have curves (and vice versa).

Choose the Pen tool and select Edit Mode. Select a node by clicking on it. If the node has control handles, they then appear, enabling you to modify the segments on either side of the node. You can also select multiple nodes with the Pen tool in Edit mode by SHIFT-clicking on each of the nodes or by dragging a box around a set of nodes. Once you've selected a node or set of nodes, you can move them or modify them.

Repositioning Nodes

To reposition a node, enter the Pen tool's Edit mode, click the node you want to move, and drag the node into place. You can also move a set of nodes as a group by selecting them all and then dragging the center handle of the bounding box that surrounds the set of nodes.

 You can move an entire path by clicking and dragging on a segment rather than on a node. When the cursor is over a segment, the cursor shape changes to a curvy line. When the cursor has this shape, you can click and drag to move the entire path, maintaining the relative positions of the nodes along the path.

Deleting and Adding Nodes

To delete a node, click the node and press the DELETE key. To delete a set of nodes all at once, select all the nodes that you want to delete, then press the DELETE key.

Another way to delete a node is to select it and then right-click anywhere in the image canvas and in the resulting context menu (shown in Figure 10-13) choose Edit | Delete.

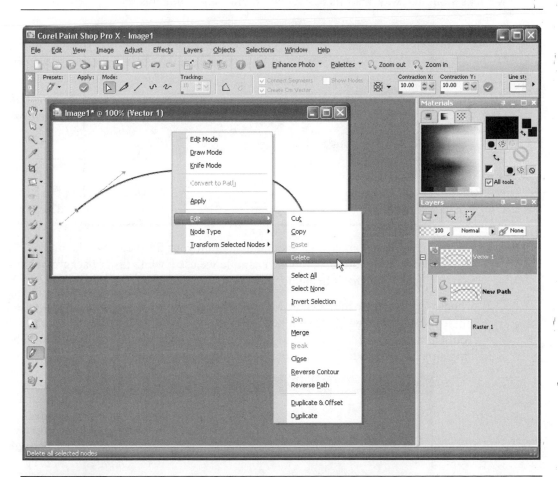

FIGURE 10-13   In the context menu available when the Pen tool is active, you can perform vector editing tasks such as deleting a node.

To add a node to a segment, position the cursor on the spot where you want your new node and then hold down the CTRL key. The cursor shape changes from a curvy line to "+ADD", as shown at right. While holding down the CTRL key, just click and a new node is added.

Project: Drawing a Key

Now let's put some of this newly acquired node-editing knowledge to use, picking up a few new tricks along the way. For this project, we'll draw a key like this one:

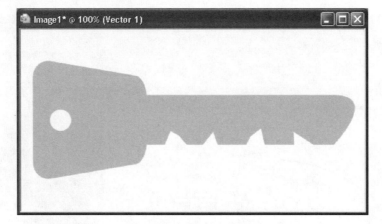

1. Open a new image that is large enough to contain your finished key. The image can have a vector background, but in the example we use a white raster background so you can better see what's being done with the vector objects.

2. Choose the Rectangle tool. On the Materials palette, set Stroke to Transparent and set Fill to the color you want for your key. (A brassy yellow is used in the example.) In the Tool Options palette, choose Rectangle as the shape, and select Create on Vector. Then drag a rectangle onto the left side of the image canvas to get something like this:

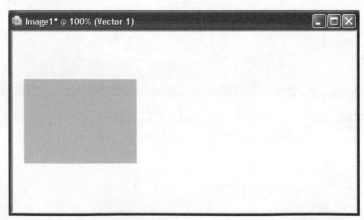

3. Switch to Edit mode on the Tool Options palette, then drag the corner handles to round the corners of the rectangle:

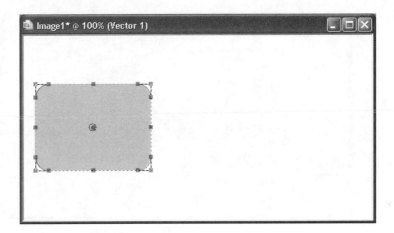

4. Convert the rectangle to a path: Right-click its object button on the Layers palette and choose Convert to Path in the context menu.

5. Choose the Pick tool. With the CTRL key held down, click and drag on one of the left corner nodes to deform your rectangle like this:

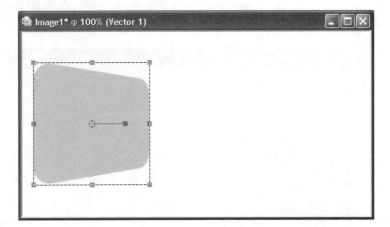

6. Go back to the Rectangle tool and draw another rectangle to get something like what's shown next. Don't worry for now if your two rectangles aren't lined up

10

perfectly. Convert the second rectangle to a path by right-clicking its object button on the Layers palette and choosing Convert to Path.

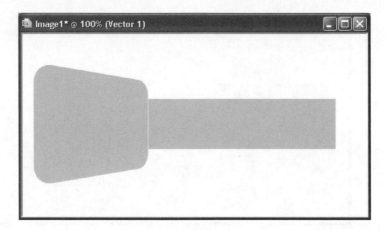

7. With the Pick tool, select one of the rectangles by clicking on it, then select the other one as well by SHIFT-clicking on it. A bounding box then surrounds both objects. Next, choose Objects | Align | Vertical Center. The two rectangles are then lined up vertically.

8. Choose the Pen tool and on the Tool Options palette select Edit mode. On the Layers palette, click the object button of the first rectangle (the one that's lower in the layer stack). You'll then see the nodes of that rectangle:

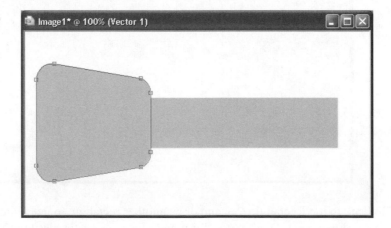

9. Click and drag around the two nodes on the right side of the rectangle, selecting these nodes. The bounding box around the nodes looks pretty much like a horizontal line, with the rotation bar and handle sticking out to the right, like this:

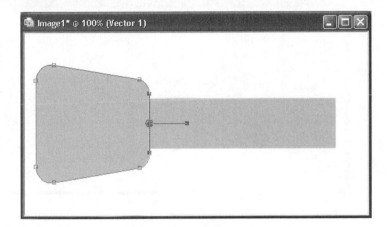

10. With those two nodes selected, right-click in the image canvas and on the resulting context menu choose Edit | Break. Now you'll see this:

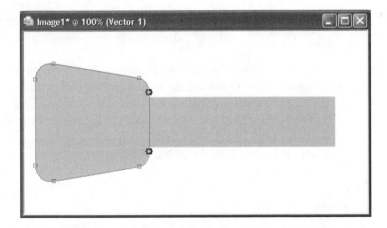

11. What Break does is split a node into two overlapping nodes. The dark, almost flower shape of the selected nodes indicates that each of these nodes overlaps another node.

Delete each of the new nodes by clicking the node and then pressing DELETE. Here's the result:

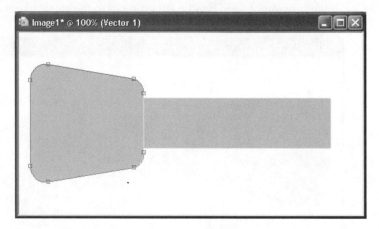

12. With the first rectangle still selected, select the second rectangle by SHIFT-clicking its object button in the Layers palette. If the Script toolbar isn't visible, choose View | Toolbars | Script. Then select the VectorMergeSelected script and click the Run button (the blue arrow) on the Script toolbar.

Notice on the Layers palette that the two rectangle objects are now merged together into a single object. The object is made up of a path with two contours (the rounded rectangle and the long narrow rectangle). With the Pen tool in Edit mode and the merged object selected, you'll see both contours in the image canvas:

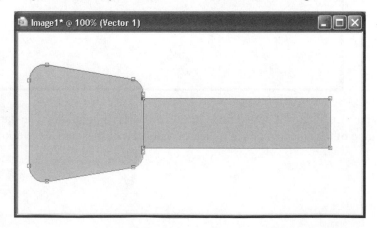

13. Select the two nodes on the left end of the long narrow rectangle. Right-click and choose Edit | Break, then click each of the "broken" nodes and delete, just as you did in steps 10 and 11. The result is this:

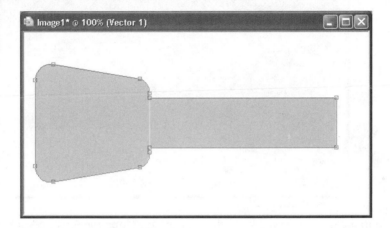

14. Now drag the top node on the right end of the rounded rectangle over the top node on the left end of the long narrow rectangle. When the cursor's shape changes so that the word "JOIN" appears, release the mouse button. Then drag the lower node on the right end of the rounded rectangle over the lower node on the left end of the long narrow rectangle. When the cursor changes to show the word "JOIN," release the mouse button.

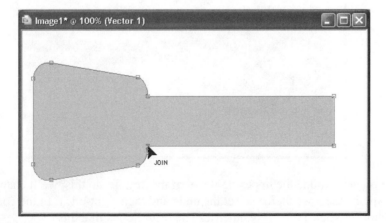

In each case, where there used to be two nodes, there is now a single node. The node you dragged and the node you dragged over are joined together as a single node. Your basic key shape is now one continuous path made up of a single contour:

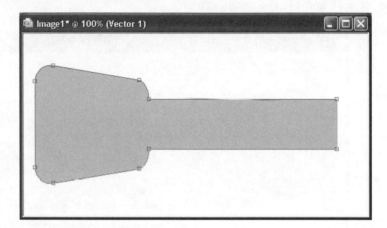

15. To make the cuts in the key, add a few nodes along the lower edge of the long narrow part of your key shape. Remember that to add a node, you hold down the CTRL key and click on the segment where you want a new node. Drag some of the new nodes to make the cuts, like this:

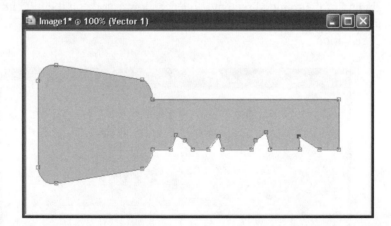

16. Now let's round the upper-right end of the key. To do this, we'll change the node type of the node there. Select the node and then right-click. In the context menu, choose Node Type | Asymmetric. The result looks like this:

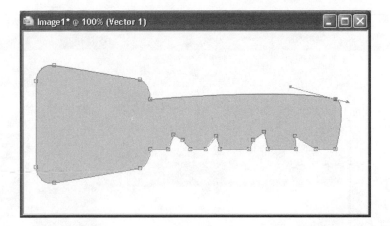

17. Refine the shape of the rounding by dragging the node's control handles. If the handle "falls off" the edge of the image canvas, click the Maximize button on the image's title bar. If you still can't see the entire control handle, zoom out with View | Zoom Out (or press the – key on the numeric keypad). Figure 10-14 shows the example image maximized and zoomed out 80%.

18. Now to cut out the hole in the key. Choose the Ellipse tool. In the Tool Options palette, set the shape to Circle, and be sure that Create on Vector is selected. Also, to be sure that you can see the circle you're drawing, select Show Nodes. With Show Nodes, you'll be able to see the nodes and segments of your circle even if the fill is the same color as the key. Drag over the key shape in approximately the position in which you want the hole.

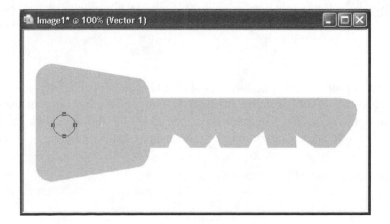

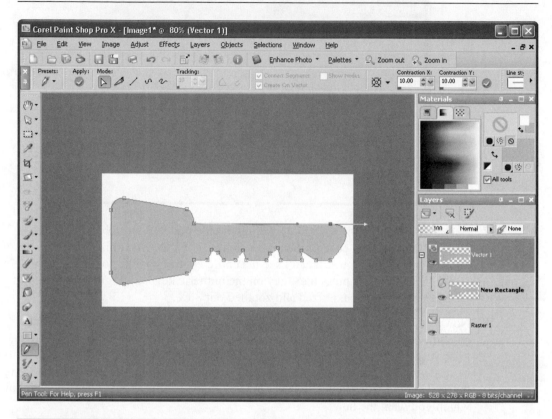

FIGURE 10-14   If a control handle "falls off" the edge of the image canvas, maximize the image and zoom out if you want to see the entire handle and be able to manipulate it.

19. Select both the circle and the key shape: On the Layers palette, click the object button of one of the shapes, then SHIFT-click the object button of the other. In the Script toolbar, select VectorMergeAndCutoutSelection and click the Run button. The circle is merged with the key shape and a cutout is made:

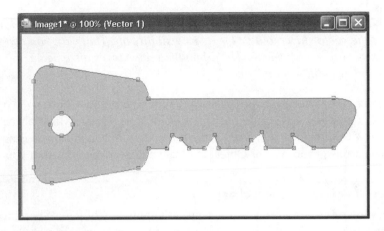

Your basic key shape is then complete. Save the key in PspImage format to preserve the layer and vector information.

NOTE *Sometimes, the VectorMergeAndCutoutSelection script inexplicably fails to produce a cutout. If this happens, choose the Pen tool in Edit mode, select exactly one of the nodes on the contour that defines the cutout area, then right-click and in the resulting context menu choose Edit | Reverse Contour.*

TIP *You can save your vector objects as preset shapes with File | Export | Shape. One important thing to keep in mind, though, is that you need to assign a unique name to any vector object or group of objects that you want to convert to a preset shape. For example, for the key shape you should change the name of the object from its default name of New Rectangle to a name of your own, such as My Simple Key. (See the Paint Shop Pro Help for more information on converting objects to preset shapes.)*

Using Vectors to Create Raster Selections

One very handy use of vector objects is to define a precise path around a figure on a raster layer. Choose the Pen tool and trace the outline of the figure using whatever mode of the Pen tool you like. Be sure that there is no stroke, only fill. Also be sure that Show Nodes is selected. Once you define the path, you can convert the path to a raster selection with Selections | From Vector Object. After creating the raster selection, you can hide the vector object using its Visibility toggle on the Layers palette or delete the vector object altogether.

> **TIP**   *When using the Pen tool to create a precise path around a figure, lower the Opacity of the vector layer to 0 or toggle its visibility off. That way, you can see the entire raster layer underneath. The fill on the vector layer disappears, but the nodes and segments still show up.*

You can also use vector shapes as the basis for a selection. Choose one of the shape tools, select Create as Vector, and uncheck Retain Style. On the Materials palette, be sure that there is a fill but no stroke. Then draw your shape. When the shape is as you want it, choose Selections | From Vector Object to create a raster selection from your shape.

Converting Vectors to Rasters

One limitation of vector objects is that you can't apply any of Paint Shop Pro's effects or adjustments to them. You can, however, convert a vector layer to raster. Once the conversion is made, you can apply any effect or adjustment you like. For example, here's the key made earlier in this chapter with Inner Bevel and Drop Shadow added after the vector layer was converted to raster.

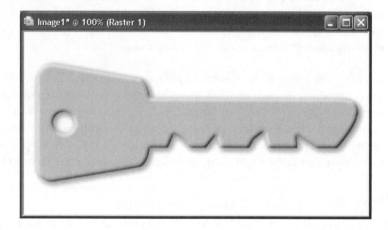

To convert a vector object to raster, select the object with the Pick tool or click the vector layer's button on the Layers palette. Next, choose Objects | Convert to Raster or right-click the vector layer's button on the Layers palette and on the resulting context menu choose Convert to Raster. All of the objects on the vector layer then become merged onto a new raster layer, which replaces the old vector layer.

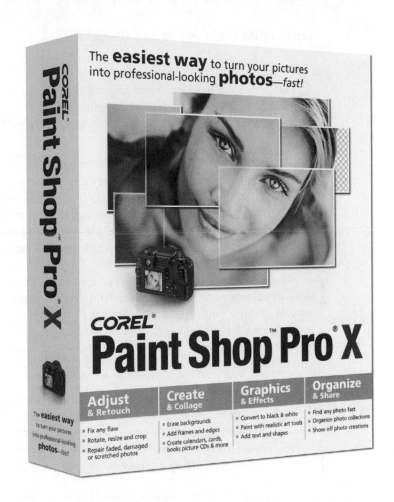

The **easiest way** to turn your pictures into professional-looking **photos**—*fast!*

COREL
Paint Shop™ Pro® X

Adjust & Retouch	Create & Collage	Graphics & Effects	Organize & Share
▪ Fix any flaw	▪ Erase backgrounds	▪ Convert to black & white	▪ Find any photo fast
▪ Rotate, resize and crop	▪ Add frames and edges	▪ Paint with realistic art tools	▪ Organize photo collections
▪ Repair faded, damaged or scratched photos	▪ Create calendars, cards, books picture CDs & more	▪ Add text and shapes	▪ Show off photo creations

CHAPTER 11
Digital Scrapbooking

Scrapbooking has become an international craze, and digital scrapping is probably at least as popular as paper scrapping. Whether you're a digital scrapper or a paper scrapper, you can use Paint Shop Pro in creating wonderful pages.

A typical scrapbook *layout* has four main elements: a background, one or more photos, text, and embellishments (that is, extras like ribbons, eyelets, and charms). Paper scrappers can use Paint Shop Pro to edit and print photos, make stickers or other printed embellishments to add to paper layouts, or print out poems, quotes, or *journaling* (text used to tell the story behind the photos). Digital scrappers can use Paint Shop Pro to do it all: edit photos; arrange the background, photos, and embellishments; add the text; and maybe even create their own backgrounds and embellishments.

Digital scrapbook pages can be printed and placed in a physical scrapbook album or used in calendars or greeting cards. You don't need to print your pages, though. Another way of sharing your digital memories is to create a digital scrapbook album that you burn to a CD or DVD using Corel Photo Album's Quick Show feature (available on Album's Share tab). Yet another alternative is to post your creations online, perhaps in a gallery at one of the many large scrapbooking Web sites.

TIP	*If you're new to scrapbooking, you can find general information about paper scrapping on the Scrapbook Basics page of the Scrapjazz Web site at http:// www.scrapjazz.com/topics/Scrapbook_Basics/. For the basics of digital scrapping, head over to the online resources listed at the end of this chapter. The Web sites listed there also provide gallery space for your scrapbook pages.*

Adding Photos to a Scrapbook Template

The easiest way to get started with digital scrapping is to add your photos to scrapbook templates. These ready-made layouts go by a lot of names, including plopper™, quick page, and scraplets. No matter what you call them, you'll find them very easy to use.

Here's an example created by Lauren Bavin, one of the designers at Digital Scrapbook Place (http://www.digitalscrapbookplace.com):

This template is a single-layered file with transparency. The background and all of the embellishments are already on the page. All you have to do is slip a photo behind the template layer and maybe add a little text.

NOTE *This template is available for free at the Osborne Web site. Head over to http://www.osborne.com/ and click on the link for this book. You'll then see a link to the download page, where you can download a zip file containing the template and its terms of use.*

1. Begin by opening your template file and your photo image.

11

2. Duplicate your photo image and the template, then close the originals. (Never work on your original images. You'll want to keep them safe and sound for future use.) To duplicate an image, choose Window | Duplicate or press SHIFT-D.

3. Do any photo editing work that's needed on the duplicated photo. You might also want to crop the photo or resize it. If the photo is not larger than the template image, hold off on resizing. You can resize the photo once you place it in the template.

4. Copy the photo by choosing Edit | Copy. Then go to the template and paste the photo into the template with Edit | Paste As New Layer. At this point, the layer structure of the layout looks like this:

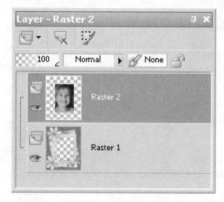

5. For a template like our example, where there's a cutout for the photo, drag the photo layer below the template layer in the layer stack on the Layers palette. The layer structure then looks like this:

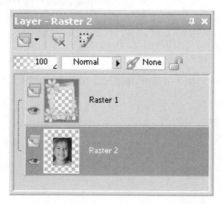

NOTE *In some templates, your photo is placed on top of an empty solid mat rather than being placed below the template and displayed in a cutout. In cases where the template has no cutout, leave the photo layer above the template layer.*

6. Position the photo using the Pick tool. You can drag in the center of the Pick tool's bounding box to reposition the photo, drag on the handle radiating from the center of the bounding box to rotate the photo, or drag on a corner of the bounding box to resize the photo.

CAUTION *You can usually shrink your photo without harming image quality. Be aware, however, that image quality can be noticeably degraded when you increase the size of a photo.*

7. Optionally, you can add some text to the template with the Text tool. See Chapter 8 for information on adding text to an image. Figure 11-1 shows an example of a finished layout made with the sample template (also shown in the color insert).

FIGURE 11-1   A finished layout using a scrapbook template

Your layout is then ready to save. If you want a copy for printing, save to a format that doesn't use lossy compression, such as TIFF. If you want a copy for display on the Web or to e-mail to your family and friends, resize the image and export the resized image as a JPEG using File | Export | JPEG Optimizer.

> **TIP** *Most digital scrapping sites provide their users with Web galleries. A good rule of thumb for sizing layouts to be displayed in a gallery is to choose a size that is no larger than 600 pixels in its largest dimension. When optimizing the resized layout with JPEG Optimizer, adjust the compression so that the file size is no more than 150K. (Different sites may have different posting rules, so if you post to a scrapping site, be sure to follow any specified rules.)*

Making a Scrapbook Page from a Kit

Once you're comfortable using templates and you want to branch out into more creative digital scrapping, it's time to enter the world of page kits. A page kit has several individual components, including one or more background papers, some frames or mats, and embellishments such as eyelets, brads, ribbons, fibers, and maybe a set of decorative letters (commonly known as *alphabets*).

Lauren Bavin has contributed a kit that you can download from the Osborne site. Let's try that kit out on a sample layout. The kit contains a number of different color-coordinated papers, ribbons, and other embellishments.

Before you begin, look over the components that are available in the kit and make a preliminary mental selection of which ones you'll want to use in your layout. Try to select what will best complement the photo or photos that will be featured in your layout. You might even want to make a rough sketch or two. When you have an idea of what you want, dive in:

1. Choose one of the papers to serve as the basic background of your layout. Open that file, duplicate it, and close the original image file. You'll do all your work on the duplicate, leaving the original untouched so it'll be ready for use the next time you need it. For this example, we'll use bg_dotty_8x10.jpg:

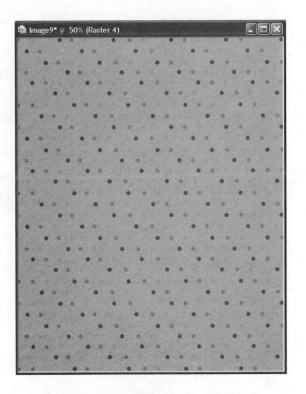

2. Decide how you want your photos displayed—maybe lying on a mat or framed in a picture frame or slidemount. In this example, let's use a piece of one of the other papers available in the kit to form a mat. Open bg_crazystripes.jpg and with the Selection tool set to Rectangle, select a piece of the paper that is large enough to form a border around the photo you want to place on the mat. Choose Edit | Copy, then close the original file. In the file containing the background, choose Edit | Paste As New Layer. Then use the Pick tool to position the mat approximately where you want it. Add a subtle drop shadow with Effects | 3D Effects | Drop Shadow, to make the mat seem to be lying above the background paper.

11

3. Open your photo, duplicate it, and close the original. Do any photo editing that you need to do on the duplicate. Crop or resize if you like, although you can hold off on resizing until after you've copied the photo into the layout.

4. Copy the photo with Edit | Copy, then close the photo. In the layout image, be sure the mat layer is the current layer and then choose Edit | Paste As New Layer. (If, when you're ready to paste, the mat layer's label isn't bold in the Layers palette, click the mat layer's label to make that layer the active layer.)

5. Use the Pick tool to position the photo over the mat. Add a subtle drop shadow to make the photo appear to be lying on top of the mat. Make sure that the direction of the shadow is the same as what you used for the mat. At this point, your layout will look something like this:

6. Add whatever embellishments you want. For each that you use, open the file in the kit, copy the embellishment image, then close the original and paste the copy as a new layer in your layout. You can move the embellishments around using the Pick tool or change their position in the layer stack by dragging the embellishment's labeled layer button in the Layers palette. When you have the embellishments where you want them, add subtle drop shadows, again being sure that the direction of the shadow is always the same throughout the entire layout.

7. If you like, you can add some text. If all of the areas of your layout are so busy that text wouldn't be readable, add a block of solid color or some simulated vellum and then place your text there. Add a subtle drop shadow to the block.

11

TIP   *Scrappers often make use of* vellum, *a semitransparent paper. Vellum lets a background, photo, or other component that it covers show through, revealing what's beneath but subduing what it covers. To make simulated vellum, add a new layer and then make a block of solid color on the layer with the Rectangle tool in raster mode. Reduce the opacity of the layer until you get the look you want.*

Your finished layout will look something like Figure 11-2 (also shown in the color insert). If you think you'll want to work on the layout again at a later time, save a copy with the layers intact in PspImage format. If you want a copy for the Web, resize the file and export to JPEG.

FIGURE 11-2   A finished layout made using a page kit

TIP
One kit can go a long way if you customize. For example, you can use the Warp brush to modify the shape of a ribbon, use one of the Geometric or Distortion effects to change the shape of an embellishment, or re-colorize a background paper or embellishment. To re-colorize, try Adjust | Hue and Saturation | Colorize or Adjust | Hue and Saturation | Hue/Saturation/Lightness.

Creating Your Own Scrapping Components

Both paper scrappers and digital scrappers can have fun creating their own components for enhancing their printed or digital pages. Simulated papers, mats, frames, eyelets, brads, and other embellishments are easy to create and use.

TIP
Paper scrappers can use photo paper, sticker paper, or printable vellum for printing out their creations for use in their paper layouts. Keep in mind that paper and ink are expensive, though. Printing can be economical for creating batches of embellishments, but for background paper it's usually less expensive to buy preprinted paper than to print your own.

Papers, Mats, and Frames

Creating papers and mats is as easy as easy can be, since they're just colored rectangles or squares. Background papers should be large enough to fill your entire layout. Common print dimensions for print layouts are 12" × 12", 8.5" × 11", 8" × 10", 8" × 8", and 6" × 6". The pixel dimensions that you need to print at those sizes depend on what resolution you want to use.

Some folks insist that 300ppi is necessary, but most people who have actually done rigorous testing agree that 200ppi or even 150ppi is perfectly fine. You should design your papers at whatever resolution suits you, but keep in mind that doubling an image's pixel dimensions quadruples the image's file size.

NOTE
The abbreviation ppi stands for "pixels per inch." Ppi in itself does not affect the file size or pixel dimensions of your image, it only tells your printer how big to print your image. For example, an image that's 300 pixels high and 600 pixels wide prints as 2" × 4" at 150ppi, 1.5" × 3" at 200ppi, and 1" × 2" at 300ppi.

The reason you might think that ppi has something to do with the pixel dimensions of your image is that if you create a new image and set Units to inches rather than pixels, PSP has to figure out how many pixels to use. It determines the pixel dimensions by multiplying the number of inches you specify by the resolution you specify (in pixels per inch): inches × pixels per inch = pixels.

11

Here's a summary of the pixel dimensions you'll need for various layout sizes at 150ppi, 200ppi, and 300ppi:

	12″ × 12″	8.5″ × 11″	8″ × 10″	8″ × 8″	6″ × 6″
150ppi	1800 × 1800	1275 × 1650	1200 × 1500	1200 × 1200	900 × 900
200ppi	2400 × 2400	1700 × 2200	1600 × 2000	1600 × 1600	1200 × 1200
300ppi	3600 × 3600	2550 × 3300	2400 × 3000	2400 × 2400	1800 × 1800

Phew! If all this does is give you a headache, don't despair. For the rest of this chapter we'll just tell you what pixel dimensions to use to make your components the right size for printing at 200ppi.

Okay, let's suppose you want a textured paper for a layout you want to print at 8" × 10". Open a new raster image that's 1600 pixels wide and 2000 pixels high. In the Image Characteristics portion of the New Image dialog, set Color to whatever color or pattern you want for your background, then click OK. The only thing left to do is add some texture to your newly created image. To do so, choose Effects | Texture Effects | Texture. Choose whatever settings give you a result you like. Here's an example in which the Sidewalk texture was used:

A mat is just a smaller version of a paper, maybe with a slight bevel added. For example, for a 4" × 6" mat, open a new raster image that's 800 pixels wide and 1200 pixels high. Set Color to the color or pattern you want for your mat. Add a texture, if you like, with Effects | Texture Effects | Texture. Then add a bevel with Effects | 3D Effects | Inner Bevel. Use either bevel 1 or bevel 2, and set Width and Depth to rather low values (just enough to make the mat appear to have a little depth). The result will look something like this:

Frames can be created as outlined in Chapter 9, in the section "Creating Your Own Picture Frames." If you want to make frames that you can share with non-PSP users, you can save your frames as PNG files instead of exporting them as Picture Frames. When you save a frame in the PNG format, it's important to enable transparency so the cutout in the frame isn't made opaque.

1. To save as a PNG with transparency, choose File | Export | PNG Optimizer.

2. On the Colors tab of the PNG Optimizer dialog, choose 16.7 Million Colors (24 Bit):

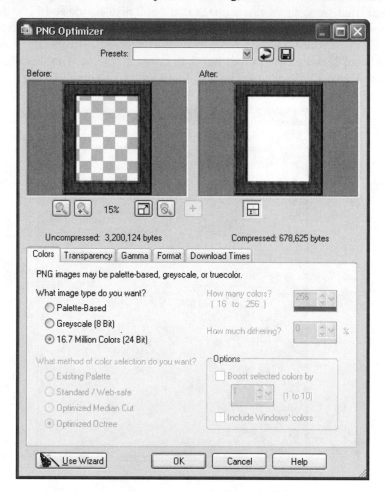

3. On the Transparency tab, choose Alpha Channel Transparency and Existing Image or Layer Transparency:

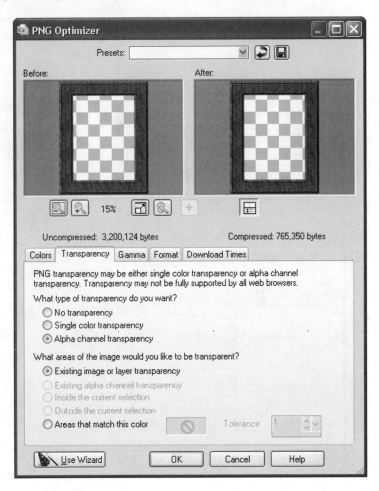

4. Leave the setting on the Gamma tab alone. On the Format tab, be sure that Non-Interlaced is selected:

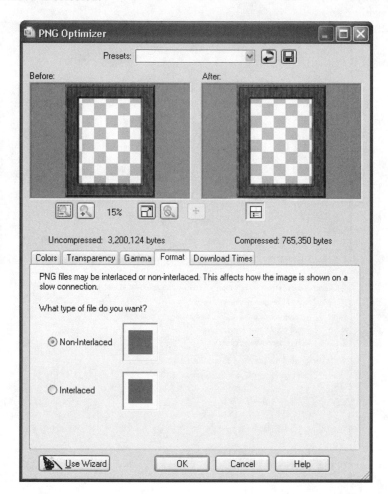

5. Click OK and in the Save Copy As dialog navigate to the folder in which you want to store your PNG file, give your file a name, and then click the Save button.

Eyelets and Brads

Paper scrappers use eyelets and brads to attach photos, mats and frames, and other components to their layouts. Simulated eyelets and brads can be used in digital layouts, too. Eyelets and brads are quite easy to make, especially if you let the Magnifying Lens and the Balls and Bubbles effects do most of the work for you.

To make an eyelet, use the Magnifying Lens:

1. Open a new raster image with a transparent background. For a quarter-inch eyelet at 200ppi, make the image 50 × 50 pixels. If you prefer, you can start with a 100 × 100 pixel image and then reduce the size later on. For this example, let's try starting with 100 × 100 pixels.

2. Choose Effects | Artistic Effects | Magnifying Lens. In the Magnifying Lens dialog, go to the Shape tab and choose Spherical as the Lens Type. Then in the left preview window drag the bounding box so that the edge of the lens's frame almost comes to the edge of the image canvas:

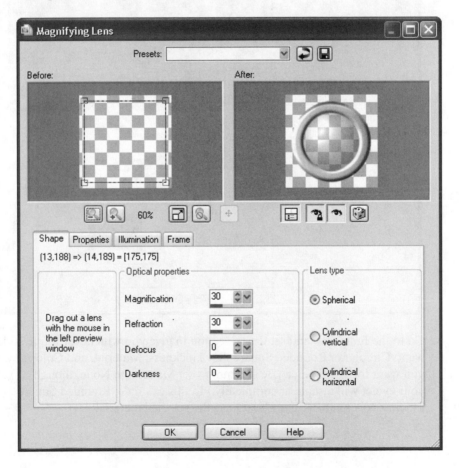

3. Go to the Properties tab and set Opacity, Shininess, and Gloss to 0. This eliminates the glass lens, leaving only the frame:

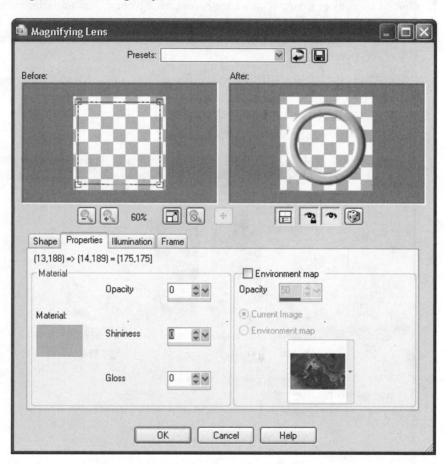

4. Go to the Frame tab and set Cross-section to give you whichever frame style you want, Circular or Rounded Square. Set Thickness, Material, and Color to whatever you want for your eyelet. (Be sure not to set Material to None, though. If you do, your eyelet will disappear completely.) In this example, Rounded Square is selected, Thickness is set to 30, and Ceramic is the selected material:

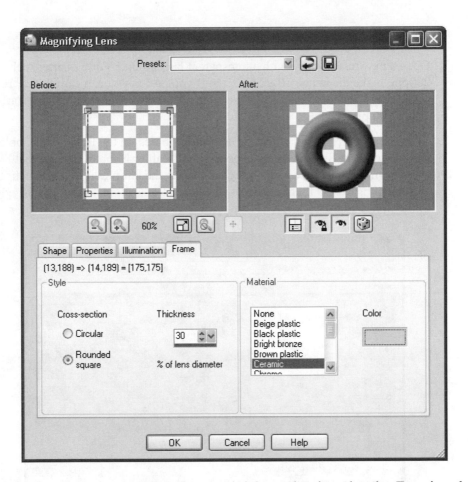

5. Click OK. Resize the image if you made it larger than it needs to be. To resize, choose Image | Resize. In the Resize dialog, set the Resample Using option to Smart Size and check Lock Aspect Ratio and Resize All Layers. Set either the Width or Height in the Pixel Dimensions portion of the dialog, then click OK.

6. Save your eyelet as a PNG with transparency or export it as a Picture Tube.

To make a brad, use Balls and Bubbles:

1. Open a new raster image with a transparent background. For a quarter-inch eyelet at 200ppi, make the image 50 × 50 pixels. If you prefer, you can start with a 100 × 100 pixel image and then reduce the size later on. For this example, let's try starting with 100 × 100 pixels.

2. Choose Effects | Artistic Effects | Balls and Bubbles. In the Balls and Bubbles dialog, go to the Shape tab and choose Single Ball or Bubble. Be sure that Maximum Possible Size is not selected, then in the left preview window drag the bounding box so that the edge of the lens's frame almost comes to the edge of the image canvas:

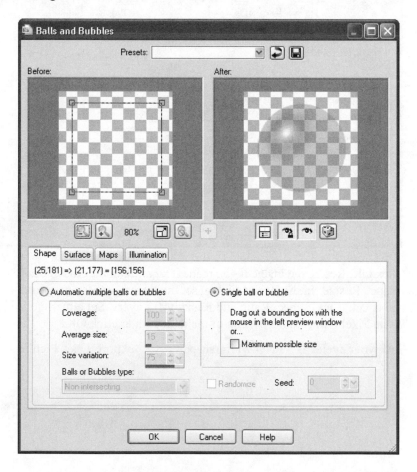

3. Go to the Surface tab and set Opacity to 100. On this tab and on the Maps and Illumination tabs, use whatever settings give you the surface that you want for your brad. Here's an example with the default settings for Maps and Illumination, and

with Material set to a solid color, Shininess set to 25, and Gloss set to 0 on the
Surface tab:

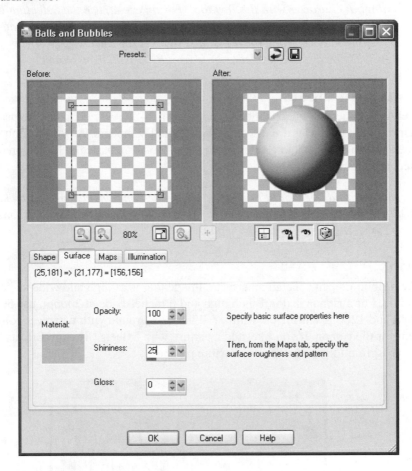

4. Click OK. Resize the image if you need to, then save your brad as a PNG with
transparency or export it as a picture tube.

| TIP | *If you have Paint Shop Pro 8, you can make good use of some of its Balls and Bubbles presets in PSP X. For example, try Brushed Metal, Christmas Ornament, Concrete Ball, Crumpled Foil, Distressed Metal, Doorknob, Galvanized, Gold Ball, Gold Filigree, Reflecting Copper, Rusty Ball, and Woven Ball. Experiment by starting with a preset and then tweaking the settings to see what you can create.* |

You can also make eyelets and brads by hand, using any shape as the basis for your eyelet or brad. Begin by creating a shape with one of the Shape tools or by entering a dingbat character with the Text tool. For an eyelet, use the Selection tool to define a hole, press the DELETE *key to create the hole, then turn off the selection with Selections | Select None (or press* SHIFT-D*). Apply Effects | 3D Effects | Inner Bevel. Then save your eyelet or brad as a PNG with transparency.*

Ribbons and Fibers

Textile embellishments—ribbons, fibers, and stitching—are very popular with paper scrappers and their digital equivalents are also a hit with digital scrappers. As you'll soon see, these components are not difficult to create. Simulated ribbons are basically just colored rectangles, and fibers are fancy brush strokes.

Ribbons and fibers aren't the only textile-like components you can make with Paint Shop Pro. Digital scrappers can create stitching using text on a path. See Chapter 10 for a discussion of text on a path.

Ribbons

To make a ribbon, open a rectangular raster image that is as high and wide as you want your image to be. For a ribbon that is 1 inch high and 6 inches wide at 200ppi, use 50 pixels for the height and 1200 pixels for the width. Fill the background with whatever color or pattern you want for the ribbon. If you like, add a texture with Effects | Texture Effects | Texture. Or create a grosgrain look with Effects | Texture | Blinds:

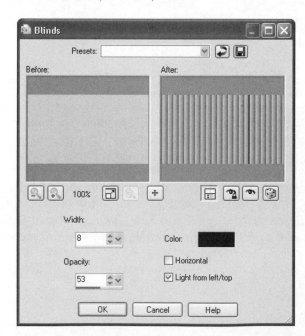

At this point, you can add a slight bevel and then save your ribbon in TIFF or JPEG format, or you can get a bit fancier like this:

1. Instead of adding a beveled edge to your ribbon, add a folded edge. Add a new raster layer above the ribbon layer, and then use the Rectangle tool in raster mode (clear the Create on Vector checkbox in the toolbar) to add the top edge of the ribbon:

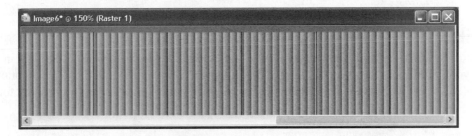

2. Copy the edge layer and apply Image | Flip to get the lower edge:

3. Now merge the two edge layers: With the topmost layer in the Layers palette active, choose Layers | Merge | Merge Down. Both the top and lower edges are now on a single layer. Add a slight Inner Bevel to the edges to get a result like this:

NOTE   *You don't need to select the edges before applying Inner Bevel. Anything surrounded by transparency on a layer is treated like a selection by Paint Shop Pro's effects.*

4. Save your ribbon as a TIFF or JPEG.

> **TIP** *You can create rickrack from a ribbon. Copy the completed ribbon to a new file that has a transparent background. Be sure that there's plenty of empty space in the image canvas above and below the ribbon. Then apply Effects | Distortion Effects | Wave. In the Wave dialog, set Amplitude in the Horizontal displacement section to 0, and set Amplitude and Wavelength in the Vertical displacement section to whatever low-valued settings give you the effect you want. For Edge Mode, choose Transparent.*

Fibers

Paint Shop Pro's Paint Brush tool is great for creating fibers. Create your fibers right in your layout. Add a new layer for the fiber, then choose the Paint Brush and in the Tool Options palette select a brush tip in the Brush Tip drop-list. Twirly Star is a nice tip to try out for fibers:

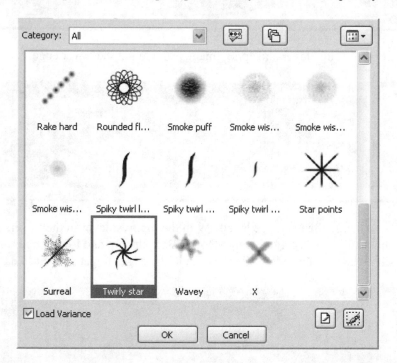

Paint your fiber on the new layer by dragging. If you like you can drag more than once, painting one line on top of another. Painting with a static brush in this way gives only so-so results, though. For more natural-looking fibers, you need to explore Paint Shop Pro's Brush Variance controls.

If it isn't displayed already, pop open the Brush Variance palette by choosing View | Palettes | Brush Variance (or press F11):

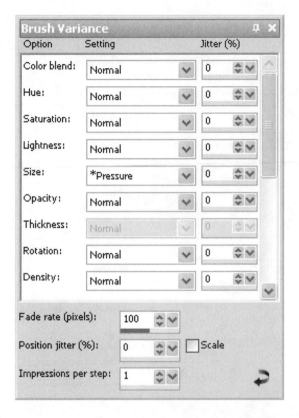

With Brush Variance, you can add variation to your brush strokes. These variations can either be random or based on particular circumstances. For example, the brush rotation can be made random by setting a Jitter value for Rotation, or the brush rotation can be made to follow the direction of the brush stroke by setting Rotation to Direction. Here are a couple possibilities using the Twirly Star brush tip:

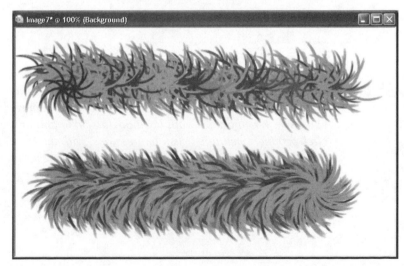

11

The top example uses the settings shown at right.

The bottom example uses the same settings except that Position Jitter (%) and Impressions per Step are also set (as shown next).

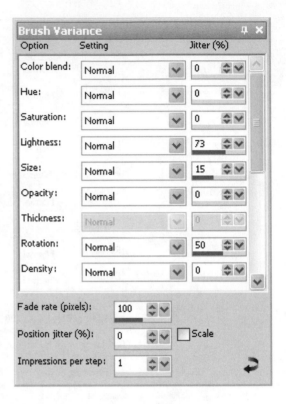

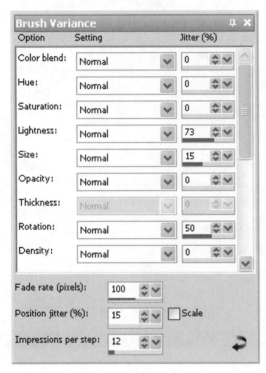

Position Jitter (%) introduces randomness in the placement of your brush impressions: Where you click won't be exactly where the brush impression appears. Impressions per Step determines how many brush impressions are created each time you click. When you set both Position Jitter (%) and Impressions per Step, each click produces multiple brush impressions, with the brush impressions scattered. The higher the value of Position Jitter (%), the farther the scattering.

Experiment with Brush Variance using different brush tips to see what kinds of fiber-like effects you can create.

> **NOTE** *In the Brush Variance palette, the options whose names begin with * are available only if you're using a graphics tablet and stylus. The other settings produce effects no matter what input device you're using.*

You're not limited to using the brush tips supplied with Paint Shop Pro. You can create your own brush tips, too. Open a new raster image that is no larger than 500 × 500 pixels with a white background. Paint with black and shades of gray to create the shape you want for your brush tip. Then choose File | Export | Custom Brush:

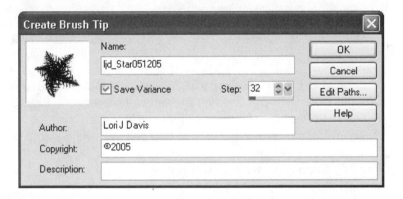

Enter a name for your brush and a default Step (where Step is the distance between brush impressions when you drag with the brush). If you want to save the current Brush Variance settings with your brush tip, check Save Variance. Click OK to export your image as a brush tip. Your new tip is then available in the Brush Tip drop-list in the Tool Options palette of any brush tool.

> **NOTE** *In your exported brush tip, areas that were black in your brush tip image will paint at full opacity, while areas that were gray will paint with semi-transparency. Any areas that were white in your brush tip image will be fully transparent when you paint with your brush tip.*

11

TIP *Brushes are good for more than just fibers. For example, you can export a string of text or a shape as a brush tip that you can use like a rubber stamp. You can also use a custom brush with Brush Variance to paint a fancy background paper.*

Plug-In Filters for Scrappers

You can create wonderful scrapping components using only Paint Shop Pro's native commands and tools. However, some component designers also make great use of plug-in filters. Alien Skin's filter sets are especially popular, particularly their Eye Candy 5: Textures, Eye Candy 5: Impact, Xenofex, and Splat! Another very popular plug-in among scrappers, and one that's pretty inexpensive, is Flaming Pear's Super Blade Pro. If you don't mind moving to the other end of the cost scale, Auto FX has some nice filter sets that are appropriate for scrapping, including Photo/ Graphic Edges and the various DreamSuite Series sets.

NOTE *In addition to their commercial plug-ins, Flaming Pear and Auto FX offer a few free filters you can download.*

Some of the smaller plug-in developers also have filters that are useful for scrappers, and their prices are quite reasonable. A few that are well worth a look are Page Curl and Puzzle Pro from AV Bros and Plaid Lite from namesuppressed Design.

There are some free plug-ins you may want to check out, too. Some of our favorites are from MuRa, including Perspective Tiling and Clouds. And be sure to look into Vizros Plugins, a formerly commercial package that is now free.

Alien Skin	http://www.alienskin.com/
Flaming Pear	http://www.flamingpear.com/
AutoFX	http://www.autofx.com/
AV Bros	http://www.avbros.com/
namesuppressed Design	http://www.namesuppressed.com/design/
MuRa's Filters	http://www.geocities.com/murakuma/mmplugins.html
Vizros Plugins	http://www.vizros.com/vp.html

TIP *For more information about plug-in filters, visit The Plugin Site's resource page at http://www.thepluginsite.com/resources/.*

Third-Party Sources of Components

There are many, many places where you can buy digital scrapping components or download some freebies. The large digital scrapbook sites are a good place to start. Here are just a few:

Digital Scrapbook Place	http://www.digitalscrapbookplace.com/
Pages of the Heart	http://www.pagesoftheheart.net/
Scrapbook-Bytes	http://www.scrapbook-bytes.com/

There are also smaller commercial sites, and these usually have a few freebies as well as items for sale. One of our favorite commercial sites is Angela M. Cable's Neocognition (http://www.neocognition.com/). The components there are so realistic that paper scrappers who happen onto Angela's site have been known to mistake the displayed components for photos of physical objects.

Some online tutorial writers also make free scrapbook components available to scrappers who visit their sites. Lori has a few herself at http://loriweb.pair.com/scraps.html. Here are a few of the things you'll find there:

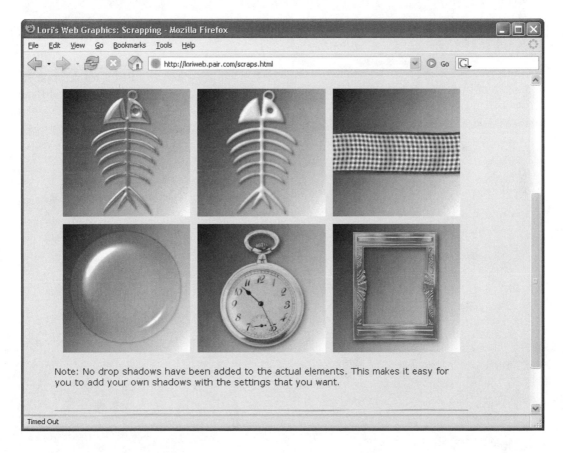

These components were all created with Paint Shop Pro (with a little help from Alien Skin's Eye Candy in the case of the chrome frame).

You can learn about other sources for scrapping components at Corel's Paint Shop Pro Scrapbooking forum at news://cnews.corel.com:119/corel.PaintShopPro_Scrapbooking. Sometimes, too, the folks there challenge each other to create components and then share the results with other members of the forum.

CHAPTER 12

Art Media

In addition to raster and vector tools, Paint Shop Pro offers special tools that simulate natural art media. These tools can be used only on a special type of layer, Art Media layers. With these special tools and layers, you can create digital works of art that resemble pencil drawings, oil paintings, and more.

Art Media Layers and Tools

To create a new image with an Art Media layer, choose File | New and in the New Image dialog select Art Media Background:

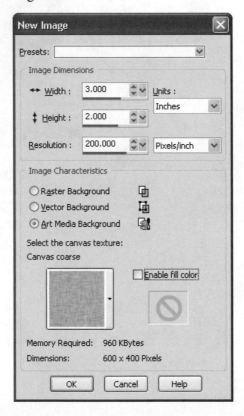

You can select from many background textures in the Canvas Textures drop-list. The different textures correspond to different natural media foundation materials, such as canvas and paper. You can also choose whether to enable a Fill Color. If Fill Color is enabled, the color chosen fills empty areas of the canvas and areas where the canvas texture shows through beneath applied pigment, as shown in Figure 12-1. If Fill Color is not enabled, empty areas of the canvas and areas where the canvas texture shows through are transparent, as shown in Figure 12-2.

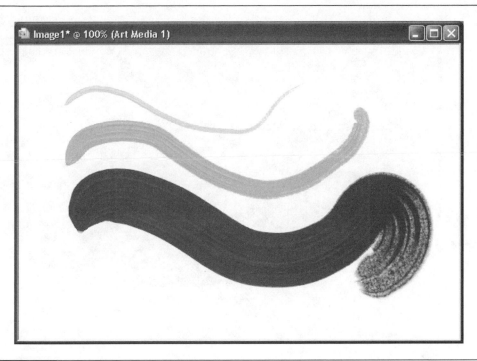

FIGURE 12-1   With Fill Color enabled, empty areas of the canvas are filled with the selected color.

NOTE   *Art Media layers can be added to existing images, no matter what other kinds of layers are present in the image. To add a new Art Media layer, choose Layers | New Art Media Layer or click the arrow for the New Layer drop-list on the upper left of the Layers palette and choose New Art Media Layer. And if you try to use an Art Media tool on a layer that is not an Art Media layer, a new Art Media layer is created automatically, with the Art Media tool then applying on the new layer.*

Once your new art media image is opened, you can start exploring the Art Media tools, located in the flyout at the bottom of the Tools toolbar. There are two basic sets of tools: dry media tools and wet media tools. The dry media tools are Chalk, Pastel, Crayon, and Colored Pencil. The wet media tools are Oil Brush, Palette Knife, and Marker. Figure 12-3 shows examples of strokes made with each of these tools.

12

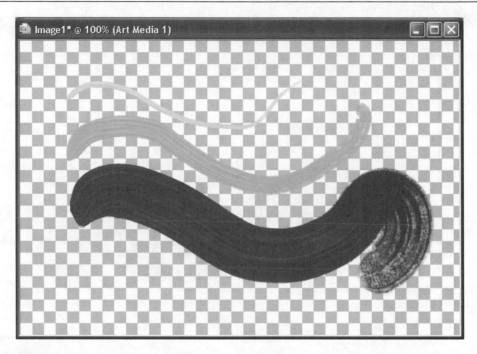

FIGURE 12-2 With Fill Color disabled, empty areas of the canvas are transparent.

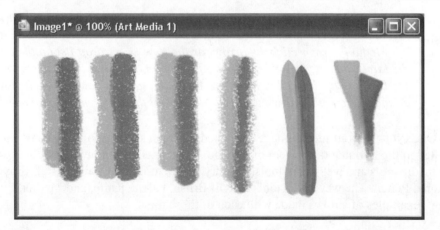

FIGURE 12-3 From left to right, pairs of strokes made with Chalk, Pastel, Crayon, Colored Pencil, Oil Brush, and Palette Knife.

In addition to the dry media and wet media tools are two additional tools: Smear and Art Eraser. Not surprisingly, Smear is used to smear applied pigment, either smudging or blending pigment already on the canvas. Art Eraser erases applied pigment. Art Eraser behaves a little differently from the raster Eraser tool, peeling off layers of pigment a little at a time.

NOTE	*The Art Media tools can be used with either a mouse or a graphics tablet and stylus. You'll have much better results using a tablet and stylus, though. The examples in this chapter are all made using a tablet and stylus, and any reference to effects that vary with pressure or tilt are relevant only if you're using a tablet and stylus.*

Drawing on Art Media Layers (Dry Media)

Chalk, Pastel, Crayon, and Colored Pencil are all dry media tools. They differ in how soft and dry the applied pigment is. For example, Pastel is softer than Chalk, and Crayon is wetter than either Pastel or Chalk. There isn't a tool specifically for charcoal, but you can get a close approximation using Pastel with the Foreground color in the Materials palette set to black or a shade of gray.

To use one of the dry media tools, click the tool's icon on the Tool palette, then select the color you want by setting the Foreground swatch on the Materials palette. You can also set various values on the Tool Options palette. Here are the tool options available for Chalk, Pastel, and Crayon:

Shape can be either round or square. (Unlike the raster Paint Brush tool, there are no fancy brush tips available with the Art Media tools.) Size is specified in pixels and can be any value from 1 to 200. Thickness is available if Head Tracking is set to Fixed Angle; setting Thickness to a value less than 100 gives you an elliptical brush when Shape is set to round or a rectangular brush when Shape is set to square. Rotation has a noticeable effect only when Thickness has a value other than 100, adjusting the angle of an elliptical or rectangular brush.

Head Tracking determines how the tool behaves when a brush stroke changes direction: with Track Path, the thickness of the stroke remains constant no matter what the direction the stroke takes, but with Fixed Angle the thickness of the stroke varies according to the tool's shape and the direction of the stroke. For example, here's the sort of effect you can

12

get with Chalk when Head Tracking is set to Fixed Angle, Thickness is set to 1, and Rotation is set to 40:

For now, ignore the checkbox labeled Trace. We'll be looking at Trace in detail later in this chapter.

In addition to these options, Colored Pencil has two others: Style and Softness. Style can be set to Tilt, Edge, or Tip, mimicking the behavior of a physical pencil. With Tilt, changing the angle of your stylus on a graphics tablet is like changing the tilt of a pencil as you draw. With Edge, the tool behaves as though you were drawing with the edge of a pencil, which is especially useful for shading. And with Tip, the tool behaves as though you were drawing with the very tip of the pencil.

Softness changes the softness or hardness of the pencil. With Softness set to a high value, you don't need much pressure to apply a lot of pigment. With Softness set to a low value, the pigment is applied only lightly unless you press down hard as you draw.

The Smear tool is used extensively with the dry media tools, especially to blend strokes together. Suppose, for example, that you started your drawing with something like this line drawing using Chalk:

After using Smear to blend together the shadows and soften the edges of the other strokes, you would get something like this:

12

Painting on Art Media Layers (Wet Media)

The wet media tools are Marker, Oil Brush, and Palette Knife. Marker resembles a marker pen. Oil Brush and Palette Knife are primarily used to simulate oil painting, Oil Brush and Palette Knife apply very wet pigment, but Marker's pigment is only semi-wet.

Marker is pretty straightforward, having the same Tool Options settings as Chalk, Pastel, and Crayon. Pigment "builds up" when new pigment is applied over pigment that has already been applied, as shown in this silly cartoon:

The most complex Art Media tool is Oil Brush. In addition to the Tool Options settings common to nearly all the Art Media tools, Oil Brush has a few added attractions. Here's Oil Brush's Tool Options palette, resized so you can easily see all the options:

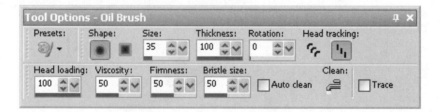

The Art Media tools we've looked at so far never run out of pigment. A single stroke made with tools like Chalk and Marker can go on and on and on. That's not the case with Oil Brush, though. Sooner or later, when you make a stroke you're going to run out of paint. Head Loading determines how much paint is loaded on the brush. Set Head Loading to a high value and your stroke can be mighty long. Set Head Loading to a lower value and you'll run out of paint sooner. You can even set Head Loading to 0, which means that there's no paint at all on the brush. In that case, you can use the brush to blend pigment that's already on the canvas without adding additional paint.

Viscosity determines how thick your paint is. As shown in Figure 12-4, high values give you a somewhat impasto effect, while low values give a thinned-out effect.

| NOTE | *All else being equal, your brush runs out of paint sooner the higher the setting for Viscosity.* |

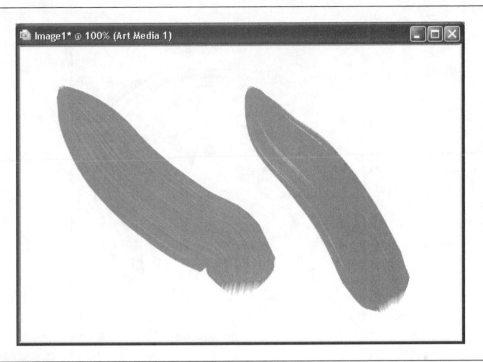

Image1* @ 100% (Art Media 1)

FIGURE 12-4 High viscosity (left) produces an impasto effect, while low viscosity (right) produces a thinned effect.

Firmness determines how well the brush keeps its shape as pressure is applied with your stylus. A firm brush retains its shape, while a less firm brush splays under pressure. Bristle Size affects the texture of the applied paint, a finer brush producing less texture than a coarser brush.

TIP   *Paint Shop Pro has no ink brush tool, but you can come close using Oil Brush. Set Head Loading to a high value and set Viscosity, Firmness, and Bristle Size to low values. The result will be something like what's shown in Figure 12-5.*

Clean and Auto Clean affect whether old paint remains on your brush when you load it with new paint. To clean the brush, removing all the old paint, click the Clean button. To automatically clean the brush between strokes, mark the Auto Clean checkbox.

The last of the wet media tools is Palette Knife. This tool is supposed to simulate a painting knife, but it's not clear that it succeeds at that. In physical oil paintings, a painting knife is often used to apply heavy dabs of paint or to create textures in previously applied paint, but you can't get either effect with Palette Knife. What you can use Palette Knife for is to apply wedge-shaped strokes of paint or, with Head Loading set to 0, to blend together paint that is already on the canvas.

12

FIGURE 12-5 An ink brush effect can be approximated using Oil Brush.

Turning Photos into Art with Trace

Even if your artistic skills are limited, you can create natural-looking drawings and paintings.

The dry media and wet media tools all have as one of their tool options a setting called Trace. With Trace selected, the tool doesn't use color from the Materials palette or Mixer palette (discussed later), but instead picks up color from layers in the layer stack that lie below the active Art Media layer. This allows you to place an Art Media layer above a photo and pick up color from the photo to use on the Art Media layer. For example, this is the layer structure of the image shown in Figure 12-6.

FIGURE 12-6 A simple painting created with Trace

NOTE *When using Trace, keep in mind that the color that the brush picks up when a stroke begins is the color that is used throughout the stroke. The color doesn't change during the stroke, even when the color changes in the image on the traced layer.*

Let's walk through an example that's a variation on the painting shown in Figure 12-6.

1. Open the photo that you want to use as the basis for your traced painting. Even an out-of-focus photo will do. Duplicate the image and close the original. In this example we used LaughingGull.jpg, which you can download from the Osborne Web site.

12

2. Before adding the Art Media layer on which to make the traced painting, let's make a "sketch" (as we did in the simulated line drawing in Chapter 9). The sketch will serve as a guide while you do the tracing. Duplicate the photo layer by right-clicking the photo layer's labeled button on the Layers palette and choosing Duplicate on the resulting context menu. On the duplicated layer, apply Effects | Edge Effects | Find All. Then apply Adjust | Brightness and Contrast | Levels to increase the contrast, eliminating any extraneous details:

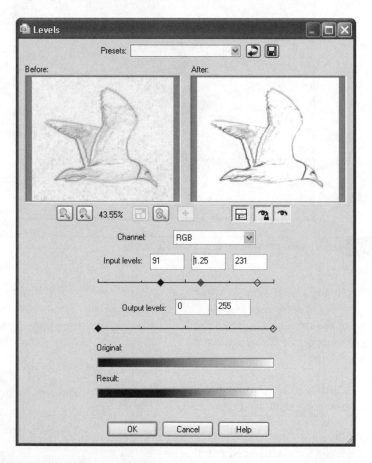

If there are still a few extra details, simply paint over them with white using the raster Paint Brush. Then set the Blend mode of the sketch layer to Darken, which makes only the dark lines of the sketch visible.

3. Make the photo layer the active layer. Add a new Art Media layer above the photo
layer with Layers | New Art Media Layer or click the arrow for the New Layer
drop-list on the Layers palette and choose New Art Media Layer. When the New
Art Media dialog appears, go to the Canvas Texture tab and mark Enable Fill and
choose a canvas texture. (In the example, Canvas Fine was used).

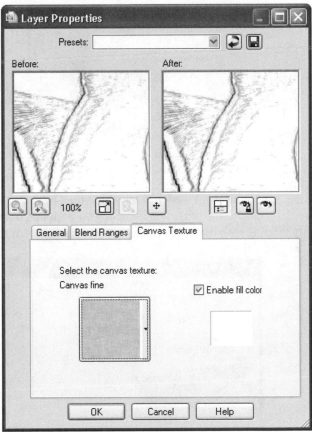

At this point, the layer structure of your image looks like this:

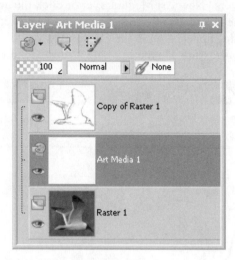

4. Be sure the Art Media is the active layer. Click the Oil Brush tool. On the Tool Options palette choose the brush settings that you want and mark the Trace checkbox. Then start painting with rather short strokes, using the lines of the sketch to guide you:

5. If you make any mistakes use Undo or the Art Eraser. Continue to paint with short strokes:

6. Continue painting until the entire figure is painted. Don't be concerned if there are small areas in the painted figure where the canvas shows through:

12

7. Choose the Smear tool and use it to blend together the strokes in your painting, being sure not to overdo the smearing (see at right).

If you like, when you're done using Smear, turn Trace off and add a few details by hand, selecting color on the Materials palette or Mixer palette.

8. At this point, you might want to delete the sketch layer to get the effect shown in Figure 12-6. Alternatively, you can keep a more subtle version of the sketch outline by lowering the opacity on the sketch layer (shown next).

To save a layered version of your painting, save it in PspImage format. For a print version, save as a TIFF. For a Web-ready version, export it as a JPEG.

Using the Mixer

Although you can work with the Art Media tools using only the Materials palette to select your colors, you'll open up far more possibilities using the Mixer palette. Think of the Mixer as an artist's palette. On the Mixer you can mix together paints to create blended colors. You can even load your brush with multiple colors to apply in a single stroke, like this:

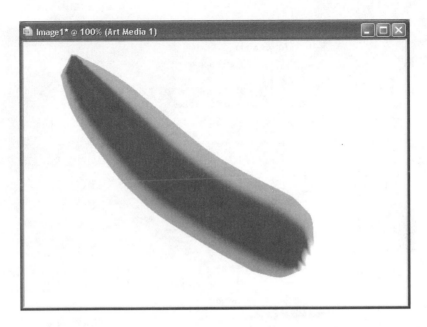

To view the Mixer, shown in Figure 12-7, choose View | Palettes | Mixer or press SHIFT-F6. The first time you open the Mixer, the Mixer area (the middle of the Mixer) will be blank. This is where you add the colors you want to add to your palette. To add a color, set the Foreground color on the Materials palette to the color you want, then click the Mixer Tube icon on the Mixer and drag in the Mixer area. Keep adding colors to the palette as you like. You can blend two colors together in the Mixer area using the Mixer Knife.

To select a color from the Mixer, click on an applied pigment in the Mixer area using the Mixer Dropper. The size of the current Art Media tool determines how much of the area is sampled by the Mixer Dropper. When you sample a color from the Mixer area, the color appears in the Foreground box on the Materials palette and is loaded on the current Art Media tool. If you want to load multiple colors to the tool, be sure that those colors are adjacent to each other in the Mixer area and that the Mixer Dropper is large enough to sample all of the desired colors at once.

NOTE   *The Mixer Dropper works only in the Mixer. If you want to sample colors from your image rather than from the Mixer area, temporarily switch from the current Art Media tool to the regular Dropper tool by holding down the CTRL key. While the CTRL key is down, the cursor changes to the Dropper cursor. Click on the part of the image that you want to sample, then release the CTRL key to switch back to the Art Media tool. The sampled color appears in the Foreground box on the Materials palette and is loaded on the Art Media tool.*

Use the icons on the bottom of the Mixer palette to load a new blank Mixer page (New Mixer Page), open a saved Mixer page (Load Mixer Page), navigate to an area of the current Mixer page that is not visible because the page is too big (Navigate), undo blending you

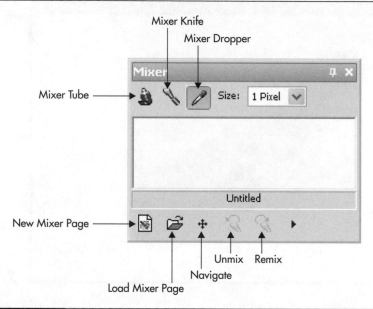

Mixer Knife

Mixer Dropper

Mixer Tube

New Mixer Page

Unmix   Remix

Navigate

Load Mixer Page

FIGURE 12-7 The Mixer palette is your digital artist's palette.

did with the Mixer Knife (Unmix), or redo an undone blending (Remix). Click the small right-facing arrow to the right of Remix to reveal a menu where you can open a new page, load a saved page, save the current page, unmix or remix, clean the page, or delete a saved page.

You now have everything you need to get started with the Art Media tools. Try your hand at your own digital paintings and drawings, creating your own works of art.

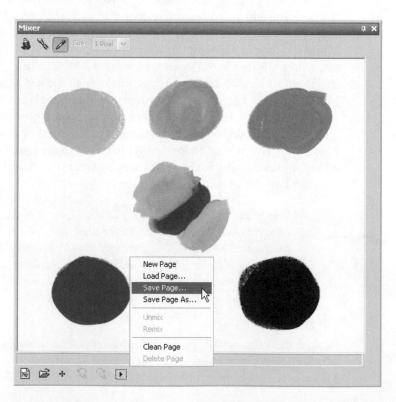

The **easiest way** to turn your pictures into professional-looking **photos**—fast!

COREL®
Paint Shop™ Pro® X

Adjust & Retouch	**Create** & Collage	**Graphics** & Effects	**Organize** & Share
■ Fix any flaw	■ Erase backgrounds	■ Convert to black & white	■ Find any photo fast
■ Rotate, resize and crop	■ Add frames and edges	■ Paint with realistic art tools	■ Organize photo collections
■ Repair faded, damaged or scratched photos	■ Create calendars, cards, books picture CDs & more	■ Add text and shapes	■ Show off photo creations

PART V

Customizing and Automation

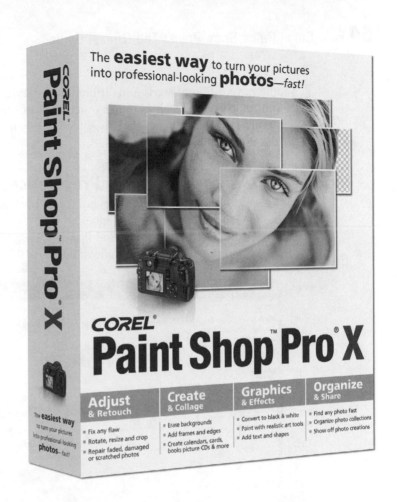

The **easiest way** to turn your pictures into professional-looking **photos**—fast!

COREL®
Paint Shop™ Pro® X

Adjust & Retouch	Create & Collage	Graphics & Effects	Organize & Share
■ Fix any flaw	■ Erase backgrounds	■ Convert to black & white	■ Find any photo fast
■ Rotate, resize and crop	■ Add frames and edges	■ Paint with realistic art tools	■ Organize photo collections
■ Repair faded, damaged or scratched photos	■ Create calendars, cards, books picture CDs & more	■ Add text and shapes	■ Show off photo creations

CHAPTER 13

Customizing the Paint Shop Pro Workspace

People have different needs and different work styles, and this is true when working in Paint Shop Pro as much as it is in other areas of life. Fortunately, Paint Shop Pro allows a wide range of customization options, enabling you to set up your workspace to suit your particular needs and style.

Modifying General Program Preferences

Some aspects of Paint Shop Pro's appearance and behavior are controlled by settings available in General Program Preferences.

Choose File | Preferences | General Program Preferences. You then see the General Program Preferences dialog. Here's the dialog with the choices for Units displayed:

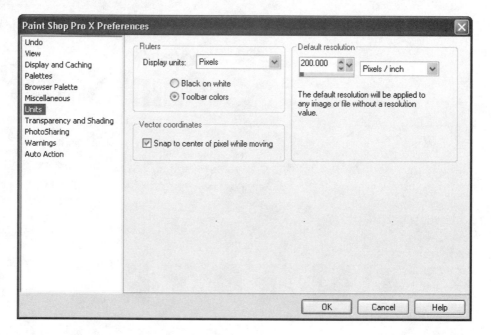

The major options in this case are the units to use when rulers are displayed (pixels, inches, or centimeters), the colors of the rulers (either black-and-white or the colors in which toolbars are displayed), and the default resolution to use for images that have no image resolution information of their own (in pixels per inch or pixels per centimeter).

There are plenty of other sorts of preferences you can set. First, select the type of program preferences you want to set by selecting from the list in the left pane of the dialog. We won't cover all of the preference options, but let's look at a couple that will probably be of interest to users of previous versions of Paint Shop Pro. First, let's try selecting Palettes and modifying some of the preference options that affect display of the Layers palette. Here's the General Preferences dialog with Palettes selected and the default settings displayed:

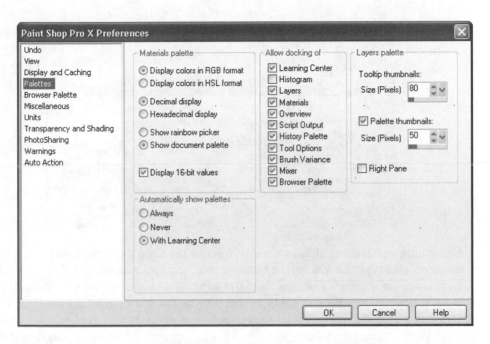

The Layers palette in PSPX is quite different from the Layers palette in previous versions. Some users who are familiar with the older Layers palette might prefer to have something closer to what they're used to, and as we'll soon see, these folks are in luck— they can choose Palette settings that will get them what they want.

In its default configuration, the Layers palette displays a thumbnail for the content of each layer and has a single pane, with controls for layer-related properties such as Opacity and Blend Mode displayed near the top of the Layers palette (see at right).

In previous versions, no thumbnails were displayed and the palette was divided into panes, layer-related controls being displayed in the right pane with a separate set of controls for each layer. To get a similar display of the Layers palette in PSPX, select Palettes in General Program Preferences and over on the right find the controls for the Layers palette. Uncheck

13

Palette Thumbnails and check Right Pane. The result will look like this, very much like the Layers palette in PSP9:

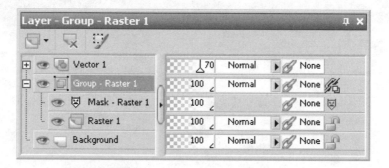

Something else that has changed in PSPX is that the Crop tool now loads with a crop rectangle of whatever size was set the last time the Crop tool was used. This is very handy if you're cropping a series of images all to the same size. However, some users find this behavior annoying, preferring to set Crop tool dimensions anew each time the Crop tool is used, just as they did in PSP9. To get the old behavior, choose File | Preferences | General Program Preferences, select Transparency and Shading, and then deselect the Automatically Display Crop Rectangle option:

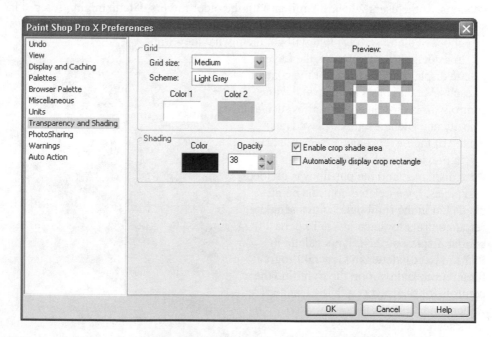

Once this change is made, the Crop tool will behave as it once did, waiting for the user to drag out a crop rectangle or enter dimension specifications in the Tool Options palette.

There are many other program preference settings you can modify: some for displaying or suppressing the display of warnings, some for applying actions automatically when you go from one tool to the next, and more. For information on these various preference options, see PSP's Help file (choose Help | Help Topics or press F1).

Changing File Locations

File Locations tells Paint Shop Pro where to look for its resource files, such as Picture Frames and Preset Shapes. For each type of resource, Paint Shop Pro looks in a subfolder of its program folder and in one or more other locations. For example, by default Paint Shop Pro looks for Picture Frames in Program Files\Corel\Corel Paint Shop Pro X\Picture Frames and in My Documents\My PSP Files\Picture Frames, but you can tell it to look in other folders in addition to these or instead of these.

To set file locations, choose File | Preferences | File Locations, which opens the File Locations dialog. For most types of resources, there are several options that you can set. For example, here's what the File Locations dialog looks like when Brushes is selected:

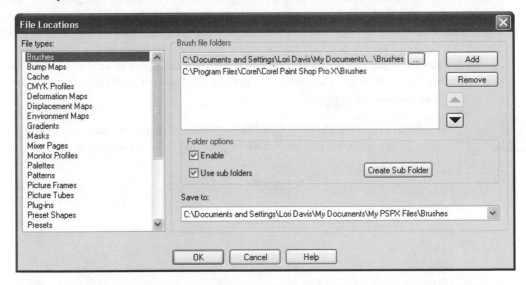

The options shown here are the sorts of options you'll find for most types of PSP resources. There's a listing of the file folders in which the resources are stored, along with buttons for adding folders to the list or deleting folders from the list. For each folder listed, you can choose to enable or disable the folder, and you can tell PSP whether to search the folder's subfolders. To enable a folder, click its path specification in the list of folders and then select the Enable checkbox. To disable a folder, click its specification in the list of folders and then deselect the Enable checkbox. To have PSP include the folder's subfolders in its search for resource files, click the folder's specification in the list of folders and then select the Use Sub Folders checkbox. Deselect that checkbox if you don't want PSP to search subfolders.

NOTE   *In most cases, the file location options will be similar to what we just saw for Brushes. For some types of resources, however, the only setting is the path specification for the resource. Resources of this sort are Cache, CMYK Profiles, Monitor Profiles, Python Source Editor, and Undo/Temporary Files.*

Rearranging the Workspace

One of the easiest but potentially most radical changes you can make to PSP is to modify the arrangement and behavior of the various palettes and toolbars. You can dock or undock individual palettes and toolbars, reposition or resize them, and show or hide them. And you can save one or more customized workspaces, loading whichever one you need for a particular task.

Showing and Hiding Palettes and Toolbars

If you don't want to display a particular palette or toolbar, you can hide it by going to the palette or toolbar's titlebar and clicking the Close button (which looks like a little "x" at the far right of the titlebar). You can also toggle the display of a toolbar off by selecting View | Toolbars and deselecting the particular toolbar that you want to hide. To toggle off a palette, choose View | Palettes and deselect the particular palette that you want to hide.

To display a toolbar that is hidden, choose View | Toolbars and select the toolbar that you want displayed. To display a palette that is hidden, choose View | Palettes and select the palette that you want displayed.

TIP   *The palettes all have shortcut keys that act as toggles, so you can easily hide them or display a particular palette simply by pressing the appropriate key:*

Brush Variance	F11
Histogram	F7
History	F3
Layers	F8
Learning Center	F10
Materials	F6
Mixer	SHIFT+F6
Overview	F9
Browser	CTRL+B
Script Output	SHIFT+F3
Tool Options	F4

Docking and Undocking Palettes and Toolbars

By default, Paint Shop Pro's palettes and toolbars are "docked" along the edges of the application window. If you prefer, you can undock any or all of the palettes and toolbars instead. For example, Figure 13-1 shows Lori's default workspace, with the Standard toolbar, Tool Options palette, Tools palette, Materials palette, and Layers palette all docked. Figure 13-2 shows the same workspace but with the Layers palette undocked.

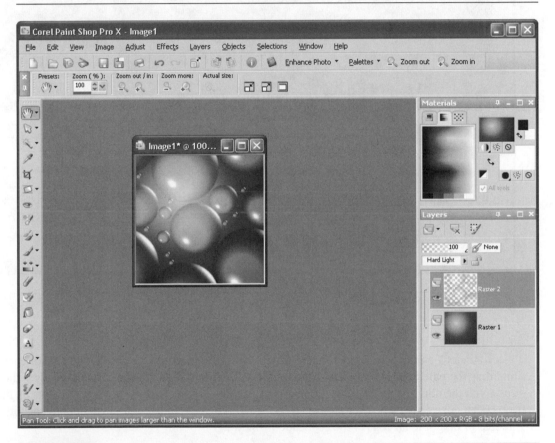

FIGURE 13-1 Workspace with the Standard toolbar, Tool Options palette, Tools palette, Materials palette, and Layers palette all docked

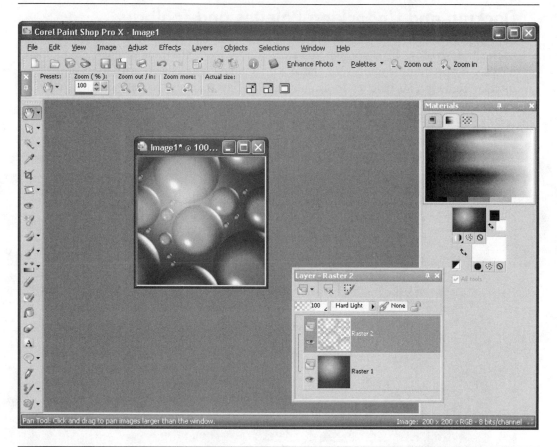

FIGURE 13-2 **FIGURE 13-2** Same workspace with the Layers palette undocked

To undock a docked palette or toolbar, double-click its titlebar or simply click on the titlebar and drag the palette or toolbar away from its docked position. If no titlebar is displayed, as is the case with the docked version of the Tools palette, double-click or drag on the series of dots on the top or left edge of the palette or toolbar. To dock an undocked palette or toolbar, double-click its titlebar or drag it to an edge of the application window.

TIP *If you want to drag a palette or toolbar near the edge of the application window without docking the palette or toolbar, hold down the* CTRL *key while you drag.*

Repositioning and Resizing Palettes and Toolbars

To reposition a palette or toolbar, click its titlebar and drag.
To resize a palette or toolbar, click and drag on the edge of the
palette or toolbar. Here's the Tools palette undocked and resized
so that the tool icons are arranged four across and five down.

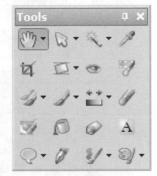

 *When the cursor is positioned in the right place for
resizing a palette or toolbar, the shape of the cursor
changes to a double-headed arrow.*

Using Rollups

You might find that palettes take up a lot of room in your workspace.
If you'd like your palettes to be automatically tucked away when you don't need them but readily
accessible when you do want them, try turning on rollups. For example, here's a workspace with
the Tool Options palette, Materials palette, and Layers palette docked and rolled up:

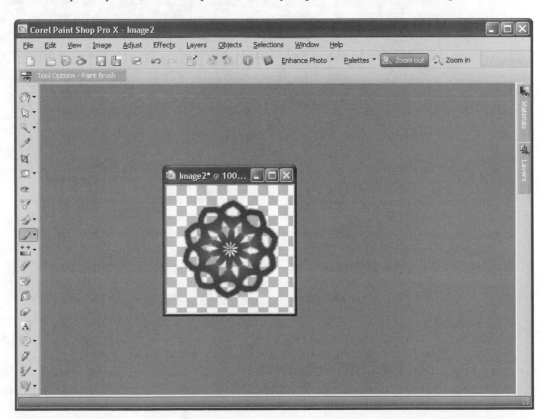

13

Undocked palettes can be set to roll up, too. Here's a workspace with the same palettes undocked and rolled up:

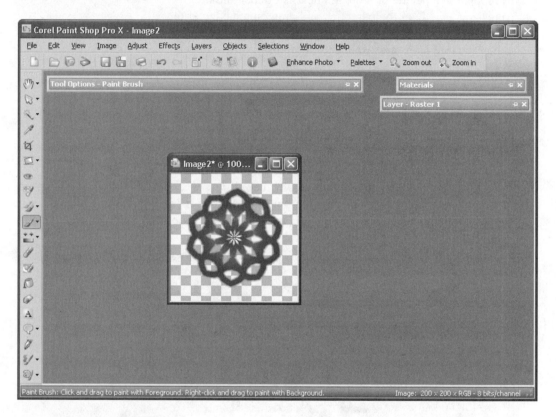

When rollup is enabled for a palette, the palette "rolls up" so that only its titlebar shows when you move the mouse cursor away from the palette. Move the cursor over the palette, and it "rolls down," revealing the entire palette until you move the cursor away again.

To enable the rollup feature, go to the right of the palette's titlebar and click the leftmost icon, which looks sort of like a small downward-pointing thumbtack. The icon then changes to look like a left-pointing thumbtack and the palette rolls up when you move the cursor away from it. To disable the rollup feature, click that left-pointing thumbtack icon. The icon changes back to a downward-pointing thumbtack and your palette stays open even when you move the cursor away from it.

Saving and Loading Workspaces

When Paint Shop Pro opens, it opens with whatever workspace you had in place when you last closed the program. This is usually convenient, but what if you had made an adjustment to accommodate an unusual situation and now would like to return to your normal workspace settings? What you can do is save a workspace that you can load whenever you need it.

Once you've set up a workspace the way you want it, save the workspace with File | Workspace | Save. This opens the Save Workspace dialog:

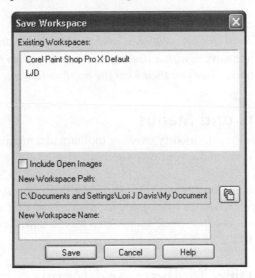

The dialog shows you a list of your existing workspaces and prompts you for a name for your new workspace. If you want the images that are currently open to be included in the saved workspace, select the Include Open Images checkbox; otherwise, deselect this checkbox. Then click Save. Your workspace can be reloaded whenever you need it.

TIP *If you want to overwrite an existing workspace, just highlight its name in the list of existing workspaces to automatically enter that workspace's name, then click Save.*

To load a saved workspace, choose File | Workspace | Load. By default, you'll be warned that if you load a new workspace, your current workspace setup will be lost. You're given the option of saving the current workspace before loading a new one. If you choose not to save the current workspace, you'll immediately see the Load Workspace dialog:

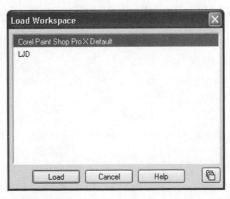

13

If you instead choose to save the current workspace, the Save Workspace dialog appears first and then the Load Workspace dialog is displayed after you save the current workspace.

 You might want a different workspace for different types of projects—maybe one for photos, one for Web page graphics, and one for vector drawing. Simply set up the first workspace, save it with a descriptive name, then do the same for each of your other workspaces. You can then load the appropriate one when you need it.

Modifying Toolbars and Menus

Paint Shop Pro enables you to modify existing toolbars and menus, deleting or adding commands. You can even create your own toolbars.

 Modified toolbars and menus are saved when you save a workspace. So, for example, if you have one workspace for photo work and another for Web graphics, these workspaces can include specialized toolbars and menus for each of these particular tasks.

Changing Existing Toolbars and Menus

You can change existing toolbars and menus in several ways, including adding or deleting commands and changing the text of menu options.

To delete a command, choose View | Customize, which opens the Customize dialog. Then go to the toolbar or menu and simply drag the label or icon for the command off the toolbar or menu. Alternatively, choose View | Customize, then go to the toolbar or menu, right-click the label or icon for the command, and select Delete from the context menu. When you're done, you can close the Customize dialog by clicking its Close button.

 You can also get to the Customize dialog by right-clicking in any empty area in the Paint Shop Pro window and choosing Customize from the resulting context menu.

To add a command to a toolbar, choose View | Customize and go to the Customize dialog's Commands tab:

Select the command type that you want in the Categories list, then click the command you want in the Commands list and drag it onto the toolbar.

You add a command to a menu in much the same way:

1. Choose View | Customize to open the Customize dialog.

2. Open the menu that you want to add the command to.

3. Go to the Commands tab of the Customize dialog and in the Categories list select the command type that you want. In the Commands list, click the command you want and drag it onto the menu, releasing the mouse button when the command is positioned where you want it in the menu.

13

You can delete tools from or add tools to the Tools palette. Delete a tool just as you would delete a command from a toolbar or menu. Add a tool by selecting Tools from the Categories selection list on the Commands tab of the Customize dialog, then drag the tool you want onto the Tools palette.

 The Layers palette has its own mini toolbar, which by default includes the Layers flyout and buttons for Delete Layer and Edit Selection. You can add other commands to this toolbar as well. A couple that you may find useful if you often use masks are Load/Save Mask and Invert Mask/Adjustment (available from the Layers category).

Creating Your Own Toolbars

In addition to the toolbars Paint Shop Pro provides, you can have your own custom toolbars. Here's how to create your own toolbar:

1. Choose View | Customize.

2. Go to the Toolbars tab and click the New button. When you're prompted for a toolbar name, enter a descriptive name and click OK. A tiny, empty floating toolbar is created, which looks like this:

3. Go to the Commands tab on the Customize dialog. Find the first command that you want to add to the new toolbar and drag the command onto it. Repeat for any other commands that you want to add. When you're done, close the Customize dialog by clicking Close.

4. Drag your new toolbar into position wherever you want it in your workspace.

Binding Commands to Keys

There are shortcut keys for many of Paint Shop Pro's commands, but you might use a command quite frequently that doesn't have a keyboard shortcut. In this case, you can bind the command to a key to use as your own custom shortcut.

To bind a command to a key, choose View | Customize and go to the Keyboard tab.

Choose the type of command you want in the Category drop-list, then choose the particular command in the Commands selection list. A description of the command is displayed in the Description textbox and any current shortcut keys for that command are displayed in the Current Keys textbox.

Press the key that you want to bind to the command. That key's name is then displayed in the Press New Shortcut Key textbox. If you want to bind the command to that key, click the Assign button.

NOTE   *If you want to eliminate an existing key binding for a command, click the key's name in Current Keys and click the Remove button. If you want to bind a key to a command but that key is already a shortcut for another command, you'll need to remove the key binding from that other command in order for your new binding to take effect.*

13

> **TIP** *To see a list of all of the currently defined Paint Shop Pro keyboard shortcuts, choose Help | Keyboard Map. In the Keyboard Map dialog select All Commands in the Category drop-list. (The listing in this dialog can come in handy for another reason, too: It gives brief descriptions of all of Paint Shop Pro's commands.)*

As this chapter shows, you have a lot of control over how Paint Shop Pro looks and how it behaves. If the defaults for any of the modifiable characteristics don't suit you, it's easy to change them. Take advantage of the flexibility of Paint Shop Pro's interface to set up one or more image editing environments that work best for you.

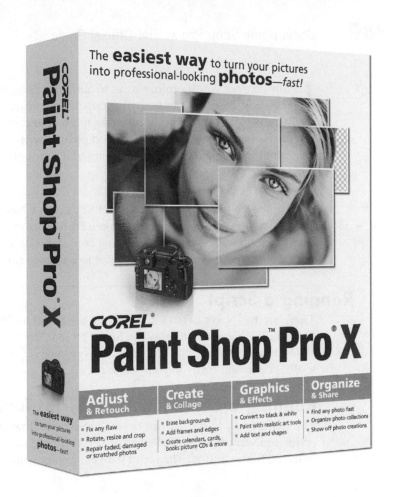

The **easiest way** to turn your pictures
into professional-looking **photos**—fast!

COREL®
Paint Shop™ Pro® X

Adjust & Retouch	**Create** & Collage	**Graphics** & Effects	**Organize** & Share
■ Fix any flaw	■ Erase backgrounds	■ Convert to black & white	■ Find any photo fast
■ Rotate, resize and crop	■ Add frames and edges	■ Paint with realistic art tools	■ Organize photo collections
■ Repair faded, damaged or scratched photos	■ Create calendars, cards, books picture CDs & more	■ Add text and shapes	■ Show off photo creations

CHAPTER 14
Scripting and Batch Processing

In this chapter you'll explore ways to automate tasks in PSP. One way to make your image-editing life easier is to use scripts. Scripts are mini-programs that run in your application. You don't have to be a programmer to create useful scripts. Although scripts can be as complex as anything an accomplished script writer can dream up, they can also be nothing more than a simple recording of a series of steps that you can then replay later on. Anyone can create useful scripts.

Another way to automate tasks in PSP is to use batch processing. In batch processing, you can perform various operations on a set of files all at once. The sorts of operation you can perform include renaming, placing copies in new locations, and converting to a different file format. You can even apply a script to a whole set of files all at once.

Running a Script

There are two ways to run a script: from the Script toolbar or from the File menu. By default, PSPX doesn't display the Script toolbar. To view it, choose View | Toolbars | Script. If you like running scripts and creating your own scripts, you'll want to have the Script toolbar open and ready in your workspace.

Running a Script from the Script Toolbar

The easiest way to run a script is via the Script toolbar, shown in Figure 14-1. Select the script you want from the Select Script drop-list. To run the selected script, click the Run Selected Script button. The script then chugs along until all the steps are completed.

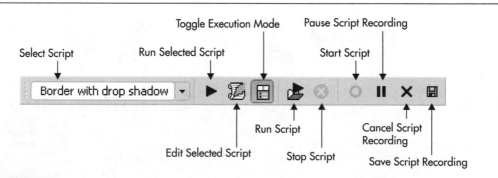

FIGURE 14-1   The Script toolbar

Running a Script from the File Menu

You can also run a script using File | Script | Run, which opens the Run Script dialog:

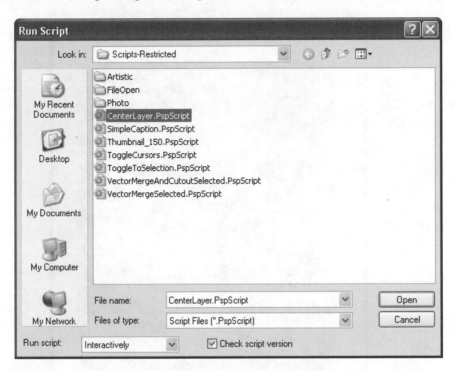

This method enables you to navigate to a particular folder that contains a script. Keep in mind, though, that you can run a script only if it's contained in a folder listed in File Locations under Scripts-Restricted or Scripts-Trusted. (See Chapter 13 for information on File Locations.)

Running a Script in Interactive Mode

Scripts can be run "silently," without any user input, or interactively. For scripts that include commands that allow user input, you can enable or disable user input by going to the Script toolbar and clicking the Execution Mode toggle.

Consider, for example, the Border with Drop Shadow script. With Execution Mode toggled off, the script runs merrily on its way, adding a 50-pixel white border to your image

14

and then adding a subtle black drop shadow falling from the lower right of the original image, like this:

Run the script with Execution Mode toggled on, though, and you can select your own border dimensions, border color, and drop shadow characteristics. The way this works is that each time the script executes a command that allows user input, the dialog box for that command appears on the screen. When you're presented with the dialog box, change any settings that you want to change and click OK. The script then continues executing. If the script comes to another command that allows user input, the dialog box for that command appears.

With Execution Mode toggled on, you open up a lot of possibilities. Instead of getting the standard result for a script, you can get all sorts of variations, such as this one for Border with Drop Shadow:

> **NOTE** *Script writers can set up scripts so that some commands always run silently and some always run interactively. In these cases, the Execution Mode toggle has no effect. Later in this chapter, in the section on modifying scripts, we'll see how to force a particular execution mode for a command.*

Sources of Third-Party Scripts

In addition to the scripts that come with PSP, there are all kinds of useful third-party scripts available online. In addition to scripts written specifically for PSPX, most scripts written for PSP8 and PSP9 should also run in PSPX.

One of the best places to start the search for scripts is http://www.psplinks.com/. To get you started, here are a few good third-party script sources:

Pixelnook	http://pixelnook.home.comcast.net/
Sheilsoft	http://www.sheilsoft.com/psp.htm
Suz's Place	http://users.adelphia.net/~suzshook/8scripts.htm
Digital Art Resources	http://www.digitalartresources.com/Scripting/psp8scripts.htm

14

Keep in mind that there are two kinds of scripts, Restricted and Trusted. Restricted scripts make use only of PSP features. Trusted scripts can make use of any of the features of Python, the programming language used for PSP scripts. To use a Restricted script, place the script in one of the folders specified in File Locations as a location of Restricted scripts (usually My Documents\My PSP Files\Scripts-Restricted). To use a Trusted script, place it in one of the folders specified in File Locations as a location of Trusted scripts (usually My Documents\My PSP Files\Scripts-Trusted). In either case, the script will then be available in the Select Script drop-list, ready to be run.

> **NOTE** *Be very careful with Trusted scripts. They're called "Trusted" for a reason. A Trusted script is a full-fledged program, and an unscrupulous script writer could produce a script that could destroy your files or wreak havoc in some other way. Even a naive script writer could accidentally include code that is irksome or even harmful. So for Trusted scripts, be sure to know your source!*

Recording and Saving a Script

Running premade scripts is fun and handy, but the real power of scripts is that they enable you to save the steps in a complex task of your own so that you can apply those steps again to other images. All you need to do is begin script recording, perform the steps to be included in your script, then save the script.

To start recording, choose File | Script | Start Recording or click the Start Script Recording button on the Script toolbar. Next, perform the steps that you want to include in your script. If along the way you want to perform some action but don't want it included in the script, choose File | Script | Pause Recording or click the Pause Script Recording button on the Script toolbar. To resume script recording, again choose File | Script | Pause Recording or click the Pause Script Recording button.

If you change your mind and decide that you don't want to save the script, choose File | Script | Cancel Recording or click the Cancel Script Recording button on the Script toolbar. Usually, though, you will want to save your script. In that case, choose File | Script | Save Recording or click the Save Script Recording button on the Script toolbar. If you choose to save the script, you'll see the Save As dialog:

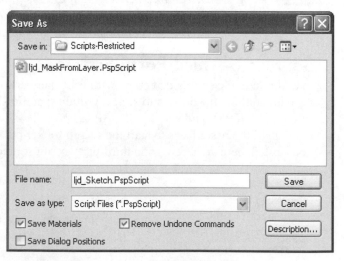

Enter a name for your script and click Save. Your script is then ready for you to use again whenever you want. Optionally, you can tweak a few things before clicking that Save button. The Save As dialog for scripts includes checkboxes labeled Save Materials, Remove Undone Commands, and Save Dialog Positions. If you want the script to always use the materials that were set in the Materials palette when you recorded the script, check Save Materials. If you want users to be able to choose their own materials, uncheck Save Materials. The Remove Undone Commands option does just what it says, eliminating from the script any command that was undone along with the associated Undo. It's usually best to keep this option selected, since it makes your script more compact and more efficient. The Save Dialog Positions option ensures that whenever the script is run interactively, any dialogs pop up in the same positions they were in when the script was recorded. This option is one that it's usually best not to select.

The Save As dialog also has a button labeled Description. Click this button to open a pop-up, shown below. As you can see, there are textboxes for three types of script information: Author, Copyright, and Description. Entries here inform other users about where the script came from and what it does. You may want to add this information even if you don't intend to share your scripts with other users. That way, you have a record of what scripts you've created and when, along with a reminder of what each of your scripts does.

Modifying a Script

You may find that there are occasions where you wish that a script would work just a *little* bit differently. Or, if you have programming skills, it may be that you've recorded a set of steps and would like to add some Python code to turn a rather ho-hum script into something special. In both cases, you're in luck! You can modify scripts with PSP's script editor or do some full-fledged script editing using any text editor.

Using PSP's Script Editor

PSP's Script Editor can be used to make simple modifications to any script that is a pure recording of PSP commands. Using the Script Editor, you can enter various sorts of information about the script or set a specific execution mode for any of the individual commands run by the script.

Let's look at an example. In the Script toolbar, select the Large Mosaic script. Instead of clicking the Run icon, click the icon just to its right, Edit Selected Script. You'll then see this dialog box:

At the top of the dialog are textboxes for Author, Copyright, and Description. If this information was entered when the script was saved, it will be displayed in the textboxes. You can also enter new text or modify existing text for any of these fields here in the Script Editor dialog.

Below the script information area of the dialog box are a set of controls for the script commands. Here's where things start to get interesting. Notice that in our example, one command is labeled Silent, one Interactive, and the rest Default. Any command marked Silent runs in the background, without displaying the command's dialog box. Any command marked Interactive opens up the command's dialog box and waits for user input. Commands marked Default run either silently or interactively depending on what the user specifies with the Execution Mode toggle.

To change the Execution Mode setting for a particular command in the script, click the right arrow near the Execution Mode label, then select the mode you want:

Some of the commands listed in our example are marked "(NOT Editable)." This indicates that the command has no settings. For these commands, it doesn't matter what you choose for the Execution Mode. In all cases, these commands run silently.

14

Editing a Script with a Text Editor

Remember that Paint Shop Pro's Script Editor can only handle scripts that are simple recordings of PSP commands. To edit more complex scripts, you need a text editor, such as Windows' Notepad. Without going into too much detail, let's look at an example. (If you're not interested in writing or editing complex scripts, just skip this section. You can always come back to it later if you want to delve into the world of complex scripts.)

In the Script toolbar, select the Border with Drop Shadow script and click the Edit Selected Script button. In this case, instead of opening up the Edit Script dialog, PSP opens your text editor and displays the code of the script there. Here's what you'd see for Border with Drop Shadow:

```
def ScriptProperties():
    return {
        'Author': 'Lori J. Davis',
        'Copyright': '(c)2003 Lori J. Davis',
        'Description': "Simulate floating an image above a background",
        'Host': 'Paint Shop Pro',
        'Host Version': '8.00'
        }

# Begin Translatable Strings
AlphaName = "Selection #1"
# End Translatable Strings

def Do(Environment):
    App.Do( Environment, 'SelectAll', {
            'GeneralSettings': {
                'ExecutionMode': App.Constants.ExecutionMode.Default,
                'AutoActionMode': App.Constants.AutoActionMode.Match
                }
            })

    App.Do( Environment, 'SelectSaveAlpha', {
            'SourceImage': 0,
            'AlphaName': AlphaName,
            'Overwrite': App.Constants.Boolean.false,
            'UpperLeft': App.Constants.Boolean.false,
            'AlphaIndex': None,
            'GeneralSettings': {
                'ExecutionMode': App.Constants.ExecutionMode.Default,
                'AutoActionMode': App.Constants.AutoActionMode.Match
                }
            })

    App.Do( Environment, 'SelectNone', {
            'GeneralSettings': {
                'ExecutionMode': App.Constants.ExecutionMode.Default,
                'AutoActionMode': App.Constants.AutoActionMode.Match
                }
            })
```

```
App.Do( Environment, 'AddBorders', {
        'Bottom': 50,
        'Left': 50,
        'Right': 50,
        'Symmetric': App.Constants.Boolean.true,
        'Top': 50,
        'Color': (255,255,255),
        'DimUnits': App.Constants.UnitsOfMeasure.Pixels,
        'GeneralSettings': {
            'ExecutionMode': App.Constants.ExecutionMode.Default,
            'AutoActionMode': App.Constants.AutoActionMode.Match
            }
        })

App.Do( Environment, 'SelectLoadAlpha', {
        'SourceImage': 0,
        'AlphaIndex': 0,
        'AlphaName': None,
        'SelectionOperation': App.Constants.SelectionOperation.Replace,
        'UpperLeft': App.Constants.Boolean.false,
        'ClipToCanvas': App.Constants.Boolean.false,
        'Invert': App.Constants.Boolean.false,
        'GeneralSettings': {
            'ExecutionMode': App.Constants.ExecutionMode.Default,
            'AutoActionMode': App.Constants.AutoActionMode.Match
            }
        })

App.Do( Environment, 'DropShadow', {
        'Blur': 20,
        'Color': (0,0,0),
        'Horizontal': 5,
        'NewLayer': App.Constants.Boolean.false,
        'Opacity': 50,
        'Vertical': 5,
        'GeneralSettings': {
            'ExecutionMode': App.Constants.ExecutionMode.Default,
            'AutoActionMode': App.Constants.AutoActionMode.Match
            }
        })
```

14

```
App.Do( Environment, 'SelectNone', {
        'GeneralSettings': {
            'ExecutionMode': App.Constants.ExecutionMode.Default,
            'AutoActionMode': App.Constants.AutoActionMode.Match
            }
        })
```

Notice that the script has several distinct parts. At the top is a set of script properties, which displays author and copyright information, along with a description of the script (assuming that this information was entered when the script was saved). Also displayed are the "host" and "host version," which in this case are Paint Shop Pro and 8.00, indicating that this script was created in Paint Shop Pro 8. The next three lines in this particular script are a comment, an assignment of a value to a variable, and another comment. The part of the script beginning with def Do(Environment): is where the real work gets done. We won't go into the details here, but you might want to note that the various code blocks that begin with App.Do run various PSP commands. For example, the block of code that begins with App.Do(Environment, 'DropShadow', { runs the Drop Shadow effect, and within that block of code, values for each of Drop Shadow's options are set:

```
'Blur': 20,
'Color': (0,0,0),
'Horizontal': 5,
'NewLayer': App.Constants.Boolean.false,
'Opacity': 50,
'Vertical': 5,
```

Here, Blur is set to 20, Color is set to 0,0,0 (which is black), the horizontal offset is set to 5, Shadow on New Layer is toggled off, Opacity is set to 50, and the vertical offset is set to 5. If you wanted to change the default behavior of the script where it applies the drop shadow, you could edit the script—replacing any of these values—and save the edited script. For example, if you wanted the script by default to apply a drop shadow with a blur of 5 instead of a blur of 20, you could change 'Blur': 20, to 'Blur': 5,.

CAUTION *Whenever you edit a script, be very careful not to change any indentation. Indentation is meaningful in Python, so inadvertent changes can make your script unusable.*

Since the details of Python programming go way beyond the scope of this book, we won't examine the code any more closely than this here. If you're interested in the guts of script writing, though, head over to http://www.python.org/ to learn about the Python programming language. And for information and user-to-user help on PSP scripting, visit Corel's Paint Shop Pro Scripting forum at newsgroup:corel.PaintShopPro_Scripting. In addition, you can download these scripting resources from Corel:

| Paint Shop Pro X Scripting for Script Authors | ftp://ftp.corel.com/pub/documentation/PSP/PSPX%20Scripting%20For%20Script%20Authors.zip |
| Paint Shop Pro X Command API | ftp://ftp.corel.com/pub/documentation/PSP/PSPXCommandAPI.zip |

Binding a Script to an Icon

If you have a script that you use a lot, you may find it handy to bind your script to an icon so you can add the icon to a palette or toolbar. To bind a script to an icon, begin by choosing View | Customize. In the Customize dialog box, click the Scripts tab:

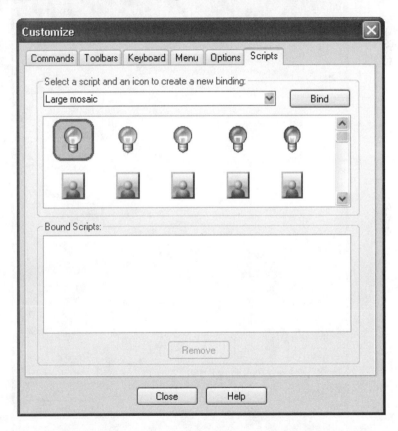

Choose the script that you want, then select the icon from the ones that are available. When you've made your selection, click Bind. The name of the script and its icon then appear in the Bound Scripts list at the bottom of the dialog box. From there, you can add the bound script to any palette, toolbar, or menu by dragging it into place. (See Chapter 13 for further information on adding commands to palettes, toolbars, and menus.)

14

Renaming Multiple Files

Now let's look at another PSP facility that helps you automate tasks: Batch Process. With batch processing, you can rename a set of files or copy a set of files to a new location, perhaps changing the file format at the same time. Let's go through an example, taking a set of files that are in PSPimage format, renaming them and converting the renamed copies to TIF format.

1. Open Batch Processing with File | Batch Process. You'll then see the Batch Process dialog box:

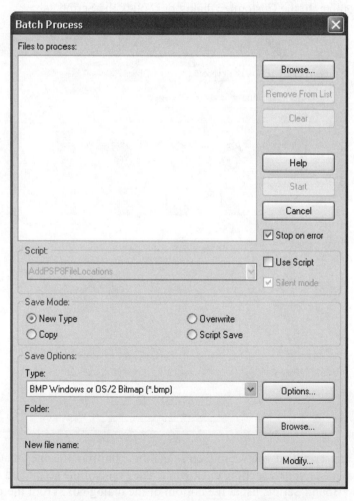

2. Click the Browse button that's near the top right of the dialog and navigate to the folder that contains the files you want to modify. Select the files you want, then click Select. (If you want to select all of the files in the folder, you can simply click Select All.)

TIP

Alternatively, you can select the files you want in PSP's browser before choosing File | Batch Process. Then when you enter Batch Process, all the files you selected in the Browser are automatically selected for processing.

3. If you want to copy the files to a new location without changing the file type, click the Copy radio button. To save as a new file type, click the New Type radio button instead. For this example, choose New Type.

4. In the Type drop-list choose the file type that you want. For this example, choose TIF Tagged Image File Format. (If you want to modify the Options for the file type, click the Options button and select the options you want.) The dialog box at this point looks like this:

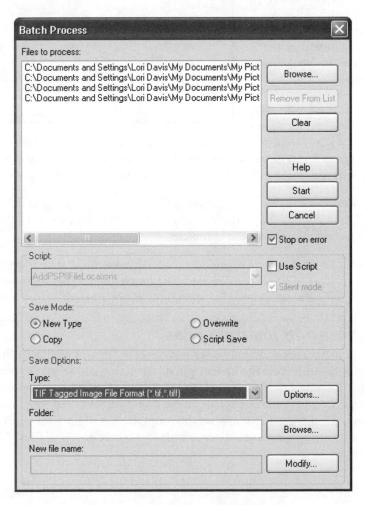

14

5. Since we want the new versions to be saved in a location different from the folder in which the original images are located, click the Browse button that's to the right of the Folder textbox. In the Browse for Folder dialog, navigate to the folder you want to save to, and click OK.

6. To rename the files, set up the specifications for the new names, and click the Modify button to the right of the New File Name textbox. This opens the Modify Filename Format dialog, where you can use various options for your files' new names.

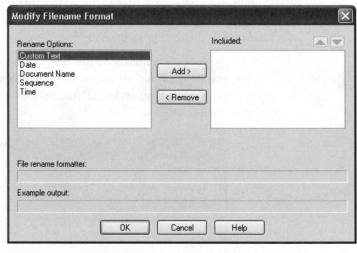

 You'll want to be sure that the specification for the new file names creates unique names for each file in the batch. You can ensure that you get unique names for each image by including Document Name or Sequence (or both) among the Rename Options that you choose.

After setting your file name and clicking OK, the only thing left to do is click the Start button! PSP then does all the work, reporting its progress along the way and letting you know when the batch processing is complete.

TIP   *If all you want to do is rename a set of files, maintaining their original file type and location, use File | Batch Rename. The Batch Rename dialog is very similar to the Modify Filename Format dialog found in Batch Process.*

Applying a Script to Multiple Files

You can use Batch Process to apply a script to a set of files. In the Batch Process dialog, click the Browse button near the upper right of the dialog and select the images that you want to apply the script to. Then select the Use Script checkbox. A drop-list to the left of the Use Script drop-list becomes active. In the drop-list, select the script that you want to run. Then click Start and PSP applies the script to each of the files you've selected.

Automatically applying a set of commands to a whole group of files? Now that's a handy feature!

INDEX